Jara Pascual

Innovation and Collaboration in the Digital Era

Jara Pascual

Innovation and Collaboration in the Digital Era

The Role of Emotional Intelligence for Innovation
Leadership and Collaborative Innovation

DE GRUYTER

ISBN 978-3-11-066511-6
e-ISBN (PDF) 978-3-11-066538-3
e-ISBN (EPUB) 978-3-11-066556-7

Library of Congress Control Number: 2021936229

Bibliographic information published by the Deutsche Nationalbibliothek
The Deutsche Nationalbibliothek lists this publication in the Deutsche Nationalbibliografie;
detailed bibliographic data are available on the Internet at http://dnb.dnb.de.

© 2021 Walter de Gruyter GmbH, Berlin/Boston
Cover image: SB/iStock/Getty Images Plus
Typesetting: Integra Software Services Pvt. Ltd.
Printing and binding: CPI books GmbH, Leck

www.degruyter.com

To Christian, Ilse and Rafael.

For my family and friends who are always there when I need support.

And for the Collabwith Community and team that inspired me to write this book with our conversations, meetings, interviews, user platform interactions and feedback.

"Innovation and collaboration are among the most important concepts that drive human society forward. Jara Pascual explores their interplay in a unique way, with the chapters walking through the richness of the topics like a Mediterranean food market, full of colour, diversity and flavours. A remarkable, engaging and satisfying read."

Johan Kestens, CIO New York Mellon Bank

"Jara's voice is rigorous and inspiring on how to manage organizations in the current era. Indeed, there are strategic reasons for diversity. And indeed, good leaders are not just smart, but emotionally intelligent. A MUST READ!"

Elena Arrieta, tech & innovation journalist. Currently working as Communications Manager at DigitalES, the Spanish Association for Digitalisation.

"Jara Pascual is opening a new box for innovation. I was intrigued about the connection of Emotional Intelligence and business in particular in a startup context. Everyone is looking for recipes for personal and professional success and this approach might be the key for both."

Sabine Stuiver, Co-founder and CMO Hydraloop

"Jara Pascual, with colleague Celia Avila-Rauch, has been able to distill and apply the ability model of emotional intelligence to the art and science of innovation and innovation leadership. In our work we note that feelings are not always facts but that emotions as a form of data. More than that, emotions can assist or facilitate with decision making, creativity and innovation rather than getting in the way, but only if leaders are "smart" about emotions and develop and deploy their emotional intelligence skills."

Dr David R Caruso, Emotional Intelligence Skills Group, Founder Yale Center for Emotional Intelligence, Research Affiliate

Preface

The opportunity to write this book arose at a time when I had witnessed the outcome of quite a number of academia/industry collaborations. Some collaborations are more difficult than originally anticipated, others become dysfunctional, and some take too long to get started. None of these scenarios is desirable, and it does not have to be this way. Hence, I was starting to look deeply into the core reasons, issues, excuses and problems surrounding these collaborations, as well as what journey academics and professionals went through to make a collaboration successful. I found that innovation is often not well understood, and in many cases, underestimated.

I wanted to write a book explaining all the secrets of how to make a collaboration successful while describing the reality and getting to the point of all the issues without excuses. The funny part is that I first created an online platform to digitize and automate the collaboration process as much as possible. Curiously, the processes, interfaces and user interactions from the platform have been a guide for designing the canvases and the structure of this book. For instance, the core of this book is the "Collaboration Journey" with the "Collaboration Canvas": this is the information architecture from the platform with its "make request" button functionality.

In this book, I have compiled, summarized and structured all the learning and opinions I received in endless conversations, interviews, and feedback sessions from professors, researchers, startup owners, entrepreneurs, innovation managers, innovation directors, students, accelerators, knowledge transfer offices, innovation consultants, partners, and policy makers (and also included my own experiences). I address this book to you, an actor inside the innovation ecosystem. You may be a professional wanting to do things differently, or an academic who wants to bring his research results to life, or you may be an innovation manager who is orchestrating the innovation ecosystem. Or you could be part of a startup which wants to change the status quo, an organization which helps society with its services. This is a book for beginners in the area of innovation and also for experts. Either way, you will learn the fundamentals and the next level on innovation leadership and rediscover the importance of innovation.

You will find years of experience condensed here into the form of best practices and canvases that will help you to transform your team, organization, ecosystem and industry in a very structured way for your collaborations, your entrepreneurship journey, your innovation projects, your research projects, your innovation consulting, your innovation development and your transformational projects.

Also, this book features more than 20 conversations with industry leaders, entrepreneurs and academics who share their perspectives in every chapter. I included these because it is particularly important to showcase role models and heroes who are doing things in a different way and who really are transforming their society, their industry and their organizations.

https://doi.org/10.1515/9783110665383-202

To start off a conversation between you and me, the reader will also find quotes from my podcast interview series "Business of Collaboration" which are worth mentioning throughout the book.

It is impossible to do innovation alone, and hence collaboration is critical to make it work and to bring innovation to the market and cause a positive impact. This book shows that if we are working together, we are going farther and faster.

Acknowledgments

I am grateful to many people and organizations. Thank you to my husband, Christian, who supports me in all the projects with his courage, time and understanding. To my two children, Ilse and Rafael, who are the best cheerleaders and support for my work and ideas, and who at times understand that I "need to work" and cannot be disturbed. To my parents, Pepe and Maribel, and to my sister Diana and my brother Eric. And to my grandparents, who always supported me, even if they did not understand what I was working on, José and Joaquina.

Special thanks to Celia Avila-Rauch because she supervised the emotional intelligence concepts and reviewed a great number of chapters in this book and provided valuable feedback and guidance on emotional intelligence skills. We wrote Chapter 4 together, and also created the "Emotional Intelligence Canvas", the "Selling Innovation Canvas" and the contribution to the guidelines to overcome fear when asking for your fee in Chapter 7. Thank you for our endless and wonderful evening conversations, lovely WhatsApp audio recordings, and tons of texts.

Thank you to Prof. Ricardo Baeza-Yates for reviewing the "bias on web" explanation in Chapter 2, and Prof. Bart de Langhe for reviewing the "behavioral economics" graphs in Chapter 7. Thank you Constantijn for our insightful and philosophical conversation.

I would like to make a special mention of my appreciation to Virginia Vila for the philosophical conversations about visualization, ecosystems and platforms. To Ginger King for being the cheerleader behind the scenes. To all my friends who are always listening to my crazy ideas and support me without questioning! Mercedes Medina, Neus Font, Raquel de la Peña, Olga Krieger, Jesús González Martí, Asun Cauhé, Jimena Saporiti, Sandra Loewe, Irene López de Vallejo and Eulalia Nadal.

Thank you to the official English reviewers Khaleelah Jones, Raquel Feliu, Paulina Samovica and Elizabeth Godynyuk, Joshua Baker and Christian Schultz. Thank you, Alejandra Nettel, for the portrait!

Thank you to Martijn Leinweber for letting me "test" the concept of "Emotional Intelligence for Innovation" and for innovation leadership, entrepreneurship, collaboration and artificial intelligence at the ESA Innovation Centre with space tech startups. Thank you to ISPIM and Ian Britan for letting me present for the first time the "Emotional Intelligence for Innovation" workshop at the ISPIM Conference in Florence in 2019, and the "Collaboration Canvas" and the "Emotional Intelligence for Entrepreneurship" as a workshop at the ISPIM Virtual Conference in 2020.

My editors from DeGruyter Steven Hardman and Maximilian Gessl for their advice and guidelines. A special mention to Prof. Daniel Schallmo for the title, and how-to-write-a-book tips. And, finally, I am grateful to all the startups I am mentoring because I am learning from them too and thank you to all the professors who are giving me the opportunity to teach and show my "canvases" as a guest lecturer at universities.

https://doi.org/10.1515/9783110665383-203

And a super thanks to all the contributors to this book for having the courage and kindness to share their experiences in every chapter!

Support Book Team

I gratefully acknowledge the "Book Breakfast Team" who gave the first direction, honest advice, critical feedback and the strategy on how to write this book.

Prof. Dr. Daniel Schallmo from Hochschule Neu-Ulm, Germany
Prof. Dr. Anton Kriz, from Australian National University, Australia
Prof. Dr. Crystal Jiang, Bryant University, USA
Prof. Dr. Christopher Tucci, Imperial College London, UK
Dr. Irene López de Vallejo, Spain
Dr. Ricardo Baeza-Yates, CTO NTENT, USA
Steven Hardman, DeGruyter, UK
Roman Meier-Andrae, Head of, TÜV, Germany
Prof. Dr. Søren Smed, Aalborg University, Denmark
Prof. Dr. Christian Haslam, Aalborg University, Denmark

Sidebars

I am infinitely grateful for the contribution of the following experts, academics, startup owners, innovation leaders, impact makers and politicians whose perspectives are included at the end of each chapter of this book.

Dr. Ricardo Baeza-Yates, CTO, NTENT on "Algorithms Bias on Web", Chapter 1
Dr. Irene López de Vallejo, on "Decentralization of Knowledge", Chapter 1
David King, CEO Exaptive on "Digitalization of Innovation", Chapter 1
Susana Solís Pérez, Member of the European Parliament on "Digital Innovation Ecosystem", Chapter 2
Marcin Plociennik, EOSC DIH Business Pilot Coordinator PSNC, on "EOSC Digital Innovation Hub", Chapter 2
Galit Bauer, Co-Founder Holiday-Sitters.com on "Digital Trust", Chapter 2
Miguel García González, Innovation Director at Bosonit on "Innovation Radar", Chapter 2
William Malek, Director SEAC Innovation Centre Stanford-Thailand on "Paradoxes of Academia/Industry Collaboration", Chapter 3
Dr. Daria Tataj, CEO Tataj Innovation on "Network Thinking", Chapter 3
Alexander Gunkel, Founder and CEO Space4Good on "Using Emotional Intelligence for Entrepreneurship", Chapter 4

Charlie Camarda, NASA Astronaut on "How important is Psychological Safety for Team Performance", Chapter 4

Carlos Lee, Director General EPIC Photonics Association on "Collaboration over Competition", Chapter 5

Karin Ekberg, CEO Leadership and Sustainability on "How to work with your competitors, case of Sustainable Apparel Coalition", Chapter 5

Martijn Leinweber, COO SBIC Noordwijk on "How to build a Space Innovation Community", Chapter 6

Juan Maldonado, Manager RSM MENTORME at RSM Erasmus University on "Creating an effective and self-maintain community of mentors", Chapter 6

Steffen Conn, Director ISPIM on "How to manage an Innovation Community at ISPIM", Chapter 6

Lana Jelenjev, founder BASE Conference on "How to create a Community", Chapter 6

Robbert Fisher, President Forum Knowledge4Innovation on "Policies and Innovation", Chapter 6

Carol Tarr, Nyenrode Business School on "Diversity for Ecosystems", Chapter 6

Kimberly Cornfield, University College London, European Research and Innovation Office (ERIO), Head of Proposal Management and

Martin Scott, University College London, European Research and Innovation Office (ERIO), Head of Innovation Management on "How to calculate Budget for Knowledge Transfer and Innovation", Chapter 7

Lina Gálvez, Member of the European Parliament on "How to calculate Budget for Innovation Ecosystems", Chapter 7

Yannick Legré, former Managing Director EGI on "The cost of Research Transfer", Chapter 7

Dominik Kufner, CEO KC Wearable Technologies on "The cost of Innovation", Chapter 7

Ivo Locatelli, Senior Expert – Team leader innovation procurement on "Public Innovation Procurement", Chapter 8

Prof. Dr. Pedro José Bueso Guillén, University of Zaragoza on "Innovation Procurement", Chapter 8

Joanne Hyland, Founding partner and President rInnovation Group, Former VP Business Ventures Group at Nortel Networks on "Corporate venturing", Chapter 8

Prince Constantijn van Oranje-Nassau, Special Enjoy Techleap.nl on "Innovation Leadership", Chapter 9

Maria Graça Carvalho, Member of the European Parliament, former Minister of Innovation and Research in Portugal on "Innovation Leadership", Chapter 9

Natalie Samovich, Head of R&I Enercoutim on "Innovation Leadership for Ecosystems", Chapter 9

Christine MacKay, CEO Salamandra on "Innovation Leadership inside Organizations", Chapter 9

Prof. Dr. Christian Haslam, Aalborg University on "Digitalization for Innovation", Chapter 10

Prof. Dr. Kimberly Houser, University of North Texas on "Ethical Algorithms", Chapter 10
Uljan Sharka, Founder and CEO at iGenius on "Design and Technology", Chapter 10
Virginia Vila, Director UX Collabwith on "The importance of UX", Chapter 10

Podcasts and Interviews

I would like to acknowledge the following people for participating in the podcast conversation "Business of Collaboration" and interviews for *Collabwith Magazine* and for giving me permission to add their amazing "quotes" as a testimonial throughout the chapters of this book.

Larry Sanger, Co-founder of Wikipedia, Chapter 1
Els De Maeijer, Researcher at Fontys University, Chapter 1
Emile Asselbergs, Head of Business Development at TNO, Chapter 1
Martin Jarolím, Head of the Retail Business Line of K&H Bank, Chapter 1
Prof. John Bessant, University of Exeter, Chapter 1, Chapter 3
Mark Phibbs, CMO CISCO, Chapter 1, Chapter 2
Jeremy Laurin, VP Business Development and Commercialization at Ontario Centres of Excellence, Chapter 2, Chapter 7
Joost d'Hooghe, VP DSM Engineering Materials, Chapter 2, Chapter 3, Chapter 4
Ragnar Ragnarsson, CIO Samskip Group, Chapter 3
Marie-Elisabeth Rusling, CEO Business Angels Europe, Chapter 3
Natalie Turner, Founder and CEO entheo, Chapter 3
Stefan Lindegaard, UPGRADE! Program, Chapter 3
William Malek, Executive Director SEAC Innovation Center and Stanford-Thailand 4.0 Research Consortium, Chapter 3
Russell O'Brien, CEO at Cognitis Innovation, Chapter 3, Chapter 4, Chapter 6
Prof. Katharina Ruckstuhl, Associate Dean Māori at the University of Otago's Business School, Chapter 3, Chapter 4, Chapter 6
Prof. Stefano Puntoni, RSM Erasmus University, Chapter 3
Dr. Irene López de Vallejo, Chapter 5
Ricardo Baeza-Yates, CTO NTENT, Chapter 5
Mieke De Ketelaere, Program Director AI at iMEC, Chapter 5
Prof. Frank Piller, RWTH Aachen, Chapter 5, Chapter 6
Prof. Anton Kriz, Australian National University, Chapter 6
Luca Emil Abirascid, Chapter 6, Chapter 8
Prof. Henry Chesbrough, UC Berkeley-Haas School of Business, Chapter 7, Chapter 8
Prof. Christopher Tucci, Imperial College London, Chapter 7
Maik Fuellmann, CEO and Co-Founder of QUIZZBIZZ Ltd, Chapter 7
Prof. Dr. Pedro-José Bueso Guillén, University of Zaragoza, Chapter 8

Joanne Hyland, Founder and President of the rInnovation Group, Chapter 8
Martin McGurk, Senior Innovation Lead at Innovate UK, Chapter 8
David Grundy, Group Head of Blockchain/DLT at Danske Bank, Chapter 9
Steve Rader, Deputy Director of NASA's Center of Excellence for Collaborative Innovation, Chapter 9
Markus Bensnes, Senior Innovation Adviser at NorConsult, Chapter 9
Rohit Talwar, CEO Fast Future Think Tank, Chapter 9
Hilligje van't Land, Secretary General International Association of Universities (IAU), Chapter 9
Jeroen Tas, Chief Innovation and Strategy Officer at Royal Philips, Chapter 10
Prof. Dr. Daniel Schallmo, Hochschule Neu-Ulm, Chapter 10
Dr. Khaleelah Jones, Founder and CEO at Careful Feet, Chapter 10

Contents

Introduction to the Collaboration Journey
for Innovation

Innovation, collaboration and entrepreneurship are much needed in the period we are living in. We need to be creative, we need to think outside of the box, we need to go out of our comfort zone, and we need to surprise ourselves with new thinking and new ideas. The solution is not to continue doing the things the same way and then add a mobile app into the mix. No. Nowadays, we have the beautiful opportunity to re-think our way of living and working. And innovation offers techniques to help us properly re-think our lives creatively, to stop and to breathe, calm down and consider what kind of present we want to live in and what kind of future we want to have, which kind of values we have now and want to continue to have. We are in a period of change, and for this period we need both leadership and creativity, we need innovation, we need positive thinking, we need innovative thinking, and we need collaborative thinking. In this book, I merged innovation with leadership, innovation with emotional intelligence, collaboration with competition, cost with knowledge, artificial intelligence with emotional intelligence, and collaboration with innovation. We need fresh ideas, we need business leaders who can execute these fresh ideas, and we need leaders who can drive our industry and our society as a whole towards this change.

Decentralization of knowledge and innovation

I have seen that knowledge is centralized and hidden in remote places both virtually and physically. The question is: How accurate and specific is the knowledge that we need to collaborate and work together to make innovation happen? Innovation might be coming from one idea or concept, maybe from a research result, and putting in the effort to make it become reality, or even still developing it before reaching the market, is not an individual effort, it's a community effort.

But the first step is to find with whom we will make this step. And understanding this decentralization is critical to realizing that there are infinite options to collaborate and to innovate together, faster. It is essential to trust people when working remotely because success is all about creating relationships.

Collaboration over competition

The Covid-19 pandemic and ensuing economic crisis are highlighting the importance of collaboration to solve global challenges, but also get to the core of what competition and collaboration really are. If you enhance support for collaboration,

https://doi.org/10.1515/9783110665383-205

then competitiveness decreases; otherwise, you reduce the chances of being competent. It seems that it is time to revisit the concept of competition

The concept of competition is different depending on whether we are talking about the field of innovation and entrepreneurship or basing our debate on the field of economics in general. But in any case, the paradox of collaboration as opposed to competition is quite interesting. On the one hand, you have the perspective of competition when there is scarcity of resources. This is the case for innovation and entrepreneurship, as can be witnessed from the fact that you are in a position to innovate better in times of crisis, and the same principle goes when choosing for entrepreneurship, starting from nothing, typically with great scarcity and no external support.

On the other hand, collaboration is happening in the face of scarcity, when trying to survive as a small group inside a bigger industry, or when a group of companies collaborate to achieve a goal within an industry. If you ask an economist, competition comes from abundance. And again, you could argue that in innovation, knowledge is infinite and the way that you as a leader can compete is to mobilize resources, but this mobilization of resources is, in the end, collaboration.

Digitalization

Digitalization is not simply doing "the same thing, but online", it's being creative when re-thinking how we are doing things. We have to surprise, we have to create new ways of working, new ways of hosting events, new ways of meeting. It's about people, not so much about technology; also, it is about creativity, about having an open mind to think and create different solutions. And this is also what innovation is all about: using your creativity to be able to create a new present. As you might know, digital transformation and digitalization of processes is not about technology, gadgets or tools, it's more about people and common sense. And also, digitalization is how we can better leverage the technology to help us in our businesses, daily work and daily life.

Collaborative innovation

Collaborating for innovation is an activity that can comprise co-brainstorming, co-creation, co-designing, co-researching, co-developing, co-prototyping, co-implementing, co-executing, co-going-to-market, co-adopting with experts, academics, startups, investors and other types of partners you can imagine in your value chain and ecosystem. Innovation cannot be done alone. You might need to collaborate with academics to understand some parts of your idea, technology or concept, or maybe you need to know who can produce your new product, so you have to be an active part of your industry and of the ecosystem you are in. Make connections and collaborate. This is the fastest and strongest choice you can make for your business to create growth. Collaboration for innovation means that you might be making a change to how current factories are producing your new product, or how companies work together, and this is innovation too. You are innovating on two levels: one is your innovative solution, and the other is that you innovate in the process. For instance, you are innovating your whole value chain from practical to transformative.

Collaboration journey

The collaboration journey is the structure, a transparent and clear process that shows which phase you are in in the course of a collaboration. It gives you a guide to what you have to do in each phase, which contracts are needed, which information is required and how to communicate to be able to go to the next phase. Since we are talking about innovation, we are dealing with the subjects of uncertainty, risk and trust. You can only succeed if you are transparent, clear, honest and every "collaborator" knows the current phase, and what information is needed. In Chapter 3 of this book, you will find Figure 3.4 detailing the "collaboration journey", with the steps from "searching phase" to "collaboration phase", and Figure 3.6 showing the "collaboration canvas", a clear framework that you can follow to know which information is important to think about and discuss with your collaborator.

Emotional intelligence

Emotions are valuable information for businesses, innovation, collaboration and entrepreneurship, not only for life or for learning. Emotions are relevant, even more relevant after having lived through a global pandemic, where a strong set of emotions came upon us in form of fear, disappointment, frustration, stress, sadness or relief, calm, joy and happiness. Emotions are information and our drivers in decision making, creativity, communication and productivity.

How much we are aware of them, and how much we are aware of the emotions of others, is the key to success in our professional and personal lives. It is very obvious that there are options to act on fear and make decisions based on that fear and panic or to calm down and understand the fear and translate this fear into positive action.

In this book, I am applying emotional intelligence for innovation, collaborations, entrepreneurship, leadership, selling innovation and creation of innovation ecosystems and communities.

Cost of knowledge

We are always talking about how to create trust, about how to communicate better, and about the worry of "talking about money". In this "all free society" where you can consume content for free on the internet everywhere, we are too used to getting free knowledge. This is creating a place where paying for knowledge or paying for co-creation is not seen as positive. In this book, you will find a different perspective, because talking about money, costs, incomes, commission fees, risks and ratios per hour is creating trust, transparency, understanding, respect and recognition of each other's value and how you create value together. Because knowledge is intangible, knowledge needs to be framed in such a way that it is possible to value it. The way to avoid anxieties about taking on budgeting, finance, tax and other financial obligations is to take action, to do calculations and to talk about the cost of doing innovation and sharing knowledge in a transparent way.

Innovation leadership

It seems it is seldom recognized that the style of leadership which is required to drive innovation is very specific, sometimes labeled "transformational leadership", "kind leadership", "feminine leadership", or "simple leadership". The levels of influence and social intelligence needed to drive change and mobilize resources, for which you might not have full responsibility, is hard and requires high levels of self-esteem, self-confidence, kindness, drive, courage, respect, learning, active listening, passion, honesty, transparency, positivity, curiosity and resilience. This is a type of leadership that has to be understood well by C-level executives, governments and entrepreneurs. Innovation leadership is embedded across corporations, SMEs, startups, governments and investors. It is a way to drive change to make innovation happen in the field with the collaboration of the whole ecosystem.

Positive impact

Taking a 360° perspective of your impact, at whose lives you are touching, we all have to accept other benefits and other effects of our actions, outside pure financial profit. This is a question that many social impact investors are asking of entrepreneurs as well – it isn't only a corporate concern. And it's difficult to answer. I remember asking an investment manager directly about how to assess impact, and she said, well, you look at the sustainable development goals. Well, this is not enough, and this is not a good answer. You can use the sustainable development goals (SDG) for doing the first categorization, to use it as a language everyone will understand. But then you have to look at your value chain, at your supply chain, at your customers, at your local area, region, country and at your industry as a whole and see if you are making a change in the behavior, market, way of working, way of operating, way of producing, way of buying, etc. Hence, apparently, we are all learning this journey of assessing impact and we have to know this – we are learning, and we can learn from those who researched this topic many years ago and re-learn and co-learn with them again because our society has changed. Then, you analyze whether this change is positive and brings a benefit and value to these actors. It is very useful as well to look at the philosophical question: What kind of future do you want to have?

———

"My career has been about decentralizing knowledge creation via the internet"

Larry Sanger, co-founder of Wikipedia (Sanger, 2019)

Chapter 1
Knowledge and Innovation are Decentralized

Summary: In this first chapter, you will get to know the basic definition of knowledge, innovation, open innovation, and decentralized innovation; and you will take the first step in the "collaboration journey" to apply decentralized innovation to your team and organization successfully.

Innovation is generating value from creativity, and it can be any kind of value from any form of creativity. You create value every time you bring something new to the market and the people use this new product, service or process you have created.

The question is: In terms of creativity, how can you be creative with the knowledge you have, or do you need extra knowledge? Do you perhaps need to be challenged to be creative? Can you "create" something new yourself? Or do you need to think together with someone else?

Myths tell us about the solo creator, or a person who is alone at his desk thinking his thoughts without any kind of interaction with the real world, and coming up with a brilliant idea, going out of the room and screaming "eureka" and then suddenly, as in 1879, everyone can purchase light bulbs for their homes. This is a good story, but far away from reality. Thomas Edison invented the light bulb with his team. In fact, Thomas Edison was the first one to create a research laboratory to invent new products. And also, he created the first partnerships for innovation with Henry Ford and Harvey Firestone. He invented and afterwards sold his inventions, and customers used his inventions, so he kept innovating.

Not to forget – we have to differentiate what is invention and what is innovation. This is a book about innovation, not invention. So, you have to remove the stress you are feeling now if you are thinking about getting innovative yourself. You do not have to create something new (that would be an invention), you have to create value and bring it to the market.

The act of co-creating and co-inspiring within your team, within your organization and with partners and other companies is called open innovation. The exact definition of open innovation is "the use of purposive inflows and outflows of knowledge to accelerate internal innovation, and expand the markets for external use of innovation, respectively" (Chesbrough, 2006). The misconceptions regarding open innovation and innovation become obvious immediately: even as the official definition of open innovation says that you are alone doing innovation at your desk, you are receiving extra knowledge from other parties and then, of course, you bring your product to the market. In practice, open innovation is about getting ideas from other people and adding them into your list of ideas, following the objective that you have to get as many ideas as you can, at the end to harvesting the creativity from others.

https://doi.org/10.1515/9783110665383-001

Knowledge is spread and decentralized which means no person owns all the knowledge. Every individual has a quantity of knowledge and that knowledge is increasing by reading books, articles, having conversation with other colleagues, listening to pitches, watching YouTube videos or training videos on other e-learning platforms, attending master classes, workshops, webinars, university courses, etc. You can see in Figure 1.1 how knowledge is everywhere. Every circle is a piece of knowledge or a person who has a piece of knowledge. This figure depicts how knowledge can be close, but it is not found together with other knowledge, nor is it linked or connected to other pieces of knowledge or people who have this knowledge. They are not related to each other. Simply, the knowledge is out there.

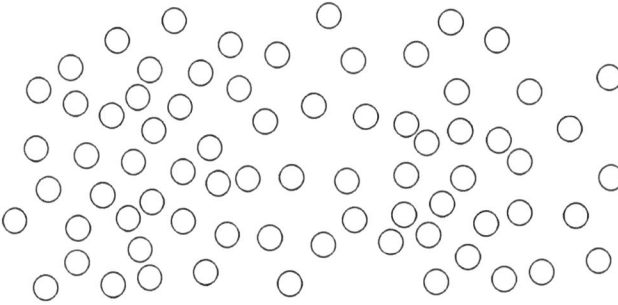

Figure 1.1: Diagram of an example of knowledge visualization.

If you assume that knowledge is spread out everywhere, you can associate knowledge with different types of links to connect the knowledge, or as Steve Jobs said, "connect the dots" of internal knowledge with external knowledge. In Figure 1.2 there are two different ways of connecting the dots. In the case of connecting your dots, you can be creative. There is the decentralized network, where knowledge is primarily connected to a knowledge hub, and then the hubs are connected. Or the distributed network, where the knowledge is connected peer-to-peer, which means one-to-one. In this case, it is a bit difficult to get a full visibility of each knowledge "dot".

The differences between a centralized network of knowledge and a distributed network of knowledge are mainly about the access to knowledge, the empowerment of the individuals, and the decision-making process of one team or organization. The decentralized network is a subset of a distributed network, which means that the decentralized network includes the properties of a distributed network. In Table 1.1 you can see a summary of power distribution between the two different types of networks.

Universities are centers of knowledge. When we look at access to knowledge at universities, the technology and knowledge transfer offices directly spring to mind. Let's look closer at the tension between the technology and knowledge transfer offices and academic professors. Tension originates from the fact that the power of the decision making is not clear and works with a hidden and often enough non-transparent

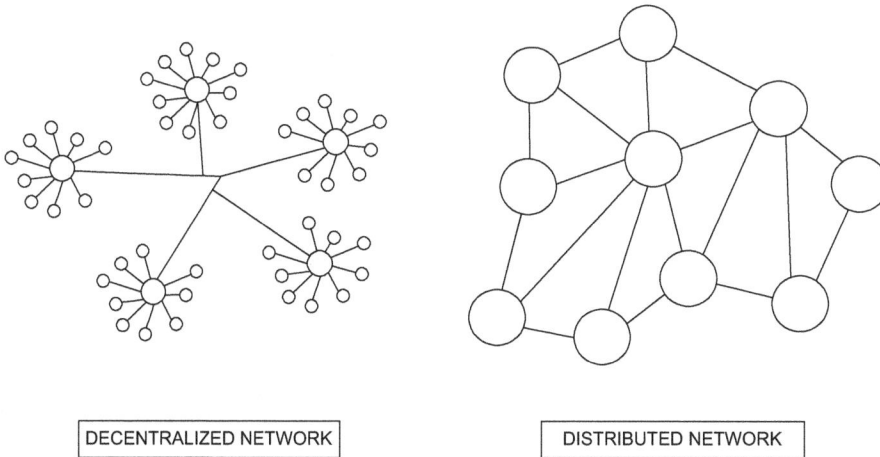

DECENTRALIZED NETWORK   DISTRIBUTED NETWORK

Figure 1.2: Examples of decentralized vs. distributed networks for knowledge connectivity.

Table 1.1: Power differences between decentralized and distributed networks of knowledge.

Decentralized Network	Distributed Network
Access to same resources and information	Everyone gets direct access to everyone's knowledge
Control is shared among independent nodes	Knowledge is distributed in different locations
Decision making is decentralized	Decision making is made locally in the node
Each node has data ownership	Cooperation between nodes is crucial

process. In some cases, the technology and knowledge office have the decision-making power, in other cases, it is the academic professor who has the power of the decision making. Who decides on the perspectives of collaborations has to be clear and has to be matched with Figure 1.2 to understand how you, as a super innovator and super collaborator, design your knowledge transfer strategy and collaboration from a university perspective in correlation with the type of network you want to have, and you are. For instance, in a case when knowledge is decentralized and owned by individual academic professors and researchers, then the power of decision making with whom to collaborate should be on the academic and researcher side.

The role of the technology and knowledge transfer office, or innovation office, should be to be an orchestrator of their own knowledge and innovation ecosystem, bringing people together, being open minded toward collaboration, as well as providing guidelines on how to properly collaborate. It also includes legal support, accounting support, business development, innovation brokerage, and organizing networking events, financial support (calls and investment opportunities), and making sure to visualize the technology and the knowledge from the university (that every company can understand and relate to), among other specific activities each office might have. The prime objective is to create a strong community from their ecosystem.

Decentralized knowledge

What exactly does the term "decentralized knowledge" mean? Its main implication is that geography doesn't matter. You do not need to be in the same room to access or share knowledge. This is possible because of the internet and thanks to the decentralized applications and tools that make it possible to share and find knowledge.

Naturally, knowledge is decentralized, and you have to understand that control of knowledge and centralization of knowledge are consequently not natural. Decentralization is an innate structure and a natural way to understand how knowledge resides inside people's minds, as well as documents, websites, books, podcasts and videos. It is important to understand that the piece of knowledge you might need is hidden somewhere and that in order to take advantage of it to innovate, you have to find it. Thus, it is key to remove barriers to access knowledge to harvest innovation potential. It is also clear that centralization of knowledge is a bottleneck for working together and innovation.

For organizations it is important to create a culture where employees can connect inside and outside of the organization with knowledge, expand on it by thinking creatively and facilitate the integration of this new knowledge into core competencies of an individual person, a team or an organization. For this, knowledge needs to be open and accessible to anyone at any given time.

And yet the question remains: What is the link between knowledge and innovation? Why is the access to knowledge important to enhance innovation? One of the major bottlenecks for creating innovation is the silo structure inside organizations. You can relate to this case whenever teams and departments are not talking to each other, when they are not sharing information and even when they created their own silos and clubs where people have difficulty entering. These silos are tightly sealed off, and in these environments innovation is impossible. Information and knowledge need to flow between teams openly, and not only inside the organizations but also outside organizations. The access to knowledge is very important for creativity (as a first step for innovation), and for knowledge sharing to happen, you have to remove the mindset of control, fear of competition, and fear of openness, and start working with the positive mindset of building a future together. This mission has to be more important than the fears of sharing and working together. It applies to small companies, departments, organizations, cities, clusters, ecosystems and countries as the clusters for knowledge are replicating the exact pattern of silos inside the organizations. Wherever the knowledge is fluent inside a small team, but not across the teams, not across the department and not across the organization.

On the contrary, where teams work together and share information, the perceived energy is higher, and the impact is greater. As already stated at the beginning of this chapter, you cannot invent alone, you cannot bring innovation to the market alone. Per default, innovation is teamwork, and the team needed for innovation may be formed within an organization, by several organizations or by individuals working together. Interleaved knowledge of individuals, and the common knowledge of organizations, which are constructed from different perspectives, different disciplines, different experiences and different knowledge, create better innovation. And you have to remember, innovation is happening whenever you bring value to people, society, industry, the market or the planet. It might be best described as bringing positive impact.

There is one recent study by RTWH Aachen University related to open innovation saying, "The majority of projects (78%) though focuses on finding the 'missing piece of knowledge'" (Piller and Diener 2019). Again, this link between knowledge and innovation is demonstrated in "open innovation" activities, through which organizations are seeking a way to find this missing piece of knowledge in the "crowd of people" with different contexts. This action might be inefficient because only the right person with the right knowledge will know about the "context" needed to solve a certain innovation challenge. And then there is the risk to talk about a real organizational problem openly where competitors can pick up on your problem. This is why open innovation challenges are more about marketing than about efficiency of finding the knowledge you need. Still, it is clear that there is a need for specific knowledge for innovation, and it is difficult to find this needed knowledge out there, inside or outside the organization, cluster and ecosystem.

How can you find the knowledge you need online?

Larry Sanger, co-founder of Wikipedia "My career has been about decentralizing knowledge creation via the internet" (Sanger, 2019)

As an example, for structured knowledge online, Wikipedia was created to "centralize" the "decentralized knowledge" of the world, as an open access encyclopedia and knowledge created by people who have a certain piece of knowledge and share it openly. Wikipedia created the framework to search for knowledge in different languages and make it easily accessible to everyone. The review process to ensure the quality of the knowledge inside Wikipedia is key to that endeavor. But Wikipedia tends to hold universal knowledge, not the highly specialized knowledge organizations need. Google was following the path of universal access to knowledge and created Google Scholar to give open access to knowledge inside books, papers and other formats where academics where writing their findings and results. Other platforms, such as Microsoft Academia, or Semantic Scholar, followed. Even if artificial intelligence technology has advanced, the search results do not provide the concrete answers in the search of knowledge, but rather a paper which has to be read and understood.

How can you create impact from knowledge?

"Cooperation and support from others is a key success factor for small companies to grow" Els De Maeijer, Researcher at Fontys University and Emile Asselbergs, Head of Business Development at TNO (De Maeijer and Asselbergs, 2018)

As another example of the impact of knowledge access and its importance, Els de Maeijer and Emile Asselbergs have worked together to analyze the power of positive and open communication during collaborations for innovation. They found out that helping each other is important, and that collaborations which work well are those where people spend time during meetings to understand each other and do not rush the conversation. This story highlights the positive mindset when working together. In the end you are working with people to create something new, because each of you has specific knowledge and experience. You have to make it work because you are there together to make it work. If there is not product on the market, if there is no service on the market and people are using it, there is no impact at all. You are sharing knowledge to make innovation work and to create impact.

How can you create solutions by sharing knowledge?

Martin Jarolím, Head of the Retail Business Line of K&H Bank "Find new ways of serving our clients better and implement new solutions that is innovation" (Jarolím, 2018)

K&H Bank of the KBC banking Group in Hungary is a great example of sharing knowledge for innovation, to create solutions together with the end consumer, employees and management. Innovative solutions originate from working together, as a result of a culture which cares about teamwork to create solutions. Martin Jarolím said, "K&H has a long history of a strong teamwork culture with loyalty and hard work at the center". An interesting manifestation of this culture are internal events: "The format is usually one or two speakers from our partners and our colleagues from other KBC Group countries, but on bigger topics, we have a whole day innovation fair with exhibitions from startups, incumbents and even student groups, we call experts via Skype and also listen to client testimonies. Last time this big topic was the future of healthcare where we see tremendous improvements and shifts. Hundreds of K&H colleagues come to these events, they experience the future and empathize with our clients: how the novelties affect their lives and start thinking about how our bank insurance group can adapt to these changes" (Jarolím, 2018).

Decentralized innovation

Decentralized innovation is happening when you are working together to make real positive impact with experts within a structure of decentralized knowledge. This impact could be created remotely by experts from academia, startups, corporates, SMEs or from other entities such as research centers and innovation agencies. Experts can be part of your organization or your local ecosystem, or outside your organization and outside your ecosystem, including from any part of the globe. This visualization of the decentralized knowledge and expertise is essential for your innovation mindset.

Decentralized innovation implies that both you and your organization are ready to be open to receive knowledge and technology from outside your network. It means that you are ready to collaborate with experts you don't know – it may even be the first time you hear about them. This is the opportunity to learn how to create trust (maybe remotely) and how to build a relationship with the expert you might need. The key point here is that relationship doesn't mean friendship, it means a healthy relationship to be able to work together, to understand each other, to be able to create a psychologically safe environment to perform on a high level. And before that, it has to be very clear what you want to do together and why you are collaborating. At the end of this chapter, you can find exercises to have an efficient decentralized innovation approach inside your team and organization.

Collaboration is the most important theme in innovation during the XXI Century (Bessant, 2020).

Differences between open innovation and decentralized innovation

But what are the differences between decentralized innovation and open innovation? At first it seems obvious. Open Innovation is working with "internal organization knowledge to make an external impact" (Chesbrough, 2006). This stemmed from the idea that innovation does not need to be part of an "innovation team" only, it is the responsibility of the entire organization to work towards it. After this, the next wave of open innovation was about "crowdsourcing", e.g., getting ideas from external people for the organization via contexts. Decentralized innovation is adding the next layer of "openness" to realize that it's not only important to work together inside the organization to bring innovation to the market, but also it is important to work and collaborate with external partners. These partners have the knowledge and the expertise that you need as a super innovator and super collaborator, and these partners could be professors from universities, researchers, or other experts hidden inside other organizations. And here it is particularly important to remark that startups, SMEs innovation agencies and research centers have technology ready to test and ready to integrate into SMEs and corporates.

"Openness" as a value is critical. This means being open to work with startups instead of using technology from the established corporates or other industry stakeholders you trust. It means partnering in creative ways with startups and innovation agencies that could bring in different business models by using and applying technology and being "open" to these opportunities for your business. If the value proposition of an ecosystem or cluster is to support collaborations for impact and exchange between "super innovators" and "established companies", this "openness" will create a different present and a different future by bringing real impact to the society.

Prof. Piller and Prof. Diener from RWTH Aachen University started talking about "collaborative innovation" as a sub-definition of open innovation where they modified the definition of open innovation. "Open Innovation is seen as collaborating with an unspecific target group, solving problems in a strategic way. Most practitioners connect activities like creating, sharing or connecting with the term open innovation" (Piller and Diener, 2019). And they continue to redefine open innovation as an "innovation system open to external input, the knowledge of the firm is extended by the large base of information about needs, applications, and solution technologies that resides in the domain of customers, users, retailers, suppliers and other external parties" (Piller and Diener, 2019). Decentralized Innovation is adding the impact of the collaboration because the objective is to bring innovative services and innovative products to the market.

DRIVE CHANGE TOGETHER	BRING VALUE
MAKE REAL IMPACT	GO TO MARKET
CO-CREATION OF INNOVATION	COLLABORATIVE INNOVATION
FIND KNOWLEDGE AND TECHNOLOGY	DECENTRALIZED INNOVATION
NETWORK OUTSIDE YOUR ECOSYSTEM	NETWORK THINKING
WORK WITH OTHERS INSIDE YOUR ECOSYSTEM	OPEN INNOVATION
INDIVIDUAL AND TEAM INNOVATION	INNOVATION

Figure 1.3: Innovation transition categories from idea to bringing value to society.

Figure 1.3 displays the innovation transition categories. The main difference is the commitment and risk of the partners who collaborate to bring the innovation together to the market. Decentralized innovation is working together to create an idea and bring it to the market in collaboration, and this is the true innovation definition we were missing until today.

The key points of decentralized innovation
- Self-organizing networks of people and resources that take action in a decentralized way.
- Understanding of a world of distributed knowledge, technology and ideas.
- Sharing knowledge of invention, such as patents or other IP, old technology, old research results shared amongst members have the potential to produce breakthrough technology and services to disrupt current markets or create new markets.
- Understanding of online communities to make decentralized connectivity and engagement possible because ecosystems and innovation should not be only about visualization.
- Crowdsourcing is only about ideation for a problem, hence it's a small part of the innovation supply chain from idea to impact.
- Connecting individuals, stakeholders and organizations and getting actively involved in ideation for discovery and in collaboration to create impact.
- Being open to gathering new knowledge and incorporating it inside the team and organization.
- Remembering the short definition of innovation: bringing value from creativity.

Benefits of decentralized innovation
- Reduce cost, save time, accelerate time to market.
- Increase difference in the market.
- Discover new opportunities.
- Share R&D and innovation investment.
- Lower risks and costs of innovation because it is distributed amongst partners.
- Early involvement in new technology and business opportunities.
- Enhance diversity and different points of view for the new products and services.
- SMEs and startups are sharing budgets and resources otherwise unavailable inhouse.
- Make the R&D and innovation process faster and reduce the time to market.
- Competitive advantage on community creating for innovation.
- Incorporate and acquire knowledge, ideas, expertise from partners and customers by increasing higher intellectual capital.
- Create new business models from the collaboration mindset instead of a competition mindset.
- Improve customer acceptance by collaborating with customers and other partners with different experiences and knowledge of the market.

Technology for decentralized knowledge and decentralized innovation

Of course, if you are going to innovate with experts who are far away from you, you will need to work and collaborate. To get an orientation, you can innovate and collaborate remotely. For this you will need to find the hidden knowledge anywhere on planet Earth. You are in luck that the internet and ever more online applications, products and services are allowing us to do this. But the thought of adopting remote collaboration as a default mode of working may not come to everyone as trivial, because many organizations still think that every employee has to be at the office every day. It is easy to say that you are living in a special time, but it's a bit more difficult for organizations to accept the new way of working and "the future of work" as a reality. For some inspiration to accept remote activities, Mark Phibbs of Cisco said, "A recent example at Cisco is that many customer events we have done have been just physical which is a huge miss. My team and I innovated to think about events as part of a campaign and an opportunity to build content. As a result, we have become a broadcaster and now all events are both online and physical. This means we can dramatically increase our reach and deliver a much greater return on investment. An example is our largest event called Cisco Live, 8,000 attendees live and now up to 1 million people watching the content online via Twitter, YouTube and WeChat." (Phibbs, 2019). While Phibbs is talking about events, this is also about the mindset and looking at the benefits of digitalization and technology instead of focusing on fear of losing control.

There are innovation platforms for corporates, open innovation crowdsourcing platforms to get ideas for a challenge, social networks for scientists, data visualization tools, data aggregators to visualize knowledge and technology like the "innovation radar", or the "startup map" from the European Union, where you can see the local ecosystems and technology clusters. And on the other hand, you can find the collaboration tools for the workplace coming from established firms like Cisco, Microsoft, Google and new brands such a Slack. Other technical platforms for digital signature or smart legal contracts like Signaturit, HelloSign or Ligo should be named here as well.

The core of using technology for knowledge; first you have to make effective use of knowledge, it needs to be classified, defined, and related in conventional terminologies. Knowledge management tools [exist for] knowledge acquisition, representation, modeling, discovery and distribution (G. Mehdi et al., 2018).

My own business, Collabwith, fits into this list of available technology to enable innovation.

Collabwith is a platform which is taking care of the whole supply chain for knowledge and innovation decentralization starting with the first step of searching knowledge from academia, startups, SMEs, corporate innovation and research teams and tech transfer offices from universities. It includes a marketplace of challenges and business opportunities to match academia and business requests and aims at removing bureaucracy and speeding up the technology and knowledge transfer from academia to industry using smart legal contracts and an automatic payment system with transparency and security.

These days we talk about Collaboration for Innovation and Ecosystem Innovation. Innovation is a huge interactive action, with knowledge being outside the organization. Now you have new digital channels to collaborate, and you have to learn new ways of collaboration for Innovation (Bessant, 2020).

The second part of every chapter in this book follows the "collaboration journey" and applies the subject of the chapter to a phase on your collaboration journey.

Collaboration journey

Not everything is about technology to find knowledge. First, you need to know what your state-of-the-art knowledge and technology are and understand what your needs are. The ultimate goal of getting knowledge is to innovate and collaborate better. In every chapter you will learn a phase of the "collaboration journey". In this chapter you start with the first phase, the "recognition phase" of your knowledge, which leads you to the answer to what kind of knowledge you need for innovation. The recognition phase has three parts: understand, discover and prioritize.

Recognition phase

How to discover which knowledge you need for innovation?

You have to be ready to think ahead. Nowadays, our society has forgotten the importance of thinking before acting. Having time to think and to be responsible for the business decisions has become a luxury. To get a general orientation, consultants or crowdsourcing can help you, but first you have to think yourself. You know your business, you know your customers, you know your team and you know what kind of future you want to have. Thinking to understand is the first step for the success of your innovation.

Understand

Innovation has one idea or several ideas as a starting point. Ideas can come from creative actions, inspiration or connecting the dots. Ideas are generated from your internal thinking and usually are triggered by a problem, an issue or a need. The first step is to understand your organization's needs by starting to ask some questions about what you need to be ready for the future. Do you need a new technology, consulting on deep tech? What do your customers need, what is the customer feedback or what is the employee satisfaction survey telling you?

Figure 1.4 shows a checklist where you can find novel issues, new problems and new needs which maybe you were not aware of. This is the first step to focus where you can innovate. Check the topic you want to focus to think.

WHERE DO I HAVE TO LOOK FOR NEW NEEDS?

☐ CUSTOMER FEEDBACK
☐ ISSUES ON COMPANY PROCESSES
☐ SERVICE DESK TICKETS
☐ USER OBSERVATION DATA
☐ BRAINSTORMING SESSIONS
☐ CONSORTIUM PARTNERS
☐ PROBLEMS TO SOLVE
☐ CHALLENGES TO OVERCOME
☐ DIGITALIZATION
☐ COMPETITOR'S PRODUCTS, SERVICES AND ADDED VALUES
☐ PARTNERS' FEEDBACK
☐ SUPPLIERS' FEEDBACK
☐ A NEW SUPPLIER TECHNOLOGY
☐ IMPROVE A PRODUCT OR SERVICE

Figure 1.4: Knowledge needs: A checklist to find blind spots and the focus for innovation.

Discover

Once you know the area and topic you are going to focus on to find needs, now it's the time to focus on how and where you can gather new knowledge and technology. You can get inspired by experts, by other products, by your customer feedback, by pictures on Instagram, by other ways of doing business in other industries. You can discover new knowledge from your internal thinking about your organization or from external sources of knowledge. Figure 1.5 is a checklist to help you with where to start looking for inspiration and discovering new sources of thinking and ideas. If you need help to think, you can co-think with your team, with employees, with customers, with consultants, but keep in mind your own thinking too. Next, you need to gather extra knowledge to make the solution happen and go to the next step in the innovation process and collaboration journey.

Prioritize

Before you go to the internet to find knowledge, you need to analyze your needs. Figure 1.6 shows a structured way to understand your priorities. You can list your needs and condense them into 3 priorities to focus. Then, analyze if you need extra knowledge or technology to solve the need. And maybe you have this

I AM JUST DISCOVERING	WHERE AM I GETTING INSPIRATION FOR NEW IDEAS FROM?
INTERNAL	**EXTERNAL**
☐ WHAT IS DAMAGING MY BUSINESS? ☐ HOW WOULD I DO MY BUSINESS IF I WANT TO START IT AGAIN? ☐ HOW CAN I HELP IMPROVE THE VISION AND THE MISSION OF MY ORGANIZATION? ☐ HOW CAN I GAIN MARKETPLACE WITH A NEW DIGITAL TOOL? ☐ HOW AND WHAT CAN I DIGITALIZE IN MY ORGANIZATION PROCESS? ☐ ...	☐ NEWSLETTERS ☐ CONFERENCES ☐ GRADUATES AND INTERNSHIPS ☐ EVENTS AND MEETUPS ☐ MASTERCLASSES ☐ WORKSHOPS AND WEBINARS ☐ INFORMAL CONVERSATIONS ☐ NETWORKING EVENTS ☐ CREATING CHALLENGE ☐ ...

Figure 1.5: Innovation and knowledge need checklists to discover new ideas.

knowledge inside the organizations, but first try to analyze further to see if you can cover your need with internal resources.

Furthermore, prioritizing what you need makes you more confident when you talk with experts. First, you have to understand your need and your need for new knowledge. Second, make a list of places where you can find this knowledge and start your search!

In the next chapters you will find the next steps in the "collaboration journey" and practical tips to make changes inside your organization and team. Thinking and understanding is the first step, before looking for the right partner to work with, because if you are bringing a disruptive innovation to the market successfully, you need the right bright minds with you and a high performing team.

Useful skills for creating a culture of knowledge sharing inside the organization
- Create structure for informal knowledge-sharing activities like innovation cafes on Friday afternoons, meet your IT events, observation days, etc.
- Enhance knowledge and innovation community effects, doing webinars and workshops by internal employees and external experts with structure (same day and time of the week).
- Influence a culture with emotional intelligence at the workplace where people are trained to be aware of themselves, aware of others, and aware of the external context to facilitate psychological safety teams.

Useful skills for creating a culture of knowledge sharing outside the organization
- Share podcasts, articles, webinars from other organizations to enhance the external knowledge gathering from inside your organization.
- Invite experts on innovation, digital transformation and other deep tech topic such as quantum, space tech, satellite, biotech, materials to come to your company every month (or do webinars – the key is to get knowledge, not to spend

LIST: WHAT DO I NEED?	SHORT LIST (3): PRIORITIES	WHERE CAN I FIND WHAT I NEED?	INTERNAL KNOWLEDGE
	Need One	Where to find knowledge and technology:	List of people inside the organization who can help.
	Need Two	My own network	Tools within your organization that you can use.
	Need Three	Local ecosystem website	Reactivate past partnerships.
		Accelerator website	...
		Google	
		Newsletters	

(List: Need One, Need Two, Need Three)

Figure 1.6: Innovation and knowledge need analysis for collaboration canvas.

your whole year's budget on one event) to open your team's mind to other perspectives and other expertise.
- Collaborate with academics, startups, SMEs, customers at different levels using webinars, workshops, brainstorming sessions, consulting, student theses, feasibility studies, innovation projects, research, PhDs, technology coaching, soft skills coaching, etc.

Ideas for creating a culture of decentralized innovation
Understand
- Create a culture of thinking, first you think to understand.
- Enhance a culture of being critical of the status quo and current situation.

Discover
- Be open to get inspiration from outside the organization everywhere.
- Go deep and discover new ways of gathering needs.

Prioritize
- Be disciplined, focus on your three main needs.
- Make structure in the way to analyze the knowledge you need and from where to get it.

Checklist for collaboration from decentralization innovation
Understand
- Take time to reflect on your needs and think of what you have.
- It's better to first use your internal knowledge.

Discover
- Make use of newsletters and other sources of knowledge (yes, even Instagram).
- Analyze the content, use your critical sense and think about connections between how the knowledge content can impact your business and how you can use it.

Prioritize
- Stop and re-think about what you really need today for operations and tomorrow for growth.
- Innovation is linked to daily operations and to the future of the organization – don't underestimate the power of innovation.

In this first chapter, I want to share with you conversations about the issue of finding the right knowledge amongst the chaos of the internet, and the importance of being knowledgeable about bias and the complexity of algorithms. Moreover, these conversations confirm the chapter's argument that knowledge is decentralized, everywhere, and innovation is created where knowledge is matched with needs.

Conversation with Dr. Ricardo Baeza-Yates about "Bias on the Web"

Director of Graduate Data Science Programs at Northeastern University, Palo Alto, USA
    CTO at NTENT, Fellow IEEE

What is the concept "Bias on the Web"?

Biases on the Web include data bias, algorithmic bias, interaction bias, evaluation bias, and our own cognitive biases when we use it. As interaction data is used by algorithms as relevance feedback, this creates a vicious cycle that can amplify bias, even more when we put content back in the Web that was created following a biased process (like searching for content and using it, reinforcing the belief of the search engine that this is good content).

How can good algorithmic design reduce the bias?

First, awareness of bias is the first step to reduce bias because you do not create more. Second, if we do data debiasing and we design algorithms that are tailored to mitigate bias, this helps to reduce it. One problem with bias is that many times we do not know the right reference value. For example, what is the right percentage of female readers for this book? Could be 50% but we do not know. However, if we do actions towards the right value, that helps.

What is the main issue of distributed data and Web biases when you try to find the right knowledge to innovate?

There are many issues: (1) the overall size of the Web, with around 200 million websites, implies that it is very hard to search fairly in those billions of pages; (2) the heterogeneity and redundancy of this data plus algorithmic biases in the design of search engines imply that the ranking algorithm will have several biases starting with popularity biases; and (3) as Herbert Simon said, "the wealth of information creates a lack of attention", because also as users we do not have enough time and we end looking at very few results (which is also due to Zipf's law of minimal effort), which biases our behavior towards popular results that reinforce them (ranking bias).

This is the Matthew effect, "the rich get richer and the poor get poorer", reinforcing (1) and (2). This is true for all topics on the Web but particularly for innovation where a lot of content might be in the long tail that received fewer visits as they appear lower in the rankings. One solution is to use very specific queries that can uniquely find this content as generic queries will only find popular content (which is correlated with quality but is not necessarily the best content) instead of the content gems that you wish to find.

Can we improve innovation search?

Yes, there are two ways. The best one is to learn how to search better, using better keywords, for example, unique and non-ambiguous. Using more than 2 words which are not semantically similar, so you match less documents. You can also restrict your search to certain domains, for example universities in the USA (site operator) or to a given university or research centre if you recall the source (e.g., site:http://cwi.nl). Another one would be to create a vertical search engine that collects the best sites in the world. This needs continuous investment to be up to date – and of course there searching would be much easier. The key issue would be to fund such search engine as the standard advertising business model may not work.

Conversation with Dr. Irene López de Vallejo about "Knowledge Decentralization"

Strategic Development and Sustainability at Disco.coop
   @ILdeV

What is decentralized knowledge?

(As this book proves) knowledge creation is not an activity to be conducted in splendid isolation. Historically, it was never a solo activity, but it certainly was centralized, with a few individuals at the top of the pyramid claiming the IP generated by many under them. Today those dynamics have changed, due to the convergence of multiple socio-cultural and techno-economic reasons, and decentralized knowledge generation is becoming the norm. We can speak of a trend that takes place in individuals heads, but only develops through interactions with others, more often than not geographically distributed, across networks of peers and other actors, in a multitude of environments, enabled by a global pervasive digital network (aka the internet). Decentralized knowledge generation is ruled by less egocentric and more collaborative principles, and is eco-centric, with people and its needs at the center.

What is decentralized innovation?

You know better than I do, Jara! Decentralized innovation rides alongside decentralized knowledge generation. This trend is open, it doesn't rely on a central authority to develop and thrive, it doesn´t ask for permission either, or leverages the power of many. Decentralized innovation happens across networks of multiple stakeholders globally distributed, interacting and learning from each other, often responding to specific local needs. Decentralized knowledge creation is an output of decentralized innovation. I believe time and place are not conditioning these processes anymore. Today, in order for innovation that enables knowledge generation to happen, this key aspect of decentralization, enabled by a combination of digital technology and new socio-economic behaviors, allow for those 2 variables to be bent at will.

Which kind of technologies could be adopted by the industry to allow innovation based on this knowledge decentralization? Which could be the technology roadmap?

First, I would like to say that I believe it is decentralized innovation that creates the conditions for decentralized knowledge generation practices to emerge. And these new innovation practices need governance, frameworks and technologies that allow the sustainability of open transparent and fair innovation dynamics. The application of these governance, frameworks and technologies can spur, for example, new ways of working and new business models that hold these principles. Disco.coop is a perfect example.

The technology to base this, as of today, advanced experiment, is a combination of Web 3.0, the next generation of internet technology that also holds the principles mentioned above, with long term work around software that is both free/libre and open-source (FLOSS) and the latest advances around Distributed Ledger Technologies (DLTs). And specifically, we need DLTs, for trusted data sharing is essential in this process. Without it, the knowledge exchanges and interactions mentioned above, that in the digital world materialize as data assets exchanges, cannot move around and be interpreted, reused, recombined, to create further knowledge. And a final word: we don´t need a technology roadmap, we need a roadmap that is inclusive of social, cultural, economic and technological aspects to support open transparent secure and fair decentralized innovation and knowledge creation practices.

Conversation with David King about "Digitalization of Innovation"

CEO Exaptive
  @dking513

What is Exaptive about?

Exaptive is a company devoted to computer-aided innovation. Instead of using technology to automate out human input, Exaptive combines data science with social science to augment and amplify human intelligence and creativity. Exaptive's software makes it easier to connect knowledge from disparate sources, experiment with tools and techniques from different disciplines in new contexts and align teams of diverse experts around complex problems.

What is the problem Exaptive is solving?

Research from Stanford and MIT suggests that clever ideas are getting harder to find (Bloom, 2017). Despite the last 30 years involving a dramatic increase in the number of researchers and knowledge workers employed, economic metrics associated with innovative output remain relatively flat. Radical innovations are still more frequently the result of serendipity than active facilitation.

How Exaptive is doing that?

Biological evolution has consistently generated innovations, called exaptation's, for millennia thanks to systems with high degrees of combinatorial modularity, fluidity, and interaction (Gould, 1982). Exaptive applies these concepts in the software domain to create virtual environments, called "Cognitive Cities", in which knowledge is modeled as a flexible and modular network instead of as the usual rigid and monolithic spreadsheet (King, 2020). On top of this knowledge graph is superimposed a social graph, so that the system knows not just "what" but also "who". Recommendation algorithms then support finding non-obvious but relevant content recommendations by mining the underlying ontology of the data, as well as facilitating the assembly of collaboration teams optimized for innovation based on the science of team science (Contractor, 2013).

What are the results? Do you have an example?

Exaptive's technology has helped both small teams of thought-partners come up with award-winning innovations as well as large-scale organizations discover untapped synergies within their existing portfolios. A humanities professor at a large university exapted techniques from genetics to develop an innovative method of textual lineage analysis. A large NGO exapted techniques from personalized medicine to develop an innovative segmentation tool for country-level health interventions.

Summary

To sum up this chapter, I will leave you with a number of exercises that help ground you in your journey to find your needs of knowledge and technology to innovate.

To practice

1. Make a plan for what kind of knowledge you need.
2. Be positive, you can collaborate remotely to create innovation!
3. You can apply decentralized innovation inside your organization. First step, review your organization's values and check if you have values such as "collaboration", "open communication" and "listening".
4. Understand the impact of changing the way you are working and innovating. You really have to change your mindset to be positive for collaboration.

In the following chapters you will find

– Tools such as a collaborative canvas to manage expectations before starting the collaboration.
– Tips on how to navigate within innovation ecosystems and technology clusters.
– More real stories from interviews with real cases, related to every chapter.

Notes

(Sanger, 2019) https://collabwith.co/2019/09/podcast-larry-sanger-cio-everipedia-and-co-founder-wikipedia-my-career-has-been-about-decentralizing-knowledge-creation-via-the-internet/
(De Maeijer, Asselbergs, 2018) https://collabwith.co/2018/12/podcast-lecture-els-de-maeijer-and-director-emile-asselbergs-on-the-impact-of-communication-in-open-innovation/)
(Jarolím, 2018) https://collabwith.co/2018/10/head-of-retail-at-kh-bank-martin-jarolim-on-innovation-culture-find-new-ways-of-serving-our-clients-better-and-implement-new-solutions-that-is-innovation/
(Bessant, 2020) https://collabwith.co/2020/01/john-bessant-crisis-driven-innovation/
(Phibbs, 2019) https://collabwith.co/2019/02/cmo-cisco-mark-phibbs-on-digitalization-we-have-become-a-broadcaster-and-now-all-events-are-both-online-and-physical/

References

Bloom, Nicholas, Charles Jones, John Van Reenen, and Michael Webb. (2017). "Are Ideas Getting Harder to Find?" https://doi.org/10.3386/w23782.

Chesbrough, Henry. Open Innovation: The New Imperative for Creating and Profiting from Technology. Harvard Business School. 2006.

Contractor N. (2013). Some assembly required: leveraging Web science to understand and enable team assembly. Philosophical transactions. Series A, Mathematical, physical, and engineering sciences, 371(1987), 20120385. https://doi.org/10.1098/rsta.2012.0385

Gould, S., and Vrba, E. (1982). Exaptation – a Missing Term in the Science of Form. Paleobiology, 8(1),4–15. doi:10.1017/S0094837300004310

King, David. (2020). Innovation-Oriented Programming: Software Development as a Medium for Exaptation and Implications for the Active Facilitation of Innovation Within Virtual Environments. 10.1007/978-3-030-45784-6_10.

Mehdi, G., Brandt, S., Roschchin, M., Runkler, T.: Semantic Framework for Industrial Analytics and Diagnostics.

Piller, Frank and Diener, Kathleen. The Third RWTH Open Innovation Accelerator Survey. The Market for Open Innovation: Collaborating in Open Ecosystems for Innovation. September 2019.

"Innovation is absolutely essential in today's world that is in the centre of digital disruption"

Mark Phibbs, CMO CISCO (Phibbs, 2019)

Chapter 2
Connecting Local Ecosystems to Create a Virtual Global Ecosystem

Summary: In this second chapter, you will discover how to search for knowledge and technology. You will get a sense of the importance of digitalization of knowledge and technology, the risk of bias on the Web, how to increase diversity within digital applications and learn how to create trust on digital platforms. This chapter presents the second phase of the "collaboration journey" which includes creating your own landscape of knowledge, technology and requests.

Innovation means impact at a local or global level. Currently, it's difficult to find the knowledge and technology you need because information on the World Wide Web has the issue of "bias on the Web", and because the knowledge and technology you need are maybe not on the same street as your business. It is very important to make visible what is invisible, and here the internet is the enabler. It is also important to digitalize what we can digitalize, for instance, the visualization of knowledge. Nowadays, innovation ecosystems are local. In essence, it is a house, a co-working space where you go to work, or maybe where your business has an office. Sometimes you have a place where the local ecosystem is organizing workshops, conferences, and after-work activities to help you to network locally. If you are lucky, they have innovation consultants and business development managers who can help you to innovate and to find your local partner to work together. Again, if you are lucky you are living in a city where there is a local commitment to innovation, organizing activities to increase the interaction of the local businesses. They may even be competing on the basis of who is the most innovative city or where one can become a successful entrepreneur. Those lucky cities, as you may know, are Berlin, Barcelona, Paris, London, Stockholm, Amsterdam, Madrid, Lisbon, and Budapest in Europe; while in the US you have the very well-known Silicon Valley, or Tel-Aviv in Israel. Of course, there are also new local ecosystems coming in, such as Cape Town in South Africa.

Nevertheless, governments are concerned about rural areas where population and services are disappearing and moving to the big cities, making an unhealthy unbalance of resources and opportunities. The idea of "geo-micro-localization" of innovation ecosystems supports the idea of inequality, forcing entrepreneurs, super innovators and other businesses to move to the "selected" and "innovative" cities. Governments have to think differently when talking about digitalization of rural areas or areas outside the "main cities". Digitalization is not only about infrastructures, which is simply the basis; digitalization means that we can live, work and create impact from any place at any time. For this reason, villages, rural areas, and cities need to create opportunities for sharing knowledge, experiences, opinions,

https://doi.org/10.1515/9783110665383-002

technology, amongst other applications which can be used with the basic infrastructure, such as internet enabled by fiber optic, 4G or 5G networks. Of course, the integration of rural areas into the city means education in respect to innovation, digitalization and entrepreneurship. It also enables people to know how to use the internet, how to have different perspectives, consider opportunities instead of focusing on the lack of resources. It is about the mindset, and how governments need to enable this open and growth-oriented mindset to make it happen.

"Coming from small geographic countries you need to understand scaling up. Canada is a very large country in terms of land, but a very small country in term of population" (Laurin, 2019). Jeremy Laurin has described what it means to scale up for rural areas. It means to connect and to have a mindset of connectivity to the rest of the world.

The European Union, with its funding opportunities, has created the European Open Science Cloud (EOSC), the Community Research and Development Information Service (CORDIS), the European startup map and the Innovation Radar, among others. Those initiatives are the first step in efforts to digitalize and visualize the knowledge and technology around Europe, including startup ecosystems, innovative projects and research projects in an easy way by getting the data from European databases and other sources. The issue with those initiatives is that they are located within European websites. They have the same look and feel, with complicated website names, and lack the appropriate outreach as few know of their existence. In some cases, these initiatives are treated as a project. This means that when project funding finishes, the tool stops operations, making the user experience terrible and the data and mission are lost.

EOSC: European Open Science Cloud (EOSC), is a portal which offers a virtual environment with open and seamless services for storage, management, analysis and re-use of research data, across borders and scientific disciplines by federating existing scientific data infrastructures, currently dispersed across disciplines and the EU member states. The portal is for European researchers and professionals in science, technology, humanities and social sciences. More information at: https://eosc-portal.eu.

Innovation Radar: The Innovation Radar is an initiative of the European Commission focused on the identification of high-potential innovation behind European-funded research and innovation projects. It covers information and communication technologies (ICT) and the best innovators get promoted through dedicated webpages to gain visibility among potential investors, users and buyers. More information at: https://www.innoradar.eu/

CORDIS: The Community Research and Development Information Service (CORDIS) is a rich and structured public repository with all the project information held by the European Commission, such as project factsheets, participants, reports, deliverables and links to open-access publications. The objective is to bring research results to professionals in the field to foster open science, create innovative products and services, and stimulate growth across Europe. More information at: https://cordis.europa.eu/

European Startup Map: The European startup map claims to visualize the European startup ecosystem with just one click. The tool has a nice visual map with a variety of colors where every startup or SME has to enter their data. The data provided is the name of the company which includes a one-line description and a link to their website. The visualization is always through the map. More information at: http://www.startupeuropemap.eu/

An issue with these initiatives is that they are stand-alone initiatives, meaning they are not connected with each other. As an innovation leader, you must visit, and know, all the different websites and where to find exactly the knowledge you need. Another issue is that these websites focus on data visualization using maps, which may be nice to look at, but it's very unfriendly to use if you don't have the time to explore all the potential connections.

Another issue is that there are not many interactions possible from the data visualization maps, despite selling the collaboration on the "front page". Additionally, an issue I encountered is that the data provided is not usable. It is missing a clear user experience (UX) and user design strategy. This is very important for innovation, for if you want users to use your products and services, they have to have a good design (including graphic design) and a good information architecture. Software developers have to work together with UX and graphic designers to understand the user journey with the user's interactions, needs and how they use the product (or if they need the product at all). You have to understand that it is not only the software developer who designs the product or service, because then the product will be terrible for the user. The popular design thinking approach is very important here. It is useful to understand how to design a good product or service. Design thinking has to be applied correctly. Firstly, good application of design thinking includes being serious and responsible about creating a new product or service. This does not refer to a team-building activity, but rather when you spend time observing your target customer (aka user). When you really spend time understanding and talking to your target customer, you collect all the unstructured data (yes, sorry, the best data is unstructured data), and once you analyze that data with your team, you consider what you want to create, what the user needs, and what are the actual issues at hand. Therefore, you think about the solutions to the problems discovered through your analysis. The brainstorming part is very serious too, as it not only applies to "science fiction" ideas. If you want to have a good product and service, you simply have to dedicate some time to thinking. Seriously think. Then you prototype your product in real life, even for software. It doesn't have to be complex, as it could be just a paper prototype which you test with a minimum of 10 target customers. From the test, you get feedback, you analyze the feedback, you think again with your team, and then you prototype again. In all those phases, the software developer is one of the participants. If you want to know more about design thinking, there are plenty of books available. Remember that the user should be at the center of all your decisions.

Let's visualize a solution for your digitalization of the innovation ecosystem. Figure 2.1 shows a perfect example of a local innovation ecosystem in a city where every actor is connected to their own "hub". You can see entities such as small businesses, universities, startups, corporates, venture capitals, and then you find the individuals such as academics, entrepreneurs, angel investors, ecosystem members and professionals, including consultants, coaches, and other experts. In order to enhance connectivity and visibility of local professionals, you have to connect the local hubs to other local hubs, or even better, you have to connect the local hubs to one virtual global ecosystem where everyone is interconnected.

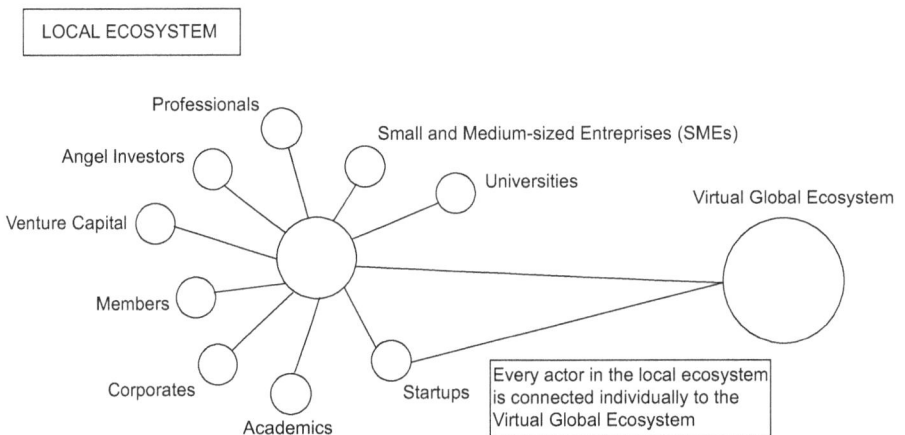

Figure 2.1: Connecting local ecosystems to a global virtual ecosystem.

Only when those local ecosystems are connected can one find hidden knowledge, technology and partners. You need local ecosystems for your business to cover your technical needs and, hence, support your ideas and bring them to the market. Technically, it is embedded in a peer-to-peer distributed network, which is then found in a decentralized network, where the global virtual ecosystem is facilitating peer-to-peer connectivity with a non-peer-to-peer network. This connection is virtual which enhances the connectivity between everyone in the ecosystem. It's a network where the actors are well connected to the local ecosystem hub. Then the hubs are connected to the global virtual ecosystem where the decentralization means that every actor can be found and potentially connected to everyone. The connections are happening based on the business needs of the individuals. Figure 2.2 shows an example of connectivity between the different local ecosystems. Every local ecosystem is connected as well as being connected to the global virtual ecosystem.

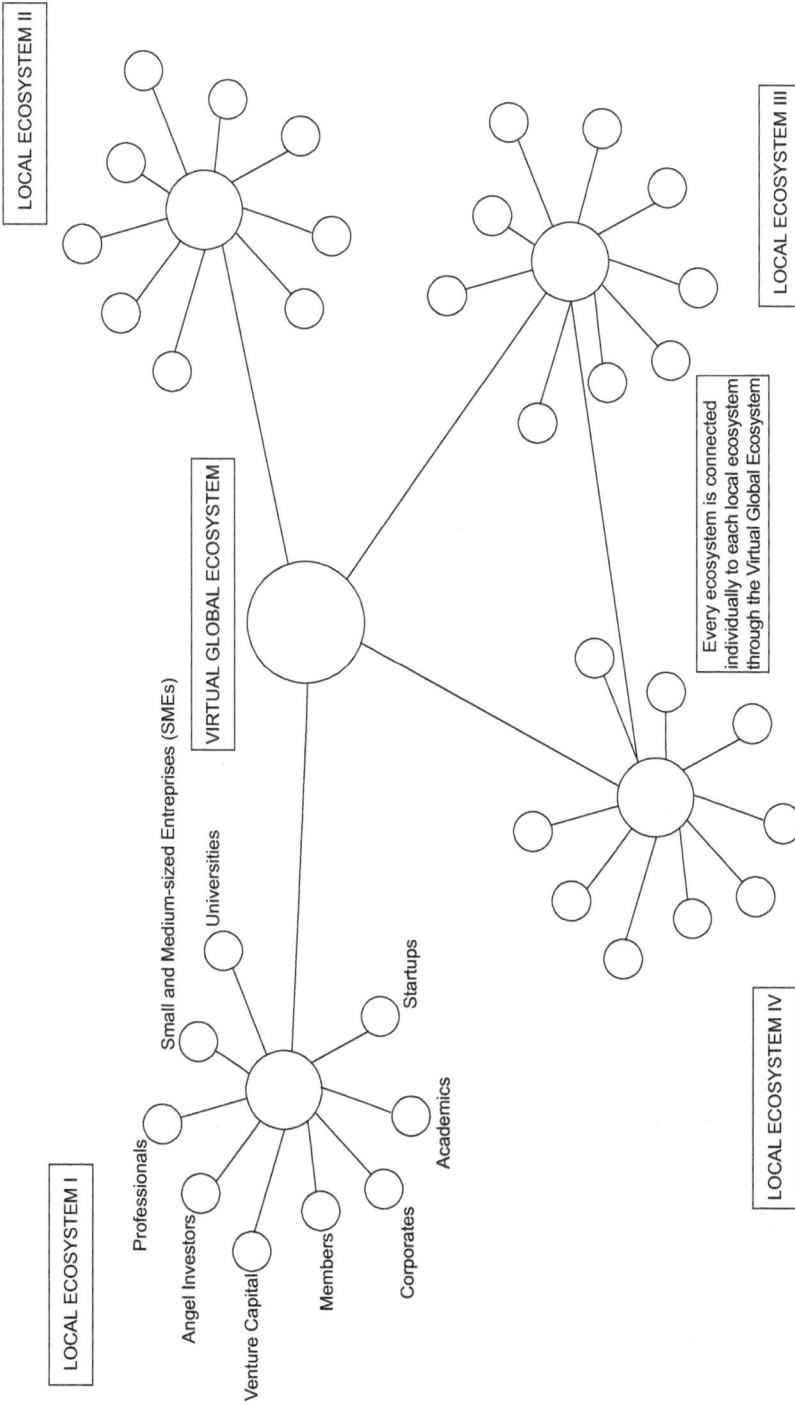

LOCAL ECOSYSTEM II

LOCAL ECOSYSTEM III

LOCAL ECOSYSTEM I

LOCAL ECOSYSTEM IV

VIRTUAL GLOBAL ECOSYSTEM

Small and Medium-sized Entreprises (SMEs)

Professionals

Universities

Angel Investors

Venture Capital

Members

Corporates

Academics

Startups

Every ecosystem is connected individually to each local ecosystem through the Virtual Global Ecosystem

Figure 2.2: Connecting local ecosystems to a global virtual ecosystem hub: more connectivity.

"You cannot solely be a domestic entrepreneur, you have to be born global," says Jeremy Laurin, VP Business Development and Commercialization at Ontario Centers of Excellence and Adjunct Professor at York University Faculty of Health, Canada (Laurin, 2019).

Let's get practical! As Jeremy Laurin remarked, if you have a business you cannot expect that your first customer lives on the same street as yourself. The same is true when you are looking for a partner to do research with. In order to find a research partner, you need to look for virtual places in which knowledge is disseminated, visible and easy to interact with. This is what is called the global virtual ecosystem. Currently, one of the issues is that only academics, startups, SMEs, or companies who are savvy with SEO tools will have a Web presence with a wide reach. Those who manage to become influencers, experts or very well-connected professionals are those who achieve visibility and get connected first for collaborations. Users face an issue of diversity and regarding the "long tail of content", either online or offline.

Diversity in networks is mainly in the long tail of the data that is hard to find on the Web

A practical example of this is when we are looking for academics in the field of nanotechnology, but you always find the same research papers, projects and professors. This is due to a popularity bias in the ranking of algorithms in Web search engines. It might be that the people in the field of nanotechnology don't spend enough time on their "visibility" on the Web. Hence, the less prominent researchers at a university who are experts in the field of nanotechnology who could provide the right material for you are not found. So, you only see the data from researchers who are active, which is known as activity bias. The same applies to technology, startups or other corporate information you need. This issue of unseen information is called the "digital desert" by Ricardo Baeza-Yates. An example of this is that 4% of the people are doing 50% of reviews on Amazon, as most of the "internet users" are passive. This is what Nielsen termed the 90-9-1 participation rule in 2006. That is, 1% of internet users generate content, 9% comment on it and 90% just look. Baeza-Yates' results show that this distribution is even more skewed, as on Twitter 2% of the active users generate half of the tweets. Therefore, online content is created by only a small percentage of internet users. Another bias is termed "presentation or exposure bias". This is illustrated when you click on content that is recommended for you, and therefore do not click on the rest of the content that is not "presented" to you, also due to popularity bias. This creates a vicious feedback loop that magnifies popularity bias if you do not mitigate it. These activity and presentation biases are the main reason for the "invisibility" of content on current digital ecosystems.

When creating the global virtual ecosystem, it is important to consider creating systems and solutions which are aware of those biases and are also aware that the data is hard to find. There is an urgency to build better applications and algorithms based on deep learning which are aware of these biases. Baeza-Yates mentions different approaches to overcome this activity and presentation bias. Those different approaches include better sampling of data, being aware of presentation and selection bias when working with personalization and contextualization, for example with matchmaking algorithms. He also mentions the need to empower diversity, novelty, and serendipity when building new Web systems to reduce the long tail and the digital desert effects.

Diversity and bias on the Web, as Baeza-Yates calls it, is about gender, geographical, economic, and linguistic biases in data and other effects caused by our cultural and cognitive biases, besides the algorithmic and behavioral biases in the interaction, such as activity and presentation bias (Baeza-Yates, 2018).

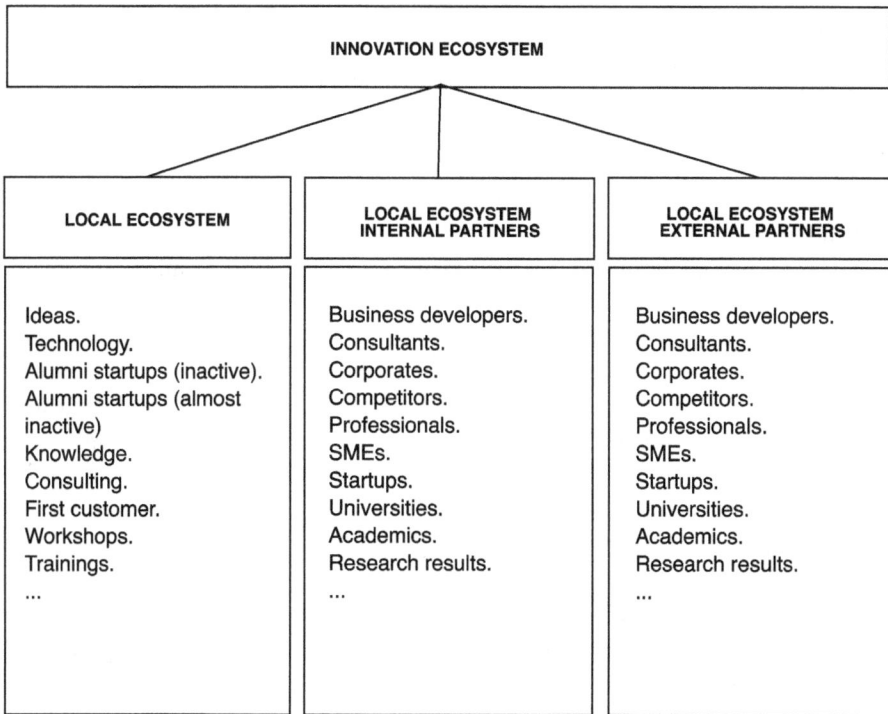

INNOVATION ECOSYSTEM		
LOCAL ECOSYSTEM	**LOCAL ECOSYSTEM INTERNAL PARTNERS**	**LOCAL ECOSYSTEM EXTERNAL PARTNERS**
Ideas. Technology. Alumni startups (inactive). Alumni startups (almost inactive) Knowledge. Consulting. First customer. Workshops. Trainings. ...	Business developers. Consultants. Corporates. Competitors. Professionals. SMEs. Startups. Universities. Academics. Research results. ...	Business developers. Consultants. Corporates. Competitors. Professionals. SMEs. Startups. Universities. Academics. Research results. ...

Figure 2.3: Local Innovation ecosystem for thinking of collaboration.

How can you avoid biases to improve finding necessary knowledge and technology?

If you are only working within a local ecosystem, you have the problem of being localized with your knowledge and technology also being localized. In this case, you can find issues of diversity and bias too. If you have a digital ecosystem, you have diversity and bias as a problem on top of long tail and digital desert issues. These problems can be solved by analyzing what in ecosystem is, keeping in mind that the collaboration and interaction among ecosystem members are the most important objectives. The core activities have to be sharing knowledge, expertise, technology, contacts, business opportunities, challenges to solve and research. It would be useful as well to create a pool of "supporters", where every member can go to resolve questions about tax, legal, accounting, patent, and policy issues along with financing opportunities. Also, an online pool of multimedia content is needed to get easy and quick access to knowledge about innovation, entrepreneurship, collaboration, networking, and how-to tips on writing pitches for investors, grants, and business models. Innovation and business development consultants together with startup coaches have to be available to every actor in the global virtual ecosystem, facilitating partnerships and interaction.

Useful skills for reducing bias in your digital ecosystem
– Create content for passive users, such as pools of "supporters" and "multimedia content" to help your ecosystem members.
– Engage your community to make the members active with education on network thinking for innovation.
– Make all your research, academics and startups visible online to improve their visibility, reducing activity and presentation bias.
– Enhance visibility of your long tail with activities dedicated for members who are not active or visible with webinars, community members' communication, interviews, etc.
– Train individuals in serendipity thinking, where members introduce other professionals to the ecosystem.

Figure 2.3 differentiates between the local ecosystem, the internal partners who are part of the ecosystem (public entity, innovation institution or co-working space), and the external partners who are not locally operating. Another type of "innovation ecosystem" is your own innovation ecosystem. Furthermore, you have to create your own network or your own ecosystem network by combining several networks (local ecosystem network and other external networks) (Figure 2.4). The information on how to create your own innovation ecosystem is further explained in Chapter 6. There are different levels of networks when you start looking for knowledge or technology. The key to the global virtual ecosystem is that you can create your own virtual ecosystem.

YOUR OWN ECOSYSTEM		
YOUR LOCAL ECOSYSTEM	**YOUR ECOSYSTEM'S OWN NETWORK**	**YOUR OWN NETWORK**
Ideas. Technology. Alumni startups (inactive) Alumni startups (almost inactive) Knowledge. Consulting. First customer. Workshops. Trainings. ...	Business developers. Consultants. Corporates. Competitors. Professionals. SMEs. Startups. Universities. Academics. Research results. ...	Business developers. Consultants. Corporates. Competitors. Professionals. SMEs. Startups. Universities. Academics. Research results. ...

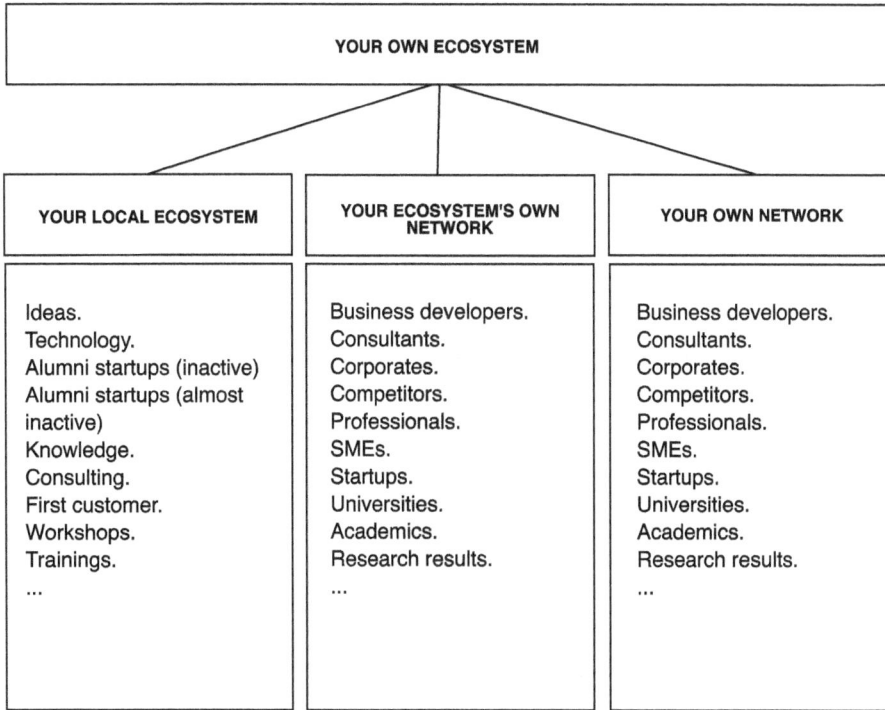

Figure 2.4: Your own innovation ecosystem for thinking of collaboration.

"Trust forms over time, through the creative input of agentic individuals. Relational forms correspond to different forms of relational risks." says Svein Tvedt Johansen, Professor at UiT The Arctic University of Norway (Johansen, 2018).

How can you trust in a digital environment?

It's a new paradigm. It's not only about trust in digital environments but also trust in people, systems, brands, etc. The creation of global virtual ecosystems implies the digitalization of local ecosystems and this digitalization opens up the question of trust: How can you create trust in a digital environment when you have to work together with partners you don't know personally for research and innovation?

There is still an issue of trust with respect to algorithms as well as recommendations for building business and innovation relationships. The interviews and conversations with Collabwith members resulted in the finding that there is a lack of trust on automatic recommended profiles on the Collabwith platform. Members preferred to have a personal recommendation to another partner or preferred to continue working with the previous partners. For instance, one marketing VP from a consulting firm mentioned that they prefer to work with the same professor from one university when doing white papers together. The risk for them to change is too high because they cannot trust a new person if they don't have any references or know them. They are afraid of failure and disappointment, or of trusting the wrong partner. For them, it's a big effort to build a new relationship and discover that they don't work well together. The approach taken by the Collabwith platform, which is building a global virtual ecosystem, is that the recommendation and matches are an offline service, instead of an automated recommendation system inside the online platform.

Let's look at another online platform whose services have a critical trust component. These online services have a sensitive approach to trust. When the trust component is mixed with risk, privacy and private lives, it concerns the most critical sense of trust in a digital environment. For instance, there are online applications dedicated to booking "grandchildren" by grandparents who want to have a companion. Alternatively, the application permits the booking of "babysitters" by parents who are on holidays or for special events, requiring someone to take care of their children. If you look at these examples of trust inside an online platform environment, you may find offline activities generate online trust. For the Papa app, an application to contract a grandchild on demand, only 4% of the "grandchild" applicants are accepted and become members of the community. They have to be empathetic, patient and skilled conversationalists. The Papa platform provides tips and support on how to socialize as well as train the elderly members to be more skilled in regard to digital and social media networks, which is essential for their online application. As trust is generated from transactions, the Papa online platform has a cost related to the service of around $15-30 per month, and $15 per hour. The pricing is related to a sense of responsibility and commitment to the service (Fast Company, 2018).

In Spain, there is a similar online platform called "Adopta un Abuelo" (adopt a grandparent). They accept only 5% of the applicants, and it's a voluntary transaction where the voluntary "grandchildren" are 90% women. "Adopta un Abuelo" has a training for the voluntary "grandchild" before spending time with the selected "grandparents". The recommendation service is done offline (El Pais, 2018).

In Norway, minTidbank is defined as a social peer-to-peer matching service that connects people who wish to share their time and services with older people who seek companionship and help. minTidbank has fully digitalized the appointment service via the online platform. Prof. Svein Tvedt Johansen researched the Norwegian platform and said "sharing time and services with strangers constitute a new type of social situation. Building trust hence also means developing mutual expectations and norms about the situation. It's about how people create trust with other people interacting on the same service-platform" (Johansen, 2018). Prof. Johansen defines trust as "how people understand the situation, as a market exchange, as a personal relationship or a combination of the two. Usually, consumer-to-consumer platforms and interactions derive from more typical market transactions in which there is a price and a specific expectation" (Johansen, 2018).

Holiday Sitters (https://holiday-sitters.com/) is a platform to book a babysitter on demand which operates in the Netherlands, Germany, Austria and Ireland. They select 7% of the babysitter applications after checking their background and references. Besides the background check, they ensure that the babysitters have first-aid training, are active with music, arts and sports, and speak several languages. Holiday Sitters includes a "Trust & Safety" manifesto on their front page. In addition, every sitter's profile inside the babysitter's directory has reviews and icons with their preferred activities and visible cost.

The examples above are successful because they create a platform including a mix of offline and online services to generate trust. The digital platform has to ensure that interactions and relationships developed between the users of the platform have a quality of interaction and enhance positive feelings towards the platform. While having a benefit for both types of users of the digital platform, in the cases above, the benefits are for the temporary grandparents and the grandchildren, and for the parents, children and babysitters. If the offline relationship and experience doesn't work, it will have a negative impact on the platform performance. You can learn from those sensitive cases and apply the best practices to your digital platform and digital ecosystem.

Useful skills for creating trust in a digital environment
- Create a mix of online and offline services. Not everything needs to be online.
- Include support training for the activities that the platform is offering and digital training to help the users to adapt to use the services in a digital way to influence trust inside the online community.
- Create clear expectations for transactions and how the online platform works.
- Ensure a positive experience with the offline and online service.
- Help create a quality relationship between the platform members.
- Trust is created over time.
- Identify risk in your digital environment and create activities to minimize the risk and increase trust.

What does trust generation mean in a new relationship and collaboration for innovation?

There is an interesting link between trust and motivation for innovation. The motivation of the relationship and collaboration is to bring a new product or service to the market or to do research together. Trust is based on this motivation to create innovation, and trust in the product that you are bringing to the market. Trust is related to your self-confidence and how good you can deal with uncertainty. As you know, innovation is how you deal with uncertainty because you don't know how your innovative solution will perform on the market. Collaboration for innovation is when you as a team can deal with this uncertainty and how self-confident you are together about your innovative solution. You need to know that only 1 in 10 startups are successful (Forbes, 2015), where a startup is defined as a small business bringing an innovative product or service to the market.

Ideas for generating trust for motivation

Goals
- What are the main motives for the collaboration?
- What are the main motives for creating the new product or service?

Decision making
- Why do you choose to pursue certain goals?
- Who is making the decision for the new product or service?

Influence
- How can you motivate yourself to work harder?
- How can you motivate your team to work harder?

Equity
- How to create balance between individual efforts and what the team is receiving from rewards?
- How to manage expectations of the team and the collaboration? (Adams, 1960).

Checklist for values for motivation to create collaboration and innovation

Innovation
- Creativity.
- Impact.
- Create value.
- Open for technology.
- Change.

Collaboration
- Working together.
- Communication.
- Transparency.
- Sharing knowledge.
- Respect.

Relationships
- Increase empathy.
- Overcome frustration.
- Create a safe psychological environment.

- Understanding of failure.
- Inspire motivation.

The second part of every chapter in this book follows the "collaboration journey" and applies the subject of the chapter to a phase in your collaboration journey.

Collaboration journey

Searching Phase: Let's apply the subject of this chapter to our "collaboration journey", as we did in the first chapter. The second phase of the "collaboration journey" is the searching phase. You have worked in the previous chapter on your business or research needs. Now, you already know what you need, and it's time to start building your strategy for searching for the technology and knowledge you described. In the previous chapter you learned about the recognition phase of the "collaboration journey". The third step, prioritize, is described in Figure 1.6. You also summarized the needs of knowledge and technology, and where to find them. In this second searching phase, you have to start searching and writing down the results of your search, including the professionals and leaders who have the knowledge and technology you need.

This visualization of your searching results will help you understand your own landscape of knowledge and technology that is required for you and your organization. Whether you are part of a local ecosystem or not, it's important to ask for information from your local consultant or institutions and also to start looking for knowledge and partners externally, outside your own network and local ecosystem network. You have to use the online tools that are mentioned in Chapter 2, such as the Innovation Radar, European startup map, EOSC, CORDIS, and Collabwith, to investigate. Alternative places to look for knowledge are the websites of each university, including research projects, academic directories, and accelerators websites where you can find the rosters of their startups. Sometimes, co-working spaces have a list of members on their websites and venture capital firms have a list of businesses and startups they are funding and engaging with. Other traditional ways to find interesting professionals with interesting knowledge is to attend networking events, conferences, workshops, webinars or accelerator events when you let serendipity help you to meet the right people. You have to keep in mind that search tools such as Google have their limitations in finding knowledge because their search results are populated with paid content (first search results are paid content too), tainted by search engine optimization (SEO), which savvy websites use to increase the activity and presentation bias that is mentioned in this chapter. Other online social media tools you can use are LinkedIn, Twitter and ResearchGate for professional work and research respectively.

Figure 2.5 illustrates the table of the second search results. The objective of this table is to help you to visualize your findings and search results. The first column

STATE OF THE ART ON TECHNOLOGY AND RESEARCH	DESCRIPTION	WHAT DO I KNOW AND HAVE?	EXTERNAL KNOWLEDGE OR INTERNAL TEAM AND ORGANIZATION	READY TO EXPLORE
Make it easy, a list of new technology and research which is interesting for you.	Define here what this technology is about and why the research is relevant for you.	Find out if you or your organization has part of the technology or knowledge already.	List of people, startups, academics and other organizations who have this technology and knowledge you need. For instance: Companies. Industry. Potential partners.	Write here an example of a request to those external people you have to reach: Title. Request description. Timelines. Budget involved (first estimation). Objectives. Priority or urgency.

Figure 2.5: Analysis of your search results before making a concrete request.

shows the description with the names of the new technology and research you found interesting. The second column is there to describe why it is relevant for you, along with a description of what the technology is about. The third column is to help you to understand that sometimes your organization has previously done a similar project or developed a similar technology that you can re-use and re-build for your current needs. The fourth column is about the people who own the knowledge and technology you need, with organization names and real professional or academic names. The last column illustrates how you will express your needs for them. This final step will help you to understand your needs and reflect on the options you have when you make a request to them. This is the first step before contacting any professional or academic. You have to have a clear overview of what you need, what your conditions are and what your expectations are.

Landscape of Knowledge: This landscape is useful for mapping your knowledge with the knowledge you and your business need, derived from the exercises in the first step ("recognition phase" of the "collaboration journey"). You have to write down the technology name, the contact details of that person, and the organization, startup, institution and academic who have this knowledge. For instance, if you are looking for data mining applications for datacenters, and you are looking for research information, you might find Prof. Dr. Fetzer from TU Dresden in Germany. You have to map every piece of required knowledge following the template in Figure 2.5.

Landscape of Technologies: The table in the Figure 2.5 helps you translate your needs into real options and real sources. This table will allow you to find your required technology for your organization and who is behind the products, services or other applications you need. This landscape is your landscape of technologies based on your needs and priorities. You visualize your state-of-the-art technology, what you already have in-house (even if it's an older version or similar product), existing or new technology and which level of development is ready for the market or still needs some development. You have to map every required piece of technology following the template in Figure 2.5.

Landscape of Requests: You should write down the structure of the requests, including title, description, timelines, objectives, informal comments, level of priority, budget involved, and purpose. Of course, the first step is to have a discussion with the person (professional, entrepreneur, academic or consultant), before signing a contract with them, but you have to mention your intention and purpose. The more explicit and detailed the request is, the faster the process of collaboration. One of the key aspects is to manage expectations from the first contact and interaction with the person you want to collaborate with. You can kick off the request by sending an email or by using the Collabwith button "Make a Request", or soon the Collabwith button on other websites and knowledge and technology directories.

Ideas for creating your landscape of knowledge and technology

Understand
- What is the exact name of the new technology you need?
- Why is this technology or knowledge relevant for you?

Discover
- Check if your organization or others have developed similar technology you can re-use.
- Who has the knowledge and who owns the technology?

Prioritize
- Structure your knowledge and technology request.
- Make clear what you need by when from whom and under which conditions.

In the next chapter on connecting innovation ecosystems, I talk with thought leaders and professionals who are currently creating a highly effective ecosystem and community. The following conversations reveal the reasons for this connectivity and open mindset and how platforms work as a key factor for growth.

Conversation with MEP Susana Solís Pérez about "Innovation Ecosystems"

Member of the European Parliament
@susanasolisp

What does it mean to have a strong European innovation ecosystem?

Having a strong innovation ecosystem for Europe means to have "more and better Europe". The foundations of the idea of Europe we have today lay on three concepts: rule of law, freedom (free market, free movements, individual rights) and welfare state. Innovation provides us with novel ways to move and connect with others. Innovation allows companies to compete, thrive and success in free markets. Innovation demands highly skilled employees and better education. Innovation ensures well-paid employments, better public services and guarantees our safety and good health (e.g., vaccines). In summary, to promote a strong innovation ecosystem for Europe is one of the ways we have within our grasp to build Europe.

What is the impact of digitalization on knowledge sharing and collaboration for innovation in Europe?

Digitalization is one of the main drivers of innovation. On the one hand, it accelerates the development of novel solutions, products and services and, on the other hand, it contributes to the democratization of innovation: digitalization enables data sharing and open access to data, thus allowing SMEs and individuals to use new sources of knowledge for their innovations.

Why is it important to have the relevant knowledge and information for increasing innovation in Europe in an accessible and digital format?

Technical innovations have led to the generation of large sets of heterogeneous data. Just as an example: our clinical data includes our clinical history, biochemical data from our blood samples, diagnostic imaging, genetic information and many other different types of data. All aspects in our daily life (the way we drive, the way we buy, even the way we feed ourselves) generate an enormous quantity of data. Digitalization helps us to gather this data, it gives us novel insights about how this data is related and allows us to better understand the challenges we face. This is the very first step to start to innovate.

How can organizations digitize their knowledge to support innovation and collaboration at European level?

FAIR principles (Findability, Accessibility, Interoperability, and Reuse of digital assets) is a good starting point for guiding organizations in how they should digitize, and public administrations should play a leading role in the adoption of these principles as they are a driving force for other organizations. Among the FAIR principles, interoperability is of utmost importance within the European context and it should be placed at the forefront of the digitalization process.

Conversation with Miguel García González about "Innovation Radar"

Innovation Director at Bosonit
    @mig_garcia

Why and how were you using the Innovation Radar?

My use of the Innovation Radar was within the context of a European H2020 project called Innovation Radar Support Services (IRSUS, www.irsus.eu). I was the coordinator of this initiative which helped startups identified via the Innovation Radar reach the market in better conditions through the provision of support services like online trainings, investment readiness programs, assistance with events, mentoring, etc.

What kind of actors and ecosystems were involved in the Innovation Radar?

We provided support to 89 startups from all corners of Europe in a project which was led by Zabala Innovation Consulting and had the participation of Innomine, IESE Business School, Docomo Digital and Etventure.

What are the results from the Innovation Radar?

Results emerging from funded actions are often unknown by stakeholders and the general public. It is essential that the results of R&D investment reach the relevant actors who can bring these innovations to the market (startups, large companies, investors, venture capitalists or business angels), so that European impact of these investments is guaranteed. The main goal of IRSUS has been to pave the road to the market for startups linked to H2020 research and innovation funding. In the framework the Innovation Radar, IRSUS project was selected to bring European startups to the next level. IRSUS aimed to bridge the gaps faced by startups to reach the market with a feasible, viable and attractive business case and strategy for users, clients, partners, and investors (Zabala, 2020).

Conversation with Marcin Plociennik about "EOSC Digital Innovation Hub"

EOSC DIH Business Pilot Coordinator, PSNC

What is the EOSC Digital Innovation Hub?

The European Open Science Cloud (EOSC) is a European initiative and digital platform for the scientific community that aims to provide seamless access to data and interoperable services for the whole research data cycle across scientific disciplines. The EOSC Digital Innovation Hub, as part of this initiative, is an international and multi-partner cooperation that supports commercial companies in accessing and utilizing the digital technologies and services offered by the EOSC. It combines different services to help companies become more competitive and those services can be grouped under the main pillars of piloting and co-design, technical services access, training, visibility and funding opportunities.

How do you enhance the innovation and research ecosystem of Europe with the EOSC Digital Innovation Hub?

Most of the digital innovation hubs in Europe are regional and domain-specific. The EOSC DIH, as part of wider European EOSC initiative, is one of the pan-European DIHs that collaborates closely not only with leading scientific research centers around Europe but also with the regional DIHs (like in Italy, Poland), while on the other hand it has established links with the wider DIH initiatives in Europe like DIHNET. The main purpose of such activities is the exchange of the innovations and knowledge to better support the companies. The EOSC DIH is referenced in a number of EOSC-related projects in the R&D area as a mechanism for exploitation and collaboration between research and the SME ecosystem.

How do you enhance collaboration for innovation with the EOSC Digital Innovation Hub?

We are engaging the companies through both direct engagement as well as open calls, providing the technical expertise and matchmaking EOSC services to be further exploited by SMEs for building new added value services. Through regular community meetings we try to engage the members to present their success stories and new ideas, give access to a network of research institutions and highlight new funding opportunities. We are present at conferences and fairs, both in the EOSC and Cloud/HPC area as well as in the industrial events, giving a way for dissemination and promotion of DIH members products, offers and services.

How do you envision the future of the EOSC Digital Innovation Hub?

The EOSC DIH is one of the important elements of the future EOSC operational ecosystem, being a natural single-entry point for the exchange of knowledge and innovation, testing and validation, and bridging the scientific world and business in EOSC. We hope that the EOSC DIH will grow constantly over the coming years, providing the platform and means for collaboration for innovation.

Conversation with Galit Bauer about "Digital Trust"

Co-Founder and COO Holiday-Sitters.com
   @holidaysitters

How do you create trust in your digital platform among parents?

We asked ourselves first: What is trust? It's very hard to define how to create trust in an online environment. We looked at the offline experience, at how parents recommend babysitters to each other. We were thinking how we can create a holy space online for this very delicate issue. For instance, Airbnb is a booking marketplace for material things such as apartments, in our case, it's your kid, it's the most precious thing in life. Our mantra states that we have to trust ourselves first and it has nothing bad to happen. Our platform is all transparent, you can see the babysitter profiles, you can chat with us and ask questions, you can see videos, it's open, you can investigate everything before booking an hour with a babysitter. We see a lot of clients, they go throughout the process, and then we ask them: what can we help you with to complete the booking? Because sometimes they need only to hear a person behind the process.

Are you using a recommendation algorithm?

Our algorithm has the basic functions to find the sitter: what the customer needs based on language, location and the age of the kid they can deal with. The search results will appear by the sitter with the most reviews. Inside the platform you can see sitters with more than 20–30 reviews written by parents. And no one of the sitters are getting less than five stars because we have a long selection process. It's very trustworthy, even the price is what you get, there are no hidden costs, everything is clear and transparent.

What is the recruiting process for sitters?

The recruiting process is very thorough, sitters have the application form with two phases, one is about their personal data and personal information and their photo. If we see the application is suitable, we schedule a video interview and we discuss their experience. In the following phase, sitters have to do a video, do a first-aid certificate online because attention and commitment are required to become a sitter. For instance, if a sitter declines a job, we call her to ask what is happening. This is a way that we are treating them very seriously and very professionally. This is part of the trust, if the sitter cannot come, then the customer will have another sitter immediately. During the recruiting process for sitters, there are a lot of drop-offs, therefore we focus on really committed sitters. Personally, I make every sitter active, as I am checking personally every sitter before adding them into the platform.

Summary

To sum up this chapter, I will leave you with a number of exercises that help to understand technology as a tool for innovation and collaboration, not as a solution.

To practice

1. Take into account the activity and presentation bias in the online tools.
2. Create your landscape of knowledge needs and sources.
3. Create your landscape of technology needs and sources.
4. Make a request for collaboration – you never know.

In the following chapters you will find

–   Tips on how to collaborate with startups, academics and other innovation organizations.
–   Tips on how to use emotional intelligence to increase the success of your research and innovation collaboration.
–   More real stories from interviews with real cases, related to every chapter.

Notes

(Phibbs, 2019) https://collabwith.co/2019/02/cmo-cisco-mark-phibbs-on-digitalization-we-have-become-a-broadcaster-and-now-all-events-are-both-online-and-physical/

(Laurin, 2019) https://collabwith.co/2019/04/podcast-ispim-ottawa-jeremy-laurin-on-scaling-start-ups-as-entrepreneurs-that-need-to-learn-that-your-very-first-customer-might-not-be-from-your-backyard

(Fast Company, 2018) https://www.fastcompany.com/90227821/the-papa-app-lets-seniors-book-grandkids-on-demand

(El Pais, 2018) https://elpais.com/cultura/2018/08/27/actualidad/1535393514_817110.html

(Zabala, 2020) https://www.zabala.eu/en/news/irsus-european-parliament

https://ec.europa.eu/research/participants/documents/downloadPublic?documentIds=080166e5c9e2f704&appId=PPGMS

(Forbes, 2015) https://www.forbes.com/sites/neilpatel/2015/01/16/90-of-startups-will-fail-heres-what-you-need-to-know-about-the-10/#78f8ff446679

(Equity Theory of Motivation, Adams, 1960), http://perpus.univpancasila.ac.id/repository/EBUPT190088.pdf#page=150

References

Baeza-Yates, R. Bias on the Web. Communications of ACM 61(6), pp. 54–61, 2018. http://www.
     websci16.org/sites/websci16/files/keynotes/keynote_baeza-yates.pdf
Johansen, ST., Foss, L. "Learning to share time: Trust in a consumer, to consumer network", 2018.

"We sometimes need outsiders to point out our strengths, such as academics"

Joost d'Hooghe, VP DSM Engineering Materials (d'Hooghe, 2019)

Chapter 3
Collaboration with Academia, Startups, Industry, Government, Suppliers, Research Centers, etc

Summary: In this chapter, you are going to learn about 360-degree collaboration, with whom to collaborate, and accepting speed and digitalization in collaboration for innovation. You will also get the first detailed tour of the collaboration canvas.

Did you know that you don't have to do everything by yourself? Innovation is one of those special areas that cannot be done alone. If you recall, innovation is creating value from creativity. This value is created when you bring your idea to the market and people or a company are using it! Even in the whole process of generating ideas, looking for problems or needs, making "concepts of solutions", making prototypes, testing, "bringing to the market", etc., there is always a "co" attached with each action. What this means includes: co-designing, co-creating, co-testing, co-prototyping, co-bringing to the market, co-communicating. The "co" means collaboration, essentially working together.

In the previous chapters, you have learned to identify your needs, to understand that knowledge is out there, somewhere, and you have to find it in a fast and efficient way. The next step is to categorize the knowledge and technology you need. In Figure 3.1 you can find the different key elements for innovation. It could apply to bringing your idea to the market, even if you are working in a small or medium-sized enterprise (SME), or if you are working in an innovation team at a

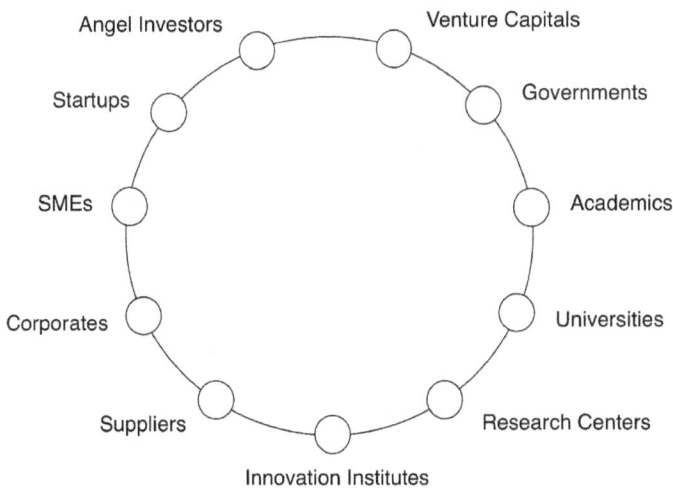

Figure 3.1: Collaboration journey opportunities and actors inside the ecosystem.

https://doi.org/10.1515/9783110665383-003

corporate organization, or even if you are an angel investor. You have to know that everyone in the circle displayed in Figure 3.1 is part of the collaboration ecosystem in society. You might need them depending on your innovation project, idea, or startup objectives, but also you might need them based on your knowledge needs. You will find it a little bit overwhelming to think about all of them. However, the objective here is to give you a new perspective and an overview of all the possibilities for collaboration. This is only an example, as maybe you have a new category in mind in which you have already collaborated.

Let's start with the example of corporates. Figure 3.2 displays connections within the circle from "corporates" to the next "nodes" in the circle. Some corporates even lack the required knowledge and the capacity to innovate in the direction they need.

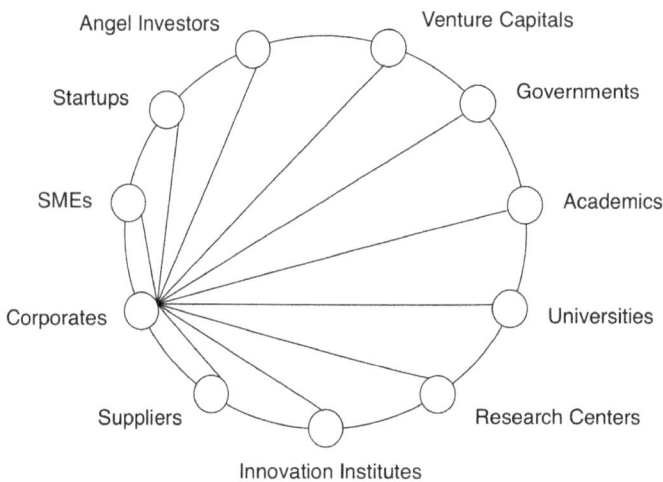

Figure 3.2: Collaboration journey connections.

Take a moment. Position yourself inside the "circle" in Figure 3.1 and find out who you are right now, and reflect on the following questions:

- How can an SME (small company) help me? Are there SMEs which are developing interesting products for my business?
- How can a startup help me with their knowledge and experience? Can I adopt their startup technology into my business?
- How can an angel investor help me understand the investment trends and interests? Can an angel investor invest in my project? Is it something for them?
- How can you collaborate with venture capitals? Can venture capital firms support you?
- Is it your idea helpful for governments? At which governmental level? Local, regional, national, international?

- If you are looking for knowledge, you can contact a professor from a university who is related to your industry and ask all the questions you have. Can you work with an academic to help you with your innovation?
- Can a university as a whole can help me to find the right professor? Can they help me to create the right collaboration journey for my business?
- Do you know whether there is research outside universities? You can go directly to research centers, understand what they are doing, what kind of products they have and think together about how you can collaborate to bring research to life!
- Innovation institutes are the best to help you to connect the dots and help you create new products and services. How can an innovation institute or ecosystem support your innovation?
- How can you collaborate with your suppliers and other partners? Can you have an open conversation about what you need or what your supplier needs or what your supplier is doing in general?

"In IT we are constantly working with our suppliers to develop new technology solutions which are deployed in our operations in many cases," says Ragnar Ragnarsson, CIO Samskip Group (Ragnarsson, 2018).

All these questions regarding each of the potential collaboration elements will help you to open your opportunities for collaboration and see the importance of every element for your innovation project. If you are not sure to what extent professionals from other areas can help you with your innovation, be open, make experiments, and have conversations with experts. You can have an open conversation, ask questions about their products, services, offerings, research and other projects they are doing or in which they are participating. You will discover the new things they are doing which may trigger a new collaboration project.

Open conversations have a significant impact on your innovation. They help you understand your needs, your business ecosystem and understand what you need exactly from high-level experts. Figure 3.3 displays the connections between all the elements of the circle at the same time. The message is clear. If you don't know where the knowledge or technology is hidden, you can collaborate with others to find that information. In the process, you have to be creative and open to collaboration in order to co-create a new future together. Co-discovery is quite interesting as to some extent you have to participate in offline or online activities. You have to use the digital tools strategically to discover new information and leave the human communication to build relationships in online or offline environments.

"Angel investors are not only for start-ups. Angel investors are investing in research projects inside Universities and in SMEs," says Marie-Elisabeth Rusling, CEO Business Angels Europe (Rusling, 2019).

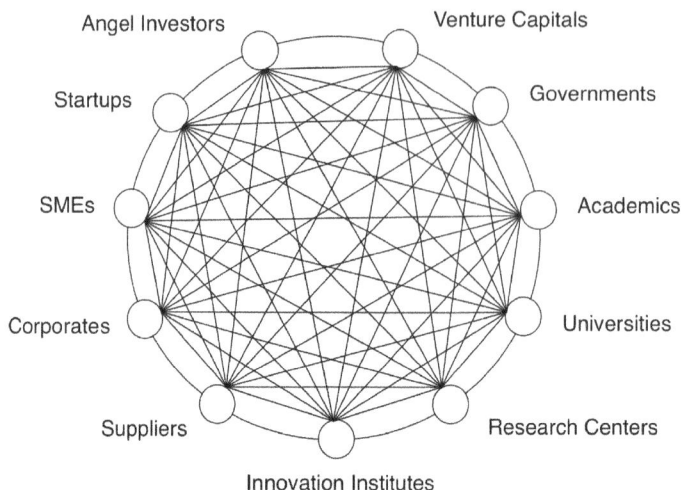

Figure 3.3: Collaboration journey ecosystem with all possible collaborations.

What is exactly collaboration for innovation?

"Collaboration for innovation means creating the value together with a common propose to bring the impact to the society," says Natalie Turner, author of the book *Yes, You can Innovate*, Founder and CEO http://entheo (Turner, 2020).

Collaboration for Innovation consists of working together with a partner in your industry or in academia to co-ideate, co-brainstorm, co-create, co-design, co-prototype, co-test, co-strategize, co-bring to the market, co-make, etc. Innovation is a space where you can be creative even in the way you are innovating, that is, in the way you are collaborating for innovation as well. You have to be open and have a look at who can bring more value to your business.

"Collaboration is a good value for your corporate culture for Innovation. You have to look at your values and see the impact they have on your Innovation activities," says Stefan Lindegaard, UPGRADE! Program (Lindegaard, 2020)

To recall the definition of innovation previously introduced in this book: "innovation is bringing value by using creativity." The collaboration for innovation has to have a shared value between the parties involved in the collaboration, and it has to have the creative component. Innovation is a change; it's something new to the market. This is quite interesting, because you can bring to the market some research or technology which was created 20 years ago but was kept in a drawer at some office or university and never brought to light. The innovation occurs when one brings to the market "lost innovation in the form of research or a ready-to-go product," hence bringing value to the industry and to people. At the same time, knowledge is often kept inside the bright minds of academics, or entrepreneurs or high-level experts inside organizations. One of the ways to valorize that knowledge is when you collaborate with them in research or innovation projects.

"Collaboration is the most important theme in innovation during the XXI Century", says Prof. John Bessant, Professor of Innovation and Entrepreneurship at the University of Exeter, UK (Bessant, 2020).

Collaborative Innovation is the means to bring better innovation to the market which is done by including diverse perspectives on the same problem, making more creative solutions with new ideas as well as merging past and present research and technology. Contrary to collaboration for innovation, a singular point of view may create a one-sided service with limited creativity, value and impact. If you want to maximize the impact of your innovation project, you have to collaborate.

Why do you need to collaborate?

"Collaboration for innovation is about how research has to be applied into the real world. Research is content but research needs context from the industry," says William Malek, Executive Director SEAC Innovation Center and Stanford-Thailand 4.0 Research Consortium (Malek, 2020).

Innovation is not ideation. But even during ideation, you might need support to build ideas on one another. Here, we are talking about real innovation, which consists of making an impact on industry and society. You have to understand that this impact results in change and transformation. The transformation is impossible to accomplish alone. Even the innovation process is impossible to do alone in a closed room, whether you are big corporate or a small business. The impact, the change and the end result (product, service, etc.) will be better when working together with experts and professionals. Of course, you might need knowledge or expertise that you might not have yourself. An innovative mindset is the enabler for being open to collaborate or create something new. The end goal is to create and to bring the innovation project to the market, with cutting-edge technology. In order to do so, you have to collaborate with the experts which have been working for more than 20 years in that particular area, such as in academia.

Benefits for academia/industry collaboration
- Academia generates a neutral and unbiased perspective on technology.
- Academia helps you to bring better products or services to the market.
- Academia gives a fresh view of projects and corporate issues.
- Academia acts as an authority behind your innovation.
- Academia contributes cutting-edge and innovative views of your ideas.
- Academia looks at the best innovative solution, not only at the commercial perspective.
- Academia helps one connect the dots and to become a visionary in their industry.

"Entrepreneurs need to learn that your very first customer might not be from your backyard," says Jeremy Laurin, VP Business Development and Commercialization at Ontario Centres of Excellence and Adjunct Professor at York University Faculty of Health, Canada (Laurin, 2019).

It's always good to open your perspective in the world. As a startup, small business or a project you keep hearing the advice to "start small", "test locally" or "prove your concept" first. As you are creating an innovative product, you might not have to test locally, or prove a small part, somewhere. You have to analyze where the product will be most useful and which market or corporation is ready to "easily" adapt your new technology. We have to explore various markets and companies as alternative options because they might be more advanced in respect to technology adoption or have a better understanding of innovation. As you are making a "new thing", you need to work with the "early adopters" which is the industry and people who like to take risks and try new things. They can be anywhere, hence you need to find them and contact them for a collaboration. First, talk to them informally, build a relationship, and make them co-creators together with you.

Benefits for industry-startups-industry collaboration
- Startups are more agile and flexible in adapting technology for your company.
- Startups are opening up new ways of using technology.
- Startups are an option for collaboration for co-designing and co-working for innovation.
- Startups can solve business problems much faster and more creatively.
- Startups have a conscious and positive way of approaching issues with solutions, as they are not only pursuing a commercial perspective.
- Startups want to make a positive impact; hence you can innovate with purpose.
- Startups help your organization be innovative.
- Startups help identify outside challenges.

Why does collaboration seem so difficult?

"Take time to get startups to understand the business, don't fear sharing problems with startups or working with them. Listen more to startups – what they have to say," says Russell O'Brien, CEO at Cognitis Innovation and former Head of Innovation and Entrepreneurship at City of Auckland in New Zealand (O'Brien, 2018).

There are plenty of excuses for making collaboration difficult, such as talking different languages, being in different cultures, having different speed of working, or different personalities or behaviors. There is another type of excuse regarding the process: that it is too long, or that the legal negotiations take months (from 6 months up to 2 years). At the end of the day, all of these are excuses are because corporates are just as slow as universities, while legal teams within corporations are just as tough as university legal teams. All the issues lie in the internal struggles over who has more power and the bigger ego. We should change this perspective, where we have a mindset which is ready for collaboration and understanding the goal of working together to create something new and better for society, industry, research or for the company.

"There is a lack of information on what is innovation, and willingness to go out of the university to engage or connect within different groups," says Russell O'Brien, CEO at Cognitis Innovation, and former Head of Innovation and Entrepreneurship at City of Auckland in New Zealand (O'Brien, 2018).

The other side is the lack of information and understanding of what innovation is and how innovation works. Innovation is not about creating "flying cars" or creating "science fiction" tech gadgets. In reality, innovation is about improving people's lives, creating new products which make sense and have a purpose. It takes time to go from idea, to concept, to prototype and then testing. Before going to market, you have to iterate several times from idea to prototype while testing with users. Innovation also consists of communication and marketing because your goal while doing innovation is to help the industry or society to adopt your new product or your innovative solution. This process is not completed in one day, but will take months or years. Innovation leaders have to understand these timelines for research, technology transfer, going to market and adoption of innovation. Consequently, you have to understand the timelines and ask questions to understand how to collaborate, how to innovate together. You have to be curious to make your joint journey to make an impact together. Or you can get research and technology that is already there, collaborate and together accelerate the process.

How can you collaborate effectively?

"It is about giving everybody an opportunity and about expanding knowledge," says Prof. Katharina Ruckstuhl, Associate Dean Māori at the University of Otago's Business School (Ruckstuhl, 2019).

Efficiency is about motivation to share knowledge and having the confidence to know what you want to do. In the next chapter, we will discuss in detail emotional intelligence for collaboration and innovation. Nevertheless, you have to ensure that the "collaboration team" is motivated. The "collaboration team" is motivated when the team is listened to, valued and when the team has a clear and transparent objective, reason for the collaboration and clarity. The faster the "collaboration team" has clear the objectives and the expectations are managed, the faster the collaboration project for innovation will be ready and productive.

"These days we talk about collaboration for innovation and ecosystem Innovation. Innovation is a huge interactive action, with knowledge being outside the organization. Now you have new digital channels to collaborate, and you have to learn new ways of collaboration for innovation," says Prof. John Bessant, Professor of Innovation and Entrepreneurship at the University of Exeter, UK (Bessant, 2020).

Digital tools assist in simplifying the process. You can refer to Chapters 1 and 2 for examples. At this stage it is the right time to adopt those tools to help you speed up your process to find and collaborate with the right experts to co-work with them during each step of the innovation process.

The experts for your collaboration for an innovation project could come from universities, institutions, or industry, including startups, SMEs, corporates, venture capital, business angels, and suppliers. The main point is that you have to accept that new digital tools are changing the process by which collaboration occurs; hence, you have to embrace change. That includes accepting automation and a reduction of time, along with increased speed and efficiency, as well as the understanding that you have to use your time for more creative tasks for collaboration instead of bureaucracy.

Ideas for managing expectations

Goals
- What are the main motives for the collaboration?
- What are the main motives for creating the new product or service?

Decision making
- Why do you choose to pursue certain goals?
- Who is making the decision for the new product or service?

Influence
- How can you motivate yourself to work harder?
- How can you support and listen more your team?

Equity
- How to create balance between individual efforts and what the team is receiving from rewards?
- How to manage the team's expectations and collaboration? (Adams, 1960)

Useful skills for using emotional intelligence for collaboration
- Identify all the goals for collaboration.
- Accept obstacles.
- Give the team permission to make mistakes.
- Do not place over-dimensional expectations on people or circumstances.
- Focus on the things you will be been able to accomplish.
- Collaboration is about motivation.
- Look for solutions instead of problems.
- Get into the mindset of "we are making a new product or service together".

Are innovation procurement and corporate venturing the same thing? Blended models

Currently, the issue is that we measure investment, but not the customer acquisition and technology adoption of innovation. In order to increase the success and impact of super innovative collaboration projects an innovation procurement process should be built inside your organization. In Chapter 8, you will find a detailed definition of innovation procurement and corporate venturing.

Corporates, as established companies and industry leaders, need to create key performance indicators (KPIs) to adapt new technology and innovation inside their organizations.

– This is the point to increase innovation created by startups or super innovators to be adopted by the industry. Usually, companies prefer to adopt Microsoft or Google products and services instead of "new" services coming from SMEs or startups.
– "Certificates of innovation" could be a solution to make sure the procurement teams have a framework and structure to monitor the adoption of new services and products from the tech industry in Europe.

The objective is to increase the number of startup products and services adopted by industry.

Policy makers should create an environment with tax benefits for corporate venturing, ready to share the risk to adopt innovative technology from startups or research universities.

– At technology readiness level (TRL) 3–6, when the startups are not ready for the market or the research is not ready, the corporate can take the risk and invest to further develop and customize the product together with the startup or research team.
– When the company is the first customer, both partners are co-creating the impact together.
– A tax benefit could be a reduction of payable taxes that correlates with the number of new products and services that are adopted inside the company from startups and research projects coming from SMEs and academia or research centers.

Knowledge and technology transfer from universities

The critical part in connecting academia with industry is that the technology offices inside universities have to help all actors find technology and innovation, not only through visualization but by enabling and facilitating collaboration and knowledge and technology transfer by reducing the legal issues across borders, and by reducing administrative bureaucracy.

The chance for the technology and knowledge transfer offices is to focus on business development, doing collaboration coaching, connecting the dots and being visionary instead of being a gatekeeper of knowledge. Those offices should reduce the bureaucracy and they have to be open to actively listening to academics to help them share their knowledge in the way they prefer to share it. The objective is to make a better and positive impact together with the innovation that could be created together with academia and industry.

It would be great to monitor and quantify the number of collaborative innovation projects across industries and academia and unify the key performance indicators (KPIs) across universities, nationally and internationally, to measure knowledge and technology transfer. Furthermore, the number of collaborations on innovation projects, on research projects where the co-creation of a new product or new service, but also the adoption or modification of existing products and services to adapt to the new needs and market, for instance:

– Number of collaborations between startups and academia.
– Number of collaborations between startups and industry.
– Number of collaborations between academia/industry.

Best practices to negotiate legal agreements for collaboration

Here, I will not give in-depth legal advice. This book's focus is to make the reader understand that you need to have a mindset for collaboration, that the objective to create a better impact together is much more important than legal discussions. Long discussions reduce the impact, increase the extended periods of bureaucracy, and focus the attention of the administration outside of the collaboration and outside of the innovation. The higher good should have priority over legal discussions about intellectual property, rights of use, patents and other issues.

However, you should use a legal template to make clear what you are doing together, who is bringing which type of knowledge to the table, and the objective of the activities you are doing together. You have to think positively, concentrate on the bigger picture, on the long-term objective and why you are doing this innovation together.

Furthermore, collaboration is easier if you are using unified templates for cross-border and cross-region agreements such as non-disclosure agreements, letters of intent, collaboration agreements, state of work agreements, consortium agreements, memorandums of understanding, etc. At the same time, it's very important to simplify payment for the collaborations, in order to reduce the time before you start working together once the contract is signed. And one of the things professionals forget is document management – to sign the contract and save it properly in the same place together with other signed collaboration agreements or legal documents.

It is highly recommended to keep track of and save all email exchanges and communications digitally, as well as all meeting minutes and decisions taken during the collaboration. The basic organization of the knowledge transfer and the decisions made during that process and during the collaboration itself is a good practice that sometimes is tedious, but it has infinite value when there are conflicts or when you have to create reports.

Checklist for strategic thinking about collaboration for innovation
Startups and SMEs
- Be creative, you can collaborate with every element of the circle in Figure 3.3.
- Keep up your confidence and motivation.
- Be curious and be open.
- Ask questions and actively listen.

Corporates and Suppliers
- Be curious to listen to startups.
- Keep positive about how startups can help you.
- Ask for help from academics.
- Understand your needs first.

Universities
- Support academics to connect the dots.
- Listen to academics.
- Bring academia and industry together and increase serendipity.
- Be creative about how academia can transfer their knowledge and research to life.
- Embrace digitalization, speed and efficiency.

Venture Capitals and Business Angels
- Learn more about innovation.
- Listen and trust academics for inspiration and expertise.
- Be open to new ways of collaboration and new ways of connecting the dots.
- Increase collaboration for your investment and startup portfolio.
- Listen actively, calmly and for a long time to every super innovator.

Governments
- Be curious about changing the process.
- Embrace efficiency and speed for administrative process.
- Create collaborative KPIs to support collaboration over competition.

- Create consistency and legal templates for standardization of collaboration.
- Support open access of research documentation, papers and innovation.
- Make intellectual property accessible to have a positive impact.

Research and Innovation Institutes
- Open your results, products and activities to facilitate connecting the dots.
- Be creative and open about different ways of collaborating for innovation.
- Embrace digitalization, speed and efficiency.
- Be curious about listening to startups.
- Be curious about changing the process.

The second part of every chapter in this book follows the "collaboration journey" and applies the subject of the chapter to a phase in your collaboration journey.

Collaboration journey

"If there is goodwill, everything can go smoothly, even when all parties are busy," says Prof. Stefano Puntoni, RSM Erasmus University (Puntoni, 2019).

Let's come back to our collaboration journey to apply this chapter's learning to it. In the following you will understand the "collaboration canvas" in the "negotiation phase" of the "collaboration journey" to create awareness of how important it is to manage expectations before starting to work together on an innovation project between academia and industry. This tool can be used by innovation ecosystems to enhance collaborative innovation through the ecosystem's actors.

When you are thinking of collaborative Innovation, the ultimate goal is getting new knowledge and new technology to better innovate through collaboration. The "collaboration journey" displayed in Figure 3.4 has distinct phases within collaborative innovation to acknowledge the key elements to shape your real innovation needs based on the knowledge you need. One of the important tools to discuss is the "collaboration canvas", which helps to manage expectations for collaborative innovation, as a key step for bringing innovation to the market successfully.

Initiation Phase

"Acknowledge the difference and find a way to take the opportunity to work together on innovation systems that can either be used by a business or in more widely terms" Prof. Katharina Ruckstuhl, Associate Dean Māori at the University of Otago's Business School (Ruckstuhl, 2019).

Figure 3.5 shows the step prior to starting to search for potential partners for collaboration. In this initiation phase:

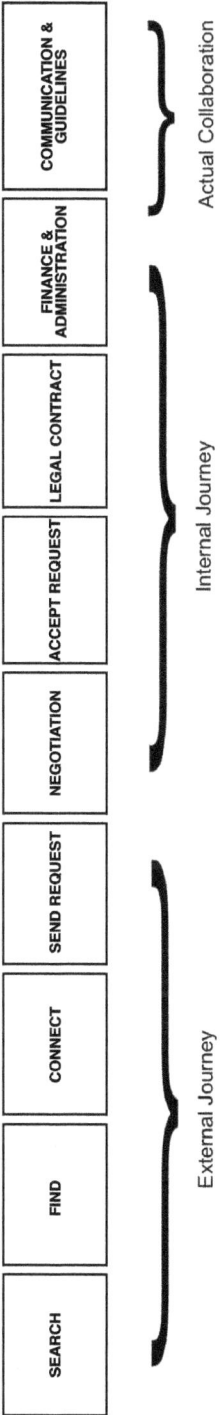

Figure 3.4: Collaboration journey overview.

LIST OF POTENTIAL COLLABORATORS	INTERESTED?	DECISION MAKING	START COLLABORATION CANVAS
Collaborator One	Yes / No / Later	What do they need to start the negotiation of the collaboration?	Use the collaboration canvas to create a clear vision of why you are working together.
Collaborator Two	Yes / No / Later	What are our common objectives?	
Collaborator Three	Yes / No / Later	Can we make a better impact together?	

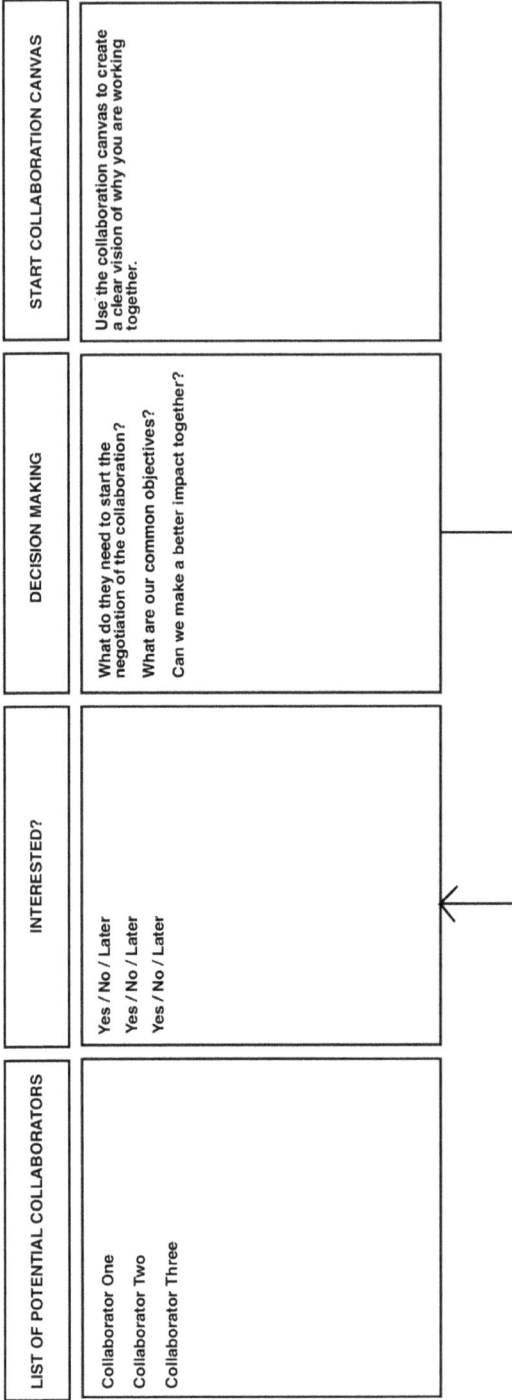

Figure 3.5: Initiation phase before you start to look for the potential partners for collaboration.

- You are looking for the core knowledge and expertise you might need to be inside the company. This knowledge might not be available yet and more of it will be needed on an ad-hoc or temporary basis.
- SMEs and innovation teams have limited or accidental access to knowledge and technology from universities.
- It is difficult to self-assess what the needs for knowledge are, and who is the right partner to collaborate with in order to gather the necessary knowledge or technology.
- There is no clear structure for how to negotiate and manage expectations between academia/industry collaboration: consequently, the parties almost always collaborate with the same experts.
- It helps to analyze how to self-assess which kind of partner you need to get the knowledge onboard in the organization.
- Leverage digital interaction and increase proximity from offline ecosystem to online presence to find the right partners.

Negotiation Phase

"This is your domain but together we're going to create something interesting," says Prof. Katharina Ruckstuhl, Associate Dean Māori at the University of Otago's Business School (Ruckstuhl, 2019).

The negotiation phase is the time to look at negotiation in a positive way. You will find in Figure 3.6 a structure to create a request for collaboration and start an open and transparent conversation. We are proposing the following solution called the "collaboration canvas":

- It's a toolkit which can be used by both parties in the collaboration, the academics and the innovation teams or SMEs representatives.
- The focus is on leveraging understanding of the key points to discuss before starting a collaboration.
- It supports you in identifying the phases where the innovation team or SMEs can identify where you lack knowledge.

In a nutshell, the "collaboration canvas" is a tool to structure the collaboration for any kind of activity you need to do to work together, to structure your request for this collaboration, to help manage expectations, to speed up the process and to have a clear and transparent conversation. It could be used at the beginning, in the middle, or at the end of the collaboration.

It's very important to make the collaboration clear and transparent from the beginning, as a starting point to speed up the process, and to help to follow the "collaboration journey" smoothly. This canvas can also be used before, during and after the collaboration as a tool to check if your objectives have been achieved or if you are missing a critical topic to address and discuss. One of the best practices is that

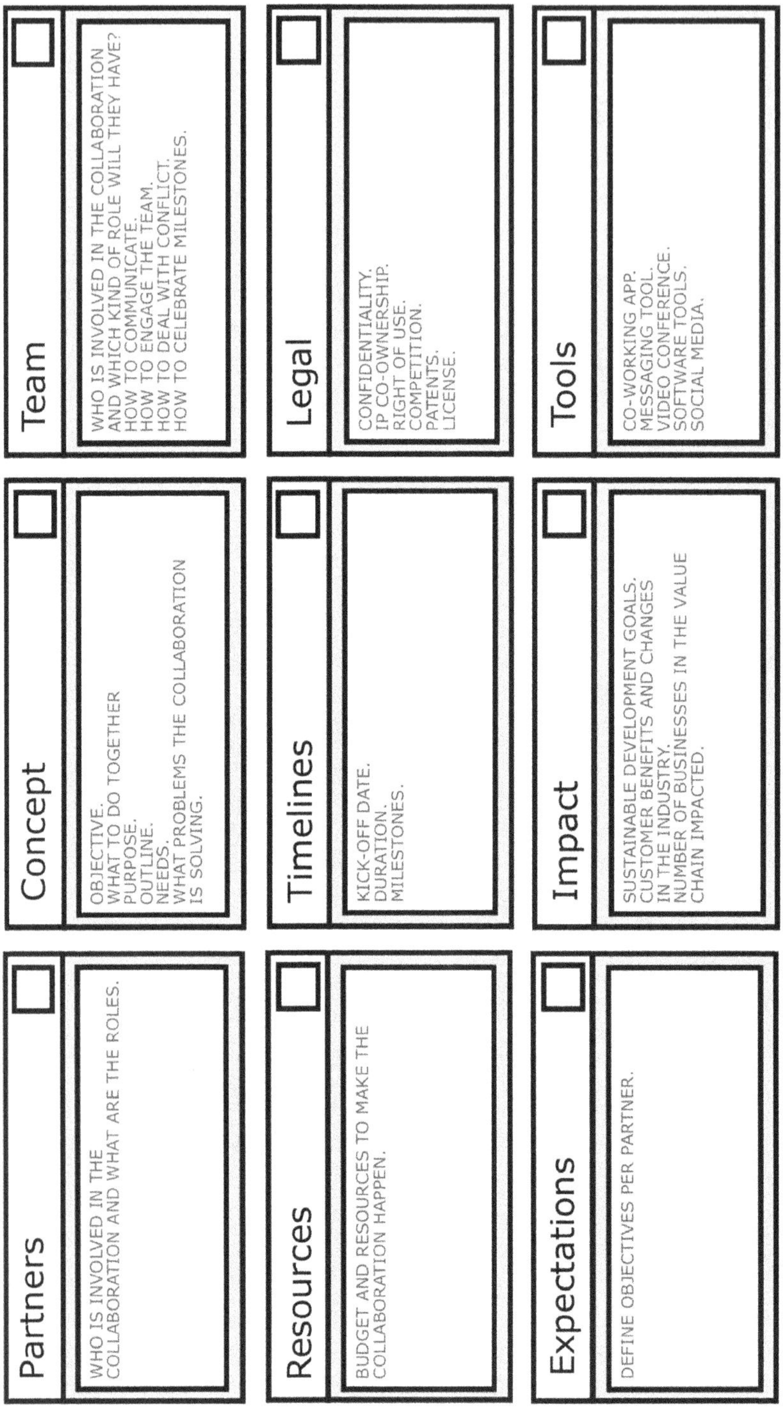

Partners

WHO IS INVOLVED IN THE COLLABORATION AND WHAT ARE THE ROLES.

Concept

OBJECTIVE.
WHAT TO DO TOGETHER
PURPOSE.
OUTLINE.
NEEDS.
WHAT PROBLEMS THE COLLABORATION IS SOLVING.

Team

WHO IS INVOLVED IN THE COLLABORATION AND WHICH KIND OF ROLE WILL THEY HAVE?
HOW TO COMMUNICATE.
HOW TO ENGAGE THE TEAM.
HOW TO DEAL WITH CONFLICT.
HOW TO CELEBRATE MILESTONES.

Resources

BUDGET AND RESOURCES TO MAKE THE COLLABORATION HAPPEN.

Timelines

KICK-OFF DATE.
DURATION.
MILESTONES.

Legal

CONFIDENTIALITY.
IP CO-OWNERSHIP.
RIGHT OF USE.
COMPETITION.
PATENTS.
LICENSE.

Expectations

DEFINE OBJECTIVES PER PARTNER.

Impact

SUSTAINABLE DEVELOPMENT GOALS.
CUSTOMER BENEFITS AND CHANGES IN THE INDUSTRY.
NUMBER OF BUSINESSES IN THE VALUE CHAIN IMPACTED.

Tools

CO-WORKING APP.
MESSAGING TOOL.
VIDEO CONFERENCE.
SOFTWARE TOOLS.
SOCIAL MEDIA.

Figure 3.6: Collaboration canvas for the negotiation phase.

you first think about all the boxes before you start the conversations with your collaborator. Consequently, the meeting or the call will be much more productive.

You have to work with the "collaboration canvas" as flexibly as you can. You start the first conversation with the basic information and get more information as long as the negotiation is advancing. This is a tool to help you discuss your expectations openly and talk about the key elements of the collaboration and innovation. Similarly, this "collaboration canvas" is supporting you to think as well about the basic infrastructure to realize the collaboration practically in your daily work activities, for instance, about communication tools.

Partners: Write here the list of partners with whom you are going to collaborate and the role they will have in the collaboration.

Resources: Describe the first approach of which resources will be needed during the collaboration, regarding budget estimation, experts and professionals.

Expectations: Define the objectives per partner and the main end goal for the collaboration. If you have a specific activity or project, you can define your new product or service which you want to create together here.

Concept: Write down the main goal for the collaboration, and what to do together, while you develop the purpose for your collaboration. Furthermore, you can write down an outline for the collaboration here, the knowledge or technology which needs to be covered during the collaboration, and what the problem is which the collaboration is solving.

Timelines: Kick-off date, collaboration's duration and if you have already milestones, you can write them down here.

Impact: You can describe the impact of your collaboration, whether it is a small workshop or a three-year research project. Refer to the sustainable development goals from United Nations to get a general idea about good areas of impact, like customer benefit, industry change, number of business impacted (suppliers, students, academics, industries, sectors, etc.). You can assess your impact from a smaller to a bigger perspective.

Team: This is about the collaboration leadership, how to communicate, how to manage the activity or project, how to engage with the team, how to deal with conflict, how to celebrate milestones.

Legal: Here, you have to think about the importance of the following legal issues for your collaboration: confidentiality, IP co-ownership, right of use, competition, patents and licenses. For instance, you have to think about whether you need a confidentiality agreement for your first conversation.

Tools: This is the part about having a common understanding of which kinds of tools you will use during the collaboration in terms of co-working apps, messaging tools, video conferencing and other software tools, such as for social media or communications.

Apart from the collaboration canvas and collaboration journey as a toolkit, there is the digital platform called Collabwith (https://platform.collabwith.co) where we make local ecosystems accessible for their main actors such as academics, startups, scaleups, SMEs, corporates, and universities. Collabwith increases the chances of success of the collaboration finding the right partner. Also, it provides an end-to-end solution, one place to find a professor or startup, talk to them, decide on the project and activity, make a proposal, create the smart legal contract and pay.

Ideas for creating your own collaboration canvas

Understand
- You have to find your right partners for collaboration.
- Start with an informal conversation and discuss the end goal.

Discover
- Understand the needs and benefits of collaboration for each partner.
- Create a psychologically safe environment for a high-performing collaboration.

Prioritize
- Make a clear difference between urgent activities and priorities.
- Embrace uncertainty, be agile and be flexible during the whole collaboration.

At the end of this chapter on collaboration, I want to share with you cases from professionals who can provide a complementary view of the journey of collaboration.

Conversation with William Malek about "Paradoxes of Academia/Industry Collaboration"

Director SEAC Innovation Center Stanford-Thailand
    @stratexe

How is your technology transfer and collaboration process?

Technology transfer opportunities themselves have become more diverse when you consider how academic research emerges and what stance professors take as they learn. The collaborations can vary widely from contract-based research to gift-funded research and this itself establishes what may or may not occur in the transfer process.

What are the paradoxes for the industry/academia collaboration?

1. Job Security
2. Personalities
3. Sense of Time
4. Intelligence Mindset
5. Metrics
6. Bureaucracies
7. Failure
8. Data
9. Publishing
10. Intellectual Property
11. Innovation
12. Culture

Do you have guidelines and best practices to overcome the paradoxes?

The paradoxes must be worked on both sides of the fence:
1. Job security for tenured professors needs rethinking especially in today's context of learning and research: the industry must fully embrace an experimentation mindset and add more incentives for more broader hypothesis testing.
2. Personalities: simply have a better onboarding of each team member and facilitate better disclosure of each personality/cultural preferences and biases.
3. Sense of Time: know the difference between research and consulting and especially the gray area in between.
4. Intelligence Mindset: appreciate the diversity of both and how this works out in deeper problem analysis (each side needs the other).
5. Metrics: probably the hardest one to deal with – if we apply circular concepts perhaps the metrics would take on a whole different feel.
6. Bureaucracies: this area needs institutional work from a contracting perspective dealing with everything from NDAs, data, to report requirements, etc.
7. Failure: the nature of research never has any guaranteed outcomes to avoid failure, in fact it is intrinsic, the better thing to do is to collaborate deeper at the beginning when the research is being framed.
8. Data: see number 6.
9. Publishing: very tricky in that sometimes both sides may have huge conflicts on this topic once the "discovery" has been validated, get this agreed to at the

beginning and lay out the decision process for what cases are not acceptable to publish on both sides.
10. IP: same answer as 6 and 9.
11. Innovation: find a common ground for "use-inspired research".
12. Culture: see number 2.

Conversation with Daria Tataj about "Network Thinking"

CEO Tataj Innovation
@dariatataj

What is the Network IQ test?

The Network IQ test is a tool to measure the Network Intelligence of individuals, teams, and social networks. We define this kind of intelligence as an ability to build two types of relations: strong ties with key collaborators, and with weak ties in key stakeholders. The Network IQ test has been designed to assess the level of managerial skills for leading high-performance virtual organizations and the power to influence the digital ecosystems.

For example, high Network IQ leaders have clarity about what is their purpose, which are the key communities they should engage with, and who are the right people to build strong, trust-based relationships with. High Network IQ teams have a balance of four digital leadership profiles, which we identity based on the Network IQ test. These four profiles are The Strategist, The Networker, The Orchestrator, and the Influencer.

Why is network thinking important for innovation?

The philosophy behind Network Thinking is about the leadership potential of every individual. Everyone connected to global networks has the power to become an influential leader through mass self-communication. The ability to leverage face-to-face and digital communication builds stronger and ever more distributed ties across an ecosystem. These ties allow every professional irrespective of age, race, gender, or physical location to recruit collaborators who join the virtual teamwork and mobilize commitment from mass supporters across the entire ecosystem who share knowledge, insights, skills, and opportunities. Thus, e-teams with a high Network IQ innovate and grow through mass co-creation.

Why is it important to be open-minded to connect to new professionals for innovation?

Being open-minded means being curious and open to learning about the world. Every professional – CEO, founder, country manager, or R&I Director – should constantly challenge the e-team to become more innovative. Our data on the Network IQ assessments shows that being open-minded is not enough. Being innovative is about a growth mindset and a skillset to build strong ties with e-teams and weak ties across the ecosystem.

What are the best practices for networking for innovation?

Our research shows that less than 20% of professionals use networking to share resources and even they declare that they are not efficient in sharing. The same research found out that while less than 20% use networking to monitor market trends and to disrupt, over 80% declared this activity brings high impact. In brief, networking is one of the strategic processes to advance innovation, validation of business ideas, getting customer insights, building awareness, building a community of early adopters. Strategic e-networking is the key to innovation in post-corona times.

Networking means making connections, building relations. Network Thinking means that you build social networks with a purpose in mind, or as we say following a Purpose – Network – Fit. In other words, every purpose requires a different network. Following this principle means that firstly, you have clarity regarding your shared purpose, secondly, you know which are the key communities you should build connections with and who are the right people to build relations with.

Summary

To sum up this chapter, I will leave you with a number of exercises that help ground you in your collaboration journey.

To practice

1. Make your list of potential partners.
2. Schedule an informal call first.
3. Create a collaboration canvas individually first, and then together with your collaboration partner.
4. Be open and listen actively to negotiate and manage expectations together for your collaboration.

In the following chapters you will find

- Tips on how to create a successful collaboration.
- Tips on emotional intelligence for collaboration.
- You will learn that innovation has a psychological part which is especially important.

Notes

(d'Hooghe, 2019) https://collabwith.co/2019/06/podcast-prof-stefano-puntoni-and-joost-dhooghte-on-collaboration/

(Ragnarsson, 2018) https://collabwith.co/2018/07/cio-samskip-ragnar-ragnarsson-on-blockchain-and-partnerships/

(Turner, 2020) https://collabwith.co/2020/02/podcast-natalie-turner-yes-you-can-innovate/

(Lindegaard, 2020) https://collabwith.co/2020/01/podcast-how-to-discuss-kpis-and-budget-for-innovation/

(Rusling, 2019) https://collabwith.co/2019/11/women-investors/

(Bessant, 2020) https://collabwith.co/2020/01/john-bessant-crisis-driven-innovation/

(Malek, 2020) https://collabwith.co/2020/02/podcast-william-malek-paradoxes-on-academia-industry-collaboration/

(Laurin, 2019) https://collabwith.co/2019/04/podcast-ispim-ottawa-jeremy-laurin-on-scaling-start-ups-as-entrepreneurs-that-need-to-learn-that-your-very-first-customer-might-not-be-from-your-backyard

(O'Brien, 2018) https://collabwith.co/2018/11/podcast-ispim-fukuoka-ceo-russell-obrien-discuss-how-to-create-a-large-scale-innovation-ecosystems/

(Ruckstuhl, 2019) https://collabwith.co/2019/03/podcast-ispim-ottawa-prof-katharina-ruckstuhl-on-inclusive-innovation-being-closest-to-each-other-thinking-and-understand-each-other/

(Equity Theory of Motivation, Adams, 1960) http://perpus.univpancasila.ac.id/repository/EBUPT190088.pdf#page=150

(Puntoni, 2019) https://collabwith.co/2019/06/podcast-prof-stefano-puntoni-and-joost-dhooghte-on-collaboration/

"Relationships are important in innovation. And the question is how we do include people thinking in knowledge to upstage science technology"

Prof. Katharina Ruckstuhl Associate Dean Māori at the University of Otago's Business School (Ruckstuhl, 2019)

Chapter 4
The Secrets of Collaboration – Using Emotional Intelligence for Innovation and Collaboration

Summary: In this chapter, you will learn the importance of emotional intelligence for innovation, entrepreneurship and collaboration. Collaboration is all about people and communication, and emotional intelligence skills are a tool for this communication and understanding about people who are key to succeeding in innovation.

Emotional intelligence is not about "being emotional" or "oversharing emotions".[1] John Mayer and Peter Salovey from Yale University first introduced the concept of emotional intelligence. They defined the concept as the ability to perceive emotions, to access and generate emotions to assist thought, to understand emotions and emotional knowledge, and to reflectively regulate emotions to promote emotional and intellectual growth. Furthermore, they described how emotional intelligence must somehow combine two of the three states of mind: cognition and affect, or intelligence and emotion (Salovey and Mayer, 1990). Mayer and Salovey went on further to define an emotional intelligence skillset: "emotional intellect implies the ability to perceive, value, and express emotions accurately; the ability to access and/or generate feelings when they contribute to thought; the ability to understand emotional emotion and knowledge; and the ability to manage emotions to foster emotional and intellectual growth. It is important to pay attention to the feelings because, if the person pays attention, he or she can learn from them" (Salovey and Mayer, 1990). David R. Caruso and Peter Salovey (Caruso and Salovey, 2004) developed a set of emotional intelligence skills in the workplace and showcased their importance. Emotions (Caruso and Salovey, 2004) flow throughout organizations. Leaders must understand the role of emotions in influencing how people decide, think, and work towards their goals.

In his book, *Emotional Intelligence* (Goleman, 1995), Daniel Goleman wrote how emotional intelligence is a set of abilities that anyone can learn. In 1995, Goleman reported that, "Emotional competence is important above all in leadership, a role whose essence is to get others to perform their respective jobs more effectively." Goleman includes emotional competencies within each construct of emotional intelligence. Emotional competencies are not innate talents, but rather learned capabilities that must be worked on. They can be developed to achieve outstanding performance. Goleman posits that individuals are born with a general emotional intelligence that determines their potential for learning emotional competencies.

---

1 This chapter has been written together with Celia Avila-Rauch.

https://doi.org/10.1515/9783110665383-004

David Caruso and Lisa Rees developed an approach in their book, *A Leaders' Guide to Solving Challenges with Emotional Intelligence* (Caruso and Rees, 2018) where they looked at EI as a skill or ability, an ability to identify, assess, and manage the emotions of oneself, of others, and of groups. After looking at my own success in driving change during my years of innovation management inside corporations, I looked within to answer questions to understand where this success came from. Why was I able to drive change and inspire people to follow innovation through the years, while others were unable to achieve the same thing? Through novel ways of applying innovation frameworks, I discovered that it was something that I naturally did. Applying empathy, active listening, bringing people together, being assertive, understanding, having fun but also looking for solutions in a positive way contributed to this framework. Many business schools are trying to teach kind leadership, or positive-impact leadership. After completing my MBA, I began to look at options for how to become a good leader. My experience showed it was not about personality or culture, it was about connecting with our human selves. I found that emotional intelligence skills were that difference between my approach to innovation and that of other innovative leaders. The focus of this chapter is to look into the connection between psychology and innovation. It is about how to apply and manage emotions during creative and innovative activities, and how one can drive innovation successfully in an organization using emotional intelligence skills to become a better leader in the process. Because emotional intelligence is applicable to innovative organizations, projects, brainstorming sessions, entrepreneurship, intrapreneurship, collaborative innovation, collaborations, high-performing teams which are creating something new, and getting the senior management on board with the required budget to make innovation happen. It is about common sense and communication.

In this chapter, we will answer why and how innovation requires emotional intelligence as a key element in the process. Before you start learning the basics of what emotional intelligence is, let's do an exercise:

What is your mood now?

You might be calm and curious because you are reading this book on a sofa, or more aware of your surroundings because you are reading this book on some form of public transportation. Or you can be happy, because someone just showed you affection and brought you a cup of tea. At the opposite end of the spectrum, you might be on a bus, someone bumped into you and you are upset. Harness what your mood tells you about yourself in this precise moment. Now look at the "The Mood Meter" in Figure 4.1 and explain, in one word, how you feel now. What is your mood, and why is this the case?

The mood meter (Figure 4.1) has four areas in different colors: red for anger, yellow for happiness, blue for sadness and green for content. You can feel a combination of these, too.

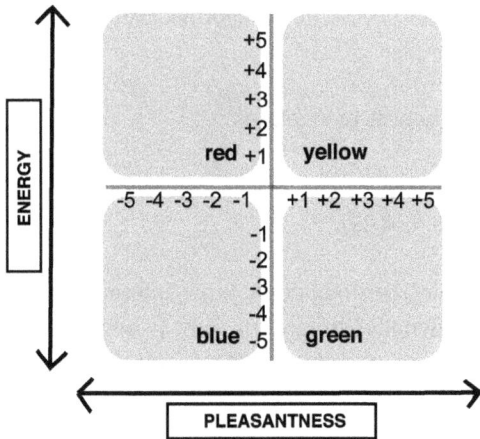

Figure 4.1: The mood meter of the Yale Center for Emotional Intelligence https://www.ycei.org/ (Caruso & Salovey, 2004).

If you want to change your mood, because you are "too excited" to concentrate and work, or "too angry" to make a decision, an excellent way to change your mood is to simply stop and breathe. You can do this on the bus, during a meeting, a brainstorming session, or before drawing up your new strategy, to help you act effectively and efficiently in any situation. You need to change your state of mind to be productive.

What is the strategy for reaching the component of emotional intelligence skills using the mood meter?

- Where are you now on the mood meter?
- What caused you to feel this way?
- What word best describes your current feeling?
- How are you expressing this feeling?
- Given how you feel, what strategy will you use to obtain the desired emotion?

Emotional intelligence is the ability to recognize, understand and regulate our emotions. How can we be healthy physically or mentally without having an effective strategy and self-awareness? There are individual differences in recognizing your own emotions. Emotions affect a lot of our decision making or judgments, and we are not conscious of all our emotions. The RULER approach was developed at the Yale Center for Emotional intelligence. The RULER approach describes how you can develop your emotional intelligence Skills. There were several people involved in its development. For example: Brackett, M.A., Caruso, D.R., & Stern, R.S. (2013). The Anchors of

Emotional Intelligence: The RULER Approach to Social and Emotional Learning. New Haven: Emotionally Intelligent Schools.
- R recognizing emotions.
- U understanding the causes and consequences of emotions.
- L labeling emotions accurately.
- E expressing emotions appropriately.
- R regulating emotions effectively (Brackett, 2019).

Everybody needs to know how to talk about their emotions. What information are people sharing? How do you connect emotionally? What do I want to accomplish? How do you match your emotional state to accomplishing what you want to achieve?

What is emotional intelligence?

Emotional intelligence is a skill or ability to self-perceive and identify, assess, and control the emotions of oneself, of others, and of groups. Emotions and cognitions are information, while data and emotional intelligence is a synthesis of three areas of scientific research which demonstrates that emotions, when used widely, supports reasoning and complex problem solving (Prof. Marc Brackett in *Permission to Feel*) (Brackett, 2019).

Caruso and Salovey created 4 areas of emotional awareness, and 4 levels of emotions (Caruso and Rees, 2018):
- *Perceiving Emotions:* the ability to recognize how you and others feel.
- *Using Emotions:* the ability to generate emotion, and to reason, think, and create with this emotion.
- *Understanding Emotions*: the ability to understand people's emotions, what causes emotions, and how emotions change.
- *Managing Emotions*: the ability which allows you to harness the power of your emotions to make effective decisions and choices.

For Daniel Goleman, the ineptitude of leaders reduces the performance of all: it wastes time, creates laziness, corrodes motivation and dedication to work, and causes hostility and apathy to accumulate. To create a good team, we must develop emotional competence, which is acquired through emotional intelligence.
- *Self-awareness* is the ability to read one's emotions and recognize their impact while using gut feelings to guide decisions.
- *Self-management* involves controlling one's emotions and impulses and adapting to changing circumstances.
- *Social awareness* is the ability to sense, understand, and react to others' emotions while comprehending social networks.

– *Relationship management* involves the ability to inspire, influence, and develop others while managing conflict.

How to apply emotional intelligence to understand creativity

"Our creativity is so closely tied to our emotional state," Marc Brackett in the book *Permission to Feel* (Brackett, 2019).

Creativity is a complex trait of human beings. One thing is certain: without creativity, humanity would not be able to improve on science and technology. As Marc Brackett states in *Permission to Feel*: "Everyday creativity is the ability to keep discovering new answers when the old ones no longer work" (Brackett, 2019). You can find creativity in art, music, fashion, and marketing, as well as in research and business. There is creativity behind every research question and answer. On the business side, you find creativity in novel ways of generating income, providing value and creating new business models. This is not limited to new technologies or products. Tesla is one of the great examples of how you can transform the automotive industry with creativity. A Tesla car is an electric car. The technology existed well before Tesla appeared on the market. Toyota Prius was a hybrid solution to make this transition, for instance. Tesla was creative in their communication to users with the message that electric cars are the most sustainable cars, creating new income streams and applying the "Kickstarter" business model for the car industry, where future customers would pay a certain percentage of the cost of the car in advance to get on a waiting list. Volkswagen did this before the Second World War in Germany as a public offering.

Another brilliant example of creativity is, as Marc Brackett said, "Whenever we make a decision or face a challenge, we have an opportunity to be creative" (Brackett, 2019). In this case, when stressed during the decision-making process, this sensation is known as fear when facing a challenge. The magic of emotional intelligence is the ability to transform these basic emotions of anger, fear, or sadness which cause you stress and frustration in your situation into contentedness, making the right decision more accessible, and making you ready to understand the situation and to think of solutions.

Along with writing this book, I also ran my company, Collabwith. Being an entrepreneur is dedicated, hard work, where working hard and smart are synonymous in the context of entrepreneurship. Sorry, there are no 4-hours-a-week successes here. It is particularly stressful when you have to manage an organization, team, customers, partners, issues, all at once. From personal experience, it is not possible to write a line when under stress. Hence, I have to be calm, relaxed, and content, to be able to write and think in frameworks, on a canvas, and connecting the dots. This book was written on my "strategy days" and "thinking days"; when I was overloaded with work, I had to have a weekend of focus towards myself and the family to be able to relax and open my mind to be able to write. In my experience, I feel connected to myself while writing. It is a meditation moment for me.

An important distinction is that creativity is not innovation. Creativity enables new ways of thinking which is one part of the innovation. Innovation creates value from this creativity and new ideas. Without action and performance, there is no innovation, only creativity. Ideas are only one step in the innovation journey.

Our society has faced the Covid-19 crisis as an external stress factor, generating fear. Many leaders have reacted with fear, eliciting a dark side of leadership where employers press employees to perform 100%, with little empathy for the situation (remote working with family around, including kids, and also friends, along with homeschooling, cooking, and working all at the same time and place without even having the opportunity to go for a walk). Some have stopped paying suppliers or small companies within their ecosystem, entirely closed factories, and held video conference meetings all day long to control their employees, removing all the budget for annual projects, etc. The light side of fear in leadership has used the fear during the Covid-19 crisis to look for solutions after analyzing the situation without panicking. Instead, they calmly acknowledge the situation, the issues, and make solutions for everyone in the company and team with elements of empathy, understanding, trust toward employees and customers, and an ability to adapt the business model and the company to the circumstances. Strategies include reducing the salary of employees down a percentage for a fixed period of time, allowing flexible working hours, focusing on objectives and not on number of working hours, making holidays mandatory in the company to reduce costs, starting digitalization of processes to make the company more virtual during and after lockdown, and looking for services and products the company can offer to help employees, customers and partners during the Covid-19 pandemic. The transformation of fear prompts new creative ways of thinking of solutions towards issues in the organization or project. As Celia Avila-Rauch states in her book *Dark and Light Side of the Fear in Leadership*, "Fear is a barometer that is telling us that we must act. The way we should act will be indicated by our self-esteem, by our ability to adapt and by our ability to be aware of facing danger, as well as knowing whether it is our ego that is affected, our values or our dignity" (Avila-Rauch, 2020). The innovative leader and the innovative organization have to be able to transform fear into creative solutions.

Why is emotional intelligence important for innovation leadership?

Marc Brackett states, "The creative process needs to be followed by concrete action" (Brackett, 2019). This concrete action is called innovation, and as Marc Brackett followed up in his book, *Permission to Feel:* "Without innovation, societies stagnate and die" (Brackett, 2019).

This book defines innovation as "generating value from creativity", the action following the idea is to generate value. The action happens when in a calm mindset. Fear can paralyze people, causing behaviors like procrastination and avoiding taking any action at all. This is one of the major issues in innovation management; the focus is mainly on idea generation and prototype development, but there is a lack of action in terms of bringing ideas to the market. Innovation is when you create value, and value is created when a product enters the market within an industry and people adopt this novelty product.

Second, when you focus on idea generation without following through with action, your organization will suffer from frustration. If your team, department or organization associate innovation with frustration, it will be difficult to manage. Innovation culture might come to have a negatively connotation, disrupting the process. Idea generation with brainstorming sessions, design thinking workshops, and idea platforms to generate ideas for problems have the danger to be only "happiness pools". The reason for this can be found in our psychology: if you are in the yellow quadrant of the mood meter (Figure 4.1) you are avoiding action. You have to have a reason behind a brainstorming session, with a budget allocated to the session and a process to implement the ideas. For instance, do you want to improve your organization's "onboarding process when a new employee is coming in"? You can bring together IT, HR, assistants, and other key stakeholders to analyze the situation and make a plan to improve the process and employee satisfaction. You need to find the issues in the process together and solve the problem as a team in an innovation project. If you don't have a budget allocated, determine who the owner of this problem is, and influence the director of that department to allocate a budget. You will have an allocated budget, you will have a sponsor, a project to focus on, a serious team of committed and responsible individuals to select the ideas and bring them to life in your organization together. If you need a tip, you can have an "employee team" of randomly selected employees to generate ideas to solve the problems you defined before with your "innovation project team". This employee team could be your user focus group, your test group, your idea generation group, and your "super user team" to create true user-centered innovation. You have to be transparent with them, you have to talk to them with clarity about your goal, process, your budget, your issues, and communicate with them after every milestone. Besides this, you could also host an informal lunch to build a relationship with your "super user team" and "innovation project team".

Innovation leadership is one of the most complex types of leadership you can face as a leader, while showing resilience. Why? Because as an innovation leader you have to manage people who are not on your team, you have to influence them without them reporting directly to you because your budget is minimal and is dependent on how you successfully sell projects to the "business owners". You are in a support function, but at the same time, you critically assess the future of the business. The whole organization has to be innovative, because an innovation leader transforms work in every project, and this implies change. You have to drive change successfully, knowing that only 30% of the change projects are successful. According to *The Heart of Change* (Kotter, 2012), change is about managing emotions. You have to bring the emotional aspect into innovation. Listening, supporting, influencing, focusing within, at the organization level, and externally, are all important factors. You have to connect the dots, so you have to know what your organization is doing, its objectives, its strategy, and its problems. Your role is in many ways like a CEO, but without having the power of a CEO. You will find a full chapter on innovation leadership in Chapter 9.

Benefits of emotional intelligence for innovation
- You create a healthy innovation culture.
- Your organization is resilient.
- Your organization accepts failure as a part of the frustration process.
- Your organization drives transformation change successfully.
- Your organization is transparent, assertive and trustful.
- Your organization provides a psychological safe space.

Ideas for creating an innovative organization through emotional intelligence
Goals
- Generate resilience.
- Value your organizational creativity and issues.

Decision making
- You have to get a budget first.
- Bring stakeholders together to analyze issues.

Influence
- Listen, listen, listen.
- Support, support, support.

Equity
- Ask more questions about what others need.
- Ask more questions about what others mean.

Why is emotional intelligence needed for successful collaboration?

Currently, you might think that academics, entrepreneurs and business professionals do not have a common language with which to discuss. Maybe they are using different vocabulary to express themselves because they are in different contexts, but all of them have one thing in common. They are not only academics, entrepreneurs or business professionals, they are friends, parents, family members. They have other hobbies and other interests. All of them are human beings, and you have to look at them as people who have a lot of knowledge to share and to connect to. The collaboration will be successful if you understand that you need to connect to every collaboration team member on a human level. Communication is key for a successful collaboration, and communication is created if you build a relationship with the collaboration partners, and here you have to differentiate between friendship and relationship. You are not a machine for executing tasks, you are a person, and so is the other partner and collaboration team member. Even if you communicate via a computer with them, you need to create a psychologically safe environment to communicate properly in an assertive way and be productive as a "collaboration team". To create a psychologically safe environment, you need to build relationships with all the members and partners. Besides that, they have to do the same thing between themselves.

A collaboration is a creation of a new team – the new team could be formed by partners, customers, suppliers, or simply team members. Team rules need to be applied for an effective collaboration. The intersection between a psychologically safe team and emotional intelligence applied together gives a new flavor to the collaborative innovation team. A collaboration is created to work together to bring something new to the market, or to create something new to bring value to the industry, to your ecosystem, or to society. Hence, the focus should no longer be on you as independent individuals, you are a team. As Amy Edmondson said, "We want to work together to make the product better" (Edmondson, 2018). You can make this slogan yours by adding your product, service, process or whatever the objective of your collaboration is to it. Amy Edmondson analyzed the characteristics of a psychologically safe team to be dependent on:
- Leadership style.
- Innovation and creativity.
- Individual and team learning effectiveness.
- Culture.
- Cohesion.
- Trust.
- Autonomy.
- Transparent communication.
- Tolerance of risk and failure.

These characteristics can be created among a new team. Emotional intelligence skills will help you to build trust, to communicate in a transparent way, to be resilient to failure, to manage fear of risk, manage creativity, encourage listening to understand other opinions or arguments, and lead with kindness.

Emotional intelligence canvas for collaboration

A collaboration team is a new team formed for a specific cause; in this case, the collaboration is for innovation. This new team is coming from different departments, organizations, backgrounds, work and communication cultures. You are creating a new team to create a new product, new services or a new process together. Your team might come from academia, other professionals or startups. You are not a group of individuals doing tasks, you are a team, and even if you are coming from different organizations, you are there together to make a new service, product, research, prototype (whatever activity you want to do) together! You must accept that you are a team now.

Communication is part of the collaboration and is critical to the success of the collaboration. If you understand that during the collaboration, you have to create relationships with your new collaboration team members, this should not be about friendship, it's about having human relationships to create cohesion, better communication, and increase engagement and motivation. For this reason, I have created the "emotional intelligence canvas" (Figure 4.2) together with Celia Avila-Rauch to help you to manage communication smoothly during the collaboration journey. After our experience working with different collaboration teams and with innovation teams, we added in this canvas the basics and the essentials to manage the team communication and experience using the emotional intelligence skills for the team. This canvas is for you and your team at the same time, it's not only for the collaboration coordinator or project manager, it's for everyone.

In a practical way, you can use the "emotional intelligence canvas" when you are in a meeting (even remotely), at the beginning of the collaboration during the kick-off meeting, at the end of the collaboration, before a major deadline, before a presentation, when you have a conflict, in every meeting. It's a practical tool to have with you every day at work as a reminder of how to handle collaborations, how you manage your emotions, how you communicate your mood and how to communicate better.

The second part of every chapter in this book follows the "collaboration journey" and applies the subject of the chapter to a phase in your collaboration journey.

You can use the "emotional intelligence canvas" with yourself, for one-to-one meetings, with your whole team, with your collaboration team, with your project team, and with your organization.

When you are hosting your kick-off meeting for a collaboration, check if you have the same values at least for the collaboration you are doing. As the "emotional intelligence canvas" has the box of "values of collaboration", everybody will be on the same page of understanding, and you can go and refer to it if necessary.
– Respect.
– Active listening.
– Understand other opinions.
– Understand other cultures.
– Learn from others and from situations.
– Appreciate your own culture.
– Avoid stereotyping people.
– Listening what others need.

ASSESSMENT	EMOTIONS	CONFLICT MANAGEMENT	VALUES OF COLLABORATION

ASSESSMENT

WHAT IS YOUR MOOD TODAY?

HOW DOES YOUR TEAM FEEL?

HOW CAN YOU CHANGE YOUR MOOD?

HOW CAN YOU CHANGE YOUR TEAM'S THOUGHTS AND BEHAVIOR?

EMOTIONS

HAPPINESS / ECSTASY / JOY / SERENITY / OPTIMISM

DISAPROVAL / GRIEF / SADNESS / PENSIVENESS / REMORSE

CALM / CONTENT / ADORATION / TRUST / ACCEPTANCE / LOVE

LOATHING / DISGUST / BOREDOM / CONTEMPT / RAGE / ANGER

TERROR / FEAR / APPREHENSION / AWARENESS / AMAZEMENT / SURPRISE / DISTRACTION

ANNOYANCE / AGGRESSIVENESS / VIGILANCE / ANTICIPATION / INTEREST

CONFLICT MANAGEMENT

IN CASE OF CONFLICT, HOW CAN YOU MAKE PHYSICAL AND MENTAL SPACE? ARE THE PEOPLE INVOLVED PREPARED TO COMMUNICATE?

HOW CAN YOU BE CALM BEFORE ADDRESSING THE CONFLICT WITH THE OTHER PERSON?

CAN YOU SPEAK UP IN A CALM WAY? WHAT IS THE CONFLICT ABOUT FOR YOU?

HOW CAN YOU UNDERSTAND THE OTHER PERSON'S ISSUE? HOW CAN THE OTHER PERSON UNDERSTAND YOU?

RECOGNIZE THE CONTEXT THAT HAS CAUSED THE CONFLICT. HOW CAN YOU MANAGE YOUR FRUSTRATION? MAKE A PLAN TO FOLLOW UP.

VALUES OF COLLABORATION

☐ RESPECT.
☐ ACTIVE LISTENING.
☐ UNDERSTAND OTHER OPINIONS.
☐ UNDERSTAND OTHER CULTURES.
☐ LEARN FROM OTHERS AND FROM SITUATIONS.
☐ APPRECIATE YOUR OWN CULTURE.
☐ AVOID STEREOTYPING PEOPLE.
☐ LISTEN TO WHAT OTHERS NEED.

EMOTIONS / **ACTIONS TO TAKE**

FRUSTRATION — BREATH, FOCUS ON YOURSELFT, DEAL WITH FEAR ACCEPT OBSTACLES, HAVE COURAGE.

LACK OF MOTIVATION — LISTEN AND VALUE WORKING WITH OTHERS, CREATE TRANSPARENCY, CLEAR OBJECTIVES, BE EMPATHETIC TO OTHER FEELINGS AND SITUATIONS.

RESILIENCE — WORK ON YOUR OWN DRIVE, KEEP A POSITIVE ATTITUDE, UNDERSTAND YOUR EMOTIONS TO COPE WITH DIFFICULT SITUATIONS, FEEL BEFORE THINKING, MANAGE YOUR EMOTIONS.

LACK OF FOCUS — DIFFERENTIATE URGENT VS. PRIORITIES FOCUS ON YOURSELF FIRST, BEFORE FOCUSING ON THE TEAM, ON YOUR ORGANIZATION, INDUSTRY, AND THE WORLD.

LACK OF CONFIDENCE — WORK ON YOUR SELF-ESTEEM, HELP YOUR CUSTOMERS TO TRUST YOU, UNDERSTAND & REMOVE FEAR FROM YOUR CUSTOMER, MAKE YOUR CUSTOMER HAPPY.

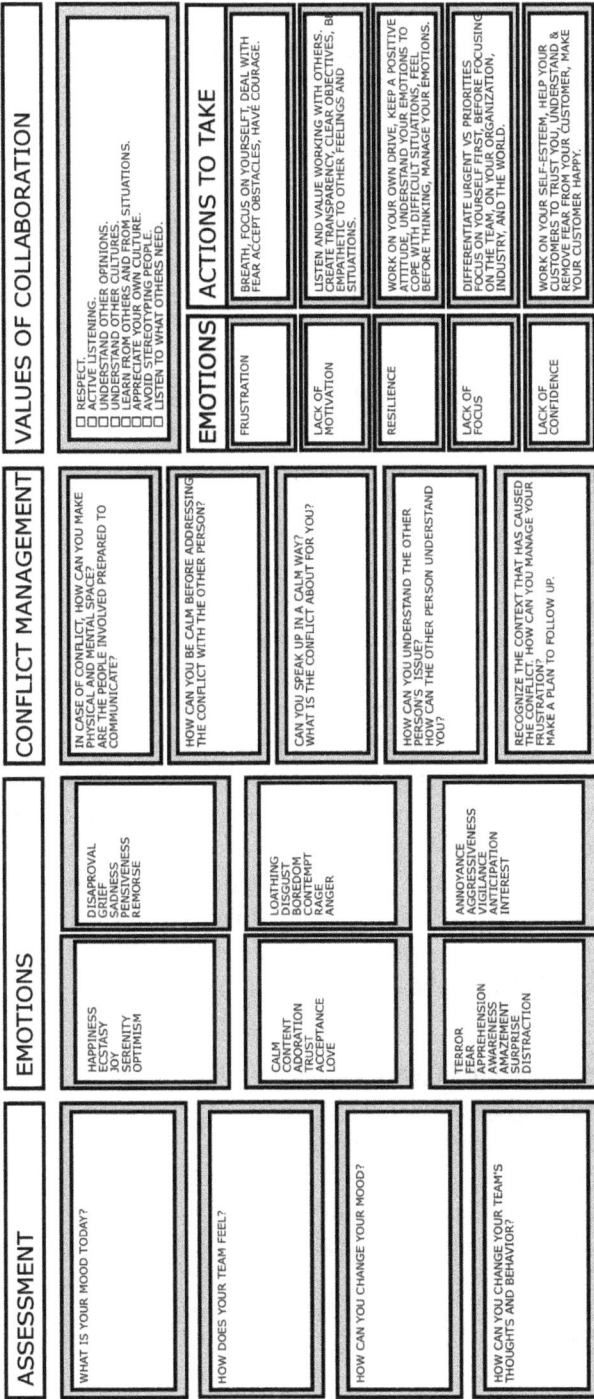

Figure 4.2: The emotional intelligence canvas for collaboration teams.

Another way to help your team to perform is to understand situations from an emotional perspective. Emotions and how you are feeling are information, and you have to receive this situation as a piece of information to take action. In the other box, you can read detailed emotions, with a specific action nearby. You just see which situation you or your collaboration team are in at the moment. For instance, if you are feeling frustrated, the action would be to take a deep breath, focus on yourself, accept the fear and the situation and see what you can do to change, and then do it! As another example, if your team is not motivated, you have to listen to them, or listen to the person who is not motivated. The action to take to motivate members is to value them, and value their work and value their role inside the collaboration.

The assessment is part of the mood meter by David Caruso, where you ask yourself the question: What is your mood now? And how is the mood of your team? (When you ask them this question and you receive an answer from your team members individually.) The answers from you and from your collaboration team need to be understood and explained between you all. Each member is responsible for answering these questions and looking at the "emotional intelligence canvas". In the other area, you find vocabulary for how you can easily express your mood, so "angry", "sad", "fine", and "happy" are not your only options to communicate.

At times when you are in conflict, know that healthy conflict is welcome to create a better team performance if it's solved in an assertive manner. With the "emotional intelligence canvas" you have a guide of questions you can follow yourself and together with your team. The objective is to use this guide to help you with the progress to communicate issues, disagreements and uncomfortable situations and look for solutions together to understand and solve the conflict. For this, first you have to assess your mood and feelings, and you have to see the mood of the other party implicated. Then you assess yourself to see whether you are in the correct mood to start a complicated conversation – you need to be calm, so if you are not calm you have to make space and distance before you approach the conflict.

Useful skills for using the emotional intelligence canvas for collaboration
– Communicate and share your values for collaboration.
– Learn how to manage your team's frustration and motivation.
– Learn how to manage conflict.
– Learn how to use the mood meter (Figure 4.1) with your team.
– Use a wide vocabulary to talk about mood and emotions.

How it works in a practical way?

Individual: You start your journey assessing yourself using the mood meter in Figure 4.1 and following the questions. Then you have to understand why you are having such a mood and understand the causes of it. You have to decide if you want to change or you want to stay in that mood. For instance, if one day you wake up tired, overwhelmed and sad, you have to understand why you are feeling that way. Maybe you are not sleeping enough hours, you are working too much, you feel stressed, you are almost burned out, you have unresolved conflicts, or you are not able to differentiate between what is urgent and what has priority. If you want to change this feeling, you have to acknowledge the feeling first, and understand the situation and then if you want to change it. In this example, you can take a break, get a cup of tea, look out the window and breathe deeply for a moment. If you feel it's difficult to do this, you have to take a walk to lower your stress levels first and feel the emotions in your body. This is the first step to see in a clear way what is happening with your emotions. Before you take action, you have to go to the "content" and "green" quadrant. Once you are "calm and content", you can think of solutions to mitigate your tiredness, such as going to sleep earlier and at the same time every night, or focusing on the urgent things and stopping procrastinating to reduce the stress levels. You need energy to act. And this is how you build resilience day after day.

Team: The first step is to make your own assessment of how your mood is, and your own understanding. The next level is the assessment of your collaboration team. Your guide should be the "emotional intelligence canvas" (see Figure 4.2) together with the mood meter in Figure 4.1 and use them with your team or collaboration partners.

Organization remotely: If you are following the "decentralized innovation" principles, you can find your collaboration team outside your office, your city and your country. Hence, you are creating a remote team per default. That may not be self-explanatory looking at the experience with lockdown during the Covid-19 pandemic: being quarantined and forced to work from home from one day to the next, often for the first time, was an experience that many companies were not ready for. In some cases, problems arose due to a lack of laptops, webmail applications or VPN connections. And those examples are the basics of IT infrastructure to provide a remote workspace with. Below, you can find the emotional intelligence checklists to be able to work remotely, because building a high-performing remote collaboration team is not only about choosing a suitable video conferencing tool, but also about leading with emotional intelligence skills, being able to empathize, understand, listen and to make clear objectives and communicate. It requires being more attentive and spending time to create and nurture the relationship, and not work only on task-based management.

Checklist for remote leadership
- Manage expectations with your team.
- Clear goals and simple objectives.
- Give direction to people.

- Build relationships outside tasks and classical meetings.
- Talk about what you are doing, how and why you are doing it and what you need every day with your team members.
- Self-management and learn how to manage healthy and toxic conflict.
- Master the emotional intelligence skills.
- Take time to relax, do sports, the day before creating your tasks for the next day.
- Listen to podcasts, or to music, for fun while working away from your team.

Checklist for remote workspace (virtual innovation ecosystem)
- Have a dedicated workspace (clean and orderly).
- Make time to walk and do sports.
- Listen to podcasts or music.
- Make time off from emails and video calls.
- Make your own to-do list for the day the day before.
- Make your own to-do list for the week before starting the week.
- Separate spaces for breakfast, lunch and work.
- Have a good headset and microphone.
- Have a laptop instead of desktop to be mobile.
- Think of having a nice background for your online calls.
- Make and provide a free choice to work from home or at the office.

Checklist for remote work during lockdowns
- Accept limitation of productivity.
- Accept the digital knowledge of others.
- Keep your team spirit, do activities together outside work.
- Build a relationship with your team remotely.
- Team with your family, now they are part of your "work team" as well.
- Focus on yourself and practice mindfulness. You can meditate while cooking, preparing your coffee or your tea and doing your laundry too.
- Learn and get energy from inside yourself.
- Increase your empathy toward the lockdown situation.
- Call your friends and family, not only your customers and partners.
- Focus on solutions.

Checklist for emotional awareness during lockdown
- Be prepared for self-motivation and discipline.
- Accept that remote work is a reality.
- Understand that family and children are around.
- Make family roles clear.
- Be aware of your pandemic stress.

- Home office is not a vacation.
- Separate tasks for personal vs. work management.
- Dedicated workplace is required.
- Keep a nice time organization and be flexible.
- Understand your fear of change.
- Learn to manage uncertainty.

Collaboration startups and organizations

"Collaborations between corporates and startups can be made on business model innovation or can be technology-driven," says Russell O'Brien from New Zealand Innovation Ecosystem (O'Brien, 2018).

"It takes time to get startups to understand your business, don't fear sharing problems with startups or working with them," says Russell O'Brien from New Zealand Innovation Ecosystem (O'Brien, 2018).

To understand the communication dance and psychology behind the relationship between startups and corporates, you have to understand the "entrepreneurship journey" and the rollercoaster of emotions of the founder, and also the emotions and complexity of the innovation team inside the organization. First, you can look at the well-described "hockey stick growth" book by Bobby Martin where it says about the blade years at the beginning of the startup: "It's an interesting stage, because it's the hardest type psychologically and physically, and it's also when the most important work is being done for the business" (Martin, 2016). "It's also a time when the founder him or herself is doing a lot of the heavy lifting and handling important aspects of the business: selling, product development, customer service and they're also learning like crazy" (Martin, 2016). It's possible to imagine a startup founder on his/her good days in a happy mood, or on a bad day feeling disappointed and frustrated, and going to pitch her startup to a potential customer in a corporate environment. It will be a drama if the founder is not able to manage his/her emotions of frustration and negativity in front of a potential customer. The founder has to be able to be resilient, to be able to overcome frustration, disappointment and fear and to translate it into drive and energy to continue the business. This is a clear example of how important it is to learn emotional intelligence skills.

On the other side, the innovation manager in the corporate organization is feeling fear of contracting a startup and trust that they will be there next year and deliver a correct product with great operational service and great customer care. In this case the corporate decision maker has several options, which are Microsoft, Google, IBM, and a no-name startup, and the innovation manager will choose the new brand innovative solution from an established American company and not the startup. Because if the established American company product fails, the established American company fails, and the innovation manager is not responsible. But if the innovation manager contracts the startup's brand-new solution and the startup fails, then the innovation manager is responsible, and he fails too. Hence, the startup founder has to be aware of this fear and responsibility of the innovation manager. The startup founder has to build trust, has to be able to manage the fear of the innovation manager, and co-work together with him/her to look for solutions and in some cases, adapt their innovative product.

Collaboration industry (including startups) and academia

A natural way of interacting and engaging between professor and research is key and helps to benefit both parties. You add value to each other when understanding each other's mind or views. For instance, we do workshops with students to see how to innovate and improve our research problems that occur at that moment (d'Hooghe, 2019).

In Chapter 3, you will find examples of different ways to collaborate for industry and academia. This chapter is about how to help you in this collaboration using emotional intelligence. The process to follow is the "collaboration journey" we introduced earlier in this book, but in the middle of managing expectations there are a lot of emotions and hidden arguments between both parties. The idea is to use the "collaboration canvas" from Figure 3.6 to support the clear communication between both parties, and the "emotional intelligence canvas" to be able to assess the emotional situation of the conversation.

Let's look at an example where one company is super exited to collaborate with a professor from university who has created footwear from a vegetable plant which is biodegradable and sustainable, and it's ready to be manufactured in a special factory next to the university. The professor is excited to collaborate and bring their research to life; however, at the same time, he does not trust what the company will do with their footwear, if the company will use it correctly. In this case, the professor is afraid, has accumulated frustration from other experiences, and he is showing control. In addition, he is not providing information about the cost or any kind of budget because he is afraid of making a wrong estimation or losing the "customer" if he overestimates the cost. On the other side, the company representative is looking for the cost to be able to request the budget for this "innovation project" to the senior management team, and the innovation manager is afraid of losing the trust of the professor, if he does not have the final agreement and a positive decision soon, which he cannot have until he has the cost estimate. This is only a basic example, and you can see here only the emotion "fear" in the scenario; however, this is enough to illustrate the importance of emotions in our behavior and decision making, and in the success of the collaboration for innovation. This case was one of the cases that did not go through because the professor was not able to provide the cost.

Emotional intelligence guidelines for collaboration
- Recognize that every human being has emotions, needs, and feelings that are as sensitive as your own.
- Try to understand the rules and norms of the culture or cultures of any person with whom you communicate.
- Respect the customs and traditions of others.
- Listen actively when someone from another culture is talking to you.
- Learn to cope with uncertainty.
- Understand and appreciate your own culture.
- Avoid stereotyping people who are different from us.
- Be aware of your own ethnocentrism.

In this chapter's conversations, I want to highlight stories I know first-hand and I want you to know why it is so important to master emotional intelligence skills for innovation, inside or outside your organization or, for instance, for entrepreneurship.

Conversation with Dr. Charlie Camarda on "How important is Psychological Safety for Team Performance?"

NASA Astronaut Space Shuttle STS-114
    Founder/CEO The Epic Education Foundation
    https://epiceducationfoundation.org

What is collaboration for innovation for you?

I will be basing my answers to this and other questions on my experiences working on teams following the Space Shuttle Columbia accident which occurred on February 1st, 2003. The teams we created were necessary because the same culture and organizational behaviors at NASA which caused the accident were preventing creativity and innovation in analysis and design to understand the technical cause of the tragedy and to rapidly develop technologies which were necessary for us to successfully return to flight.

Many problems we face are complex, not complicated. They are the result of non-linear, dynamic interactions of many disciplines and the result of these interactions renders the problems to be nondeterministic. This means the exact results cannot be calculated to 100% certainty. To solve such problems requires multiple researchers with expertise in several disciplines to work very closely in a converged fashion to solve these highly coupled problems. Many of the issues which must be understood are the result of these unknown interactions and requires the collective intelligence and coordination of teams of experts to conduct numerous experiments, to explore the boundaries of that knowledge by testing to failure; and to be able to correlate re-sults and predict failure analytically (using physics-based models).

Collaboration for technical teams solving such problems means that each team member must feel psychologically safe to express their ideas without fear of per-sonal risk, and to candidly critique the ideas of other team members. The informa-tion the teams need must be open, transparent, and shared with every team member. If the teams do not have the required expertise, they must be willing to explore out-side their team to obtain the necessary expertise.

What were the cases where psychological safety was especially important for your teams and for innovation?

Every one of the teams that were successful during the return-to-flight (RTF) period following Columbia maintained a high degree of psychological safety. One team, which I refer to as the Research and Development Impact Dynamics Team (R&D IDT), was a collection of research engineers from two NASA Research Centers, Langley and Glenn and impact dynamics experts at Boeing Philadelphia. The R&D IDT was instru-mental in understanding the dynamics of the foam impact to the Shuttle Orbiter vehi-cle which was determined to be the technical cause of the accident. I initiated this team against the wishes of the Space Shuttle Program Office (SSPO) because the origi-nal SSPO team did not have the expertise and were, in fact, incapable of predicting severity of the foam strike while the crew of STS-107 was in orbit. The researchers who composed the R&D IDT were raised and mentored in a psychologically safe envi-ronment and used a rigorous, building block approach to understand the physics of this complex problem. In only three months' time, they were able to exactly predict the full-scale impact test which simulated the conditions of foam impact to STS-107 during launch. Imagine if the Shuttle Program knew this expertise existed within their own Agency. We had experienced large pieces of foam debris since the begin-ning of the Shuttle program in the early 80's!

Another team which was formed during RTF was the research and develop-ment reinforced carbon-carbon on-orbit repair team (R&D RCCOORT). This team was formed to develop an on-orbit repair capability for the Shuttle crews in the event of damage to the Orbiter wing leading edges. We formed a small team to brainstorm new ideas to help solve problems the formal SSPO teams were strug-gling with. The R&D RCCOORT team conducted its analysis and testing in a se-cret laboratory offsite from the Johnson Space Center (JSC) specifically so that it could maintain a psychologically safe environment and be allowed to try numer-ous ideas, fail fast, and rapidly learn and mature ideas which proved to be suc-cessful. These are the principles we used to develop the innovative solutions which I flew on the first flight following the accident. The methodology we developed, called innovative conceptual engineering design (ICED) are the same principles we use in the Epic Challenge Program with students around the world.

Conversation with Alexander Gunkel about "Emotional Intelligence for Entrepreneurship"

Founder and CEO Space4Good

www.space4good.com

Space4Good uses space technology to support social and environmental impact projects all over the world.

What is innovation for you? How are you innovating in your organization?

For me "innovation" means the process of using creativity with action to improve the status quo. As such I don't think innovation needs to be technical but aimed to change something for the better. At Space4Good we decided to do this with the help of space technology, in particular satellite earth observation, which we combine with new processing methods, models and talents to support meaningful initiatives through geospatial insights. While space technology somehow implies a strong focus on technical innovation, we actually feel that our diverse backgrounds and motivations contribute the most to our clients.

How are you applying emotional intelligence skills in your entrepreneurship journey?

Being trained as a mechanical engineer, emotional intelligence actually never appeared on my curriculum nor at my first jobs. Only once I started my entrepreneurial journey, I was looking for ways on how to better understand and collaborate with my teammates for which personality profiles helped me a big deal. Even more so this kicked off a process of self-understanding which forms the prerequisite to support others. I'm still very inclined towards an analytical, numerical mindset but learned to complement it with an additional layer of emotional intelligence skills and hope to expand on them even further.

What are the key benefits of managing your team with emotional Intelligence skills?

I believe that EI skills help to not only address the functional needs of a team but indeed also the emotional ones which include purpose, recognition and safety. I actually see my job as helping my teammates grow professionally and personally within the vision and mission of Space4Good. This includes setting rules and making sure that they are followed but after all it feels much less "managing" than supporting which I believe is a key benefit of EI skills.

What did you change in your routine after learning emotional intelligence skills?

I think I take a bit longer for important decisions since I try to gather more viewpoints and not only consider the practical consequences but also the emotional ones. This also includes checking in with me more frequently since it got easy to get carried away with practical "to-dos" once our company started growing. As such I didn't change anything with my routine – just expanded it with an additional layer and recommend everyone to do so as well!

Summary

To sum up this chapter, I will leave you with a number of exercises that help form the basis of your journey toward increasing your emotional intelligence skills for innovation and collaboration.

To practice

1. Be aware of your own emotions and feelings.
2. You have to build relationships with your collaboration team to make a high-performing collaboration.
3. Use the "emotional intelligence canvas" to assess yourself and your collaboration team.
4. Keep in mind the collaboration values.

In the following chapters you will find

– Tips on how to manage collaboration vs. competition.
– Tips on how to talk about money during and for a collaboration.
– You will learn that collaboration has a process for each part of the deal.

Notes

(Ruckstuhl, 2019) https://collabwith.co/2019/03/podcast-ispim-ottawa-prof-katharina-ruckstuhl-on
-inclusive-innovation-being-closest-to-each-other-thinking-and-understand-each-other/
(O'Brien, 2018) https://collabwith.co/2018/11/podcast-ispim-fukuoka-ceo-russell-obrien-discuss-
how-to-create-a-large-scale-innovation-ecosystems/
(d'Hooghe, 2019) https://collabwith.co/2019/06/podcast-prof-stefano-puntoni-and-joost-dhooghte-
on-collaboration/

References

Avila-Rauch, C. "Dark and light side of the fear in leadership". 2020.
Brackett, M. Permission to Feel: Unlocking the Power of Emotions to Help Our Kids, Ourselves, and
Our Society Thrive. 2019.
Caruso, D. and Salovey, P. The Emotionally Intelligent Manager: How to Develop and Use the Four
Key Emotional Skills of Leadership. 2004.
Caruso, D.R., Rees, L.T. A Leader's Guide to Solving Challenges with Emotional Intelligence. EI
Skills Group. 2018.
Edmondson, A. The Fearless Organization: Creating Psychological Safety in the Workplace for
Learning, Innovation, and Growth. 2018.
Kotter, J. and Cohen, D. The Heart of Change: Real-Life Stories of How People Change Their
Organizations. 2012.
Martin, B. The Hockey Stick Principles: The 4 Key Stages to Entrepreneurial Success. 2016.
Salovey, P., and Mayer, J. D. (1990). Emotional intelligence. Imagination, Cognition, and
Personality, 9(3),185–211.

―――――

"Being patient, listening to others, and trying to find opportunities for win-win situations"

Dr. Irene López de Vallejo (López de Vallejo, 2018)

Chapter 5
Co-opetition: Collaboration vs. Competition. Sharing and Receiving: Two Sides of Innovation

Summary: In this chapter, you will learn the importance of collaboration vs. competition and how to speak up when it's necessary to balance the ethical and legal imperatives of collaboration for innovation.

Competition is a "struggle for existence," according Darwin's survival theory from a biological and ecological perspective. Competition is a term that is frequently used for entrepreneurship because, officially, surviving is the state or fact of continuing to exist, typically despite an accident, ordeal or difficult circumstance. This is the case for many entrepreneurs (as well for well-established organizations) in times of crisis. Competition could be defined as a scenario in which an individual or organization is trying to win something or to be more successful than another. Conversely, collaboration is a process where two individuals or organizations work together to realize shared goals. Innovation has had a very competitive approach rather than a collaborative perspective that makes it possible to work together to bring a specific innovation to the market.

Competition in nature is realized in the sense of resources first, and status second. Resources such as sunlight, nutrients, water, air, and space, to name a few, are critical. The same definition of competition is attached to anthropology. According to Marvin Harris, war is a fight for resources, because there are too many or too few of them for group survival. Darwin explained that if a mutation in an individual was suitable for the environment, that individual was better adapted. A mutation is a change in the individual, while the environment could be the same or the environment could adjust as well. You can interpret from the studies by Charles Darwin and Marvin Harris that competition was defined as a successful adaptation to the new context, which suffered from lack of resources. It was called "competition", but maybe our society is misusing the word "competition" instead of "competence". The better word might be "resilience" as a way to adapt to adverse circumstances to continue our evolution. Here, it's important to differentiate resilience and persistence, which could be seen as adaptation to the new circumstances to achieve a goal, versus resistance, which is doing the same thing over and over again without looking at the environment.

Charles Darwin's theory of "survival of the fittest" claimed that the power of adapting and changing was key to survival. He said that "better-adapted individuals" had the "fitness" to survive and breed, and therefore, these "better-adapted individuals" passed their "changes" to the next generation. Hence, the whole next generation is "fitted" and "adapted" to the environment. The concept of "adaptation" and "legacy" (next generation still has the change adopted) could be related to business, and how market changes

https://doi.org/10.1515/9783110665383-005

make businesses stronger or fitter if they can adapt to new circumstances consistently until the environment changes again. Change is a part of innovation, because innovation is bringing something new to the market or something new for a person or a process. Innovation generates new value through creativity; this new value is a change in process, or in society, or somewhere in the value chain or supply chain of industries. Change is deviance from some norm, difficulties, and problems.

If an organization accepts change as a part of their evolution, the organization will get stronger and fit for the next generation. You can see a clear example during the Covid-19 crisis: some companies died, and some companies became stronger. The Covid-19 crisis has been proof of how fast an organization can adapt their business model and way of operating to adapt to a new environment, situation and circumstances. Currently, governments are looking at this case as "business resilience" instead of "business recovery", because organizations were not likely to go back to their pre-Covid-19 operational status, instead evolving and adapting to the new situation, and further future situations. Hence, organizations have to be resilient. And in some cases, there is confusion between "surviving", as related to startups and entrepreneurs, and being competent and resilient within the change in the environment.

Darwin explained his theory inside an ecosystem, and here it's the most interesting part of the theory – individuals are not alone. The ecosystem and the context around them are what make them "adapted" or "not adapted". You can see the impact and the role of the ecosystem within individuals during the process of adaption and evolution. This is what in biology is called "ecology". And this is the bridge between "competition" and collaboration. Ernst Haeckel in 1866 defined ecology as the "whole science of the relations of the organism to the environment including, in the broad sense, all the conditions of existence." Ecology as a complex interaction between the organisms and habitat, could be used today as a term for the complex interaction between organizations and their context. In the case of a virtual innovation ecosystem, the ecology is the remote interaction between organizations and their context. The organizations are described in Figure 3.1 in the "collaboration journey" as actors. Habitat is a mix between the local environment in which they are living and the virtual context where they can create new opportunities for collaboration to adapt and evolve. In Chapter 6 we will explain in detail the essence of ecosystem and community.

Let's rethink our understanding of collaborations as co-adaptation, co-change, co-work, co-design, and work together to become stronger and resilient. As a part of the "ecology", those interactions between organizations are relationships, partnerships and collaborations to adapt better to the environment and market. This adaptation is a consequence of the change of the environment or the realization that the organization has to change to be better adapted. And this is what makes an ecosystem perform, to have individuals inside the ecosystem who are ready to collaborate and interact with each other to make each other stronger together. The goal is to overcome adverse circumstances in new environments via cooperation and reciprocity as a form of survival and positive evolution.

In the long history of humankind (and animal kind, too) those who learned to collaborate and improvise most effectively have prevailed Charles Darwin (Darwin, 1859).

In a practical and modern way, you have to change your mindset from a losing/winning/competition mindset to an adaptive/learning/resilience mindset. If competition is coming from the idea of scarcity and lack of resources, collaboration is coming from an abundance mindset. Abundance thinking in innovation is learning, resilience, adaption and evolution. If you are on the side of abundance, you are on the side of working together towards a goal, a mission, because you want to bring value, and this is the only objective that matters. Of course, if you want to bring value you have to generate value and income for your organization. In Chapter 7, we describe the value and money concept of knowledge sharing and innovation. Collaboration for innovation means that collectively we are learning and evolving together, and we are all better adapted to the new environment.

Innovation is all about competition, let's change it to collaboration

"We always have competition, and we need innovation and change to encourage it," says Ricardo Baeza-Yates, CTO NTENT (Baeza-Yates, 2018).

Innovation is creating value from creativity; this definition has nothing to do with lack of resources or competitiveness. But there is a front-end innovation framework which includes a funnel of selection of ideas. And this sense of "selection of the best" gets misinterpreted as being equal to the competition from Darwinian theories. Again, it's not the best idea which is selected for prototyping, or for implementing, it's a variety of circumstances, biases and decision making which define the selection process. You can see that not the best ideas are selected at all times because the success on the market may be very low, and this is again another story to explain. Currently, innovation is not considering the critical and complex factors of the market for successfully bringing the innovation to the market and to the consumer. But success is all about marketing, storytelling, collaborations, partnerships and the right investment decisions.

There are "idea contests" in the form of challenge campaigns, or startup pitch competitions to select ideas, projects or startups. This "natural" competition is too early, it's impossible to say and predict the success of an idea on the market from a 3-minute pitch or a paragraph describing an idea. This is an issue for the reputation of innovation, and a misunderstanding of innovation. The consequence is that it has created a systemic problem in the investment-innovation ecosystem that "one idea" is equal to innovation or success. This type of contest is helping to enhance the competitiveness between the ideators and leaving them alone on the innovation and entrepreneurship journey. Here, entrepreneurship is defined as the process to bring the innovation to the market. The real approach from Darwin's theory is that the better-adapted ideators who are collaborating will be successful in the ecosystem and environment. The better-adapted ideators will understand what they need to change and adapt and with whom. The innovation ecosystem has to ensure the interaction between the ecosystem members to ensure the evolution of their ideas into products and services that people will use. And the innovation ecosystem has to offer support in all the areas needed to bring people together with the required knowledge, technology and investment.

The resilience of the theory is when the ideator can adapt the idea through adverse circumstances and evolve the idea to be better adapted, co-working together with other partners or customers and in a full interactive mode with the members of the ecosystem (see Figure 3.1) adversity can be overcome every time.

Change is an act or process through which something becomes different, and of course not everybody is prepared for changes or uncertainties. People in general do not want to face problems. Problems must be seen, not ignored. You should be prepared to look for a solution and not a problem. To approach a problem, you need:

– A clear definition of the problem in concrete terms.
– An investigation of the solution attempted so far.
– A clear definition of the concrete change to be achieved.
– The formulation and implementation of a plan to produce this change.

For instance, if you are looking at startups when they are looking for funding, they are in competition for funds. The lack of available investment is the reason for the competition, when in reality when you talk to investors and venture capitals, their perception is that there is enough money, and for them the issue is to find the good investments, so there is a lack of good startups. You can add a little bit of common sense and understand that the issue is an ecosystem issue of understanding how to do business (a startup is not only an idea on paper) and investment is one factor in a company's success. Therefore, the investments should focus more on how to create impact with good innovations, not only to add something trendy to the market. This is one of the dilemmas regarding the definition of competition and its correlation with scarcity or abundance in the environment. Investors should look for entrepreneurs who are resilient and who know where they are going with a purpose.

"Academics also face internal competition," says Mieke De Ketelaere (De Ketelaere, 2018).

Academia is suffering from competition because of the lack of public grants that make it possible for academics to perform public research. The selection process of patents and recognition of inventions and the selection process of publications are further reasons for competitive behavior Again, there is a lack of resources, in this case, public funding for research, recognition of invention and a limited number of scientific magazines and publishers. The consequence is that researchers have limited resources, they have to select which projects could perform better in the public selection, and they are faced with reviews to be able to publish. This is a negative circle of competition and the basis of a competitive ecosystem within academia. The rest of the ecosystem members (see Figure 3.1) are mostly excluded. Here we can observe a clear loss of the common mission and goal of the ecosystem.

How to transform your mindset from competition to collaboration?

"Academia/industry collaboration is not about contracts; it is about trust and being mentally prepared. To start with, you have to trust people and have an open mind" says Prof. Frank Piller, RWTH Aachen (Piller, 2020).

Let's transform your mindset from competition to collaboration. Instead of looking at the current situation through a negatively-biased lens, Table 5.1 shows the difference in values that apply to competition or collaboration. This visualization of the different set of values will help you understand what your values are and in which context you are feeling more comfortable. Thinking and talking about values is one of the solutions for overcoming the bias in relationships.

Table 5.1: The different values for competition and for collaboration.

Values of competition	Values of collaboration	Values of Innovation
Individual	Openness	Innovation
Closed mindset	Transparency	Creativity
Control	Negotiation	Impact
Unclear	Abundance	Knowledge
Creation of conflict	Trust	Technology
Lack of resources	Respect	Change
Scarcity	Togetherness	Collaboration
Limitations	Regime of reciprocity	Working together
Insufficient	Co-creation	Transparency
Inequality	Reduce conflict	Communication
Homogeneousness	Reduce transaction costs	Courage
		Learning
		Openness

If you are looking at the competition values in Table 5.1. you will see values with a negative connotation, while innovation has values on the positive spectrum, the same as collaboration. It is quite interesting to note how humanity often favors a competitive innovation process and a competitive perspective on innovation when the reality is that innovation is about creating value, and it's impossible to bring value alone or in an isolation mode.

To take a practical example from the tech world, we can have a look at how Google, LinkedIn or Stripe are making their "apps" available to be integrated into other systems and applications through application programing interfaces (APIs). This allows everyone to "collaborate" with these companies in a super easy way even without talking to managers inside Google, LinkedIn or Stripe. This type of tech-collaboration is making Google bigger and stronger as an organization and it's a new way of creating extra impact with users that might not be users of Google at first, but thanks to the API integration, now these collaborations are expanding Google values, and Google services to other systems, customers and industries.

Checklist for having a collaboration mindset
- Think about your own values and make a list of your important values.
- Be open minded toward different options for collaboration.
- Be resilient, adapt your project and organization.
- Be patient, listen and understand the issues and needs.
- Create trust among your team and organization.
- Look at your customers and your supply chain to find opportunities for collaboration.
- The objective is to make something together which is a new innovation.
- Have a win-win mindset when you think of collaborating.
- Reputation is about how you manage conflict.
- Transparency brings wealth and positive impact for innovation.
- Remember: stronger together and further together.

What exactly does it mean to have a collaboration mindset? Let's take the example of a managing director of an accelerator or the technology transfer manager for a university. People in these roles often understand their position as the gatekeeper of startups, academics, research and technology. But they should not act as a gatekeeper! Saying, "I am protecting my startups", or "I am allowing only collaborations with trusted companies" (knowing that trust takes months and years to build!) is plain wrong. This kind of "gatekeeper" is only doing business and allowing collaborations with partners who are actually sponsors of the ecosystem. Do you see the injustice of the situation? It is unfair to the startups, and shows disrespect for the research which is never applied to the organizations which really need it. This mindset is an obstacle to knowledge sharing, knowledge transfer, technology adoption, research application, value generation, growth of the industry, growth of the ecosystem and growth of the country's economy. Likewise, this sends out the message that you need to become a paid partner of the accelerator or university to be able to access their technology and knowledge. This weakens SMEs and startups, but also other organizations that might not have the capacity to sponsor every university or accelerator before they know they need it.

Universities and accelerators as organizations where knowledge and technology are created via research or innovation have to be open. This means that they have to open their research publications, research projects, research partnership opportunities, and make every academic accessible to the rest of the world. Universities do not have to be afraid of "overwhelming" academics with nonsensical proposals. When corporates and SMEs reach out to an academic, it's because they really need him or her! And if they see cases of nonsensical requests, academics can refer their contacts directly to the tech transfer office for details and follow-up. It's important to create a structure and a clear process that everyone is feeling positive about and that provides the tools to manage every situation. The same is true for the accelerators, which need open their startups and technology to the industry in a transparent and clear way, where organizations can find them easily to make business and innovation. Do you remember the "bias on Web" issue of finding knowledge on Google, and how difficult is to find information on internet? Make it easy!

First steps and guidelines for building an open ecosystem
- Make research publications open to the public (past research).
- Make it easy to find a directory of startups.
- Make it easy to find a directory of academics with their current and past research (kept up to date).
- Make academics visible with interviews, videos, podcasts and other online events (not only your closest contacts, but everyone also has to have the chance to be visible).
- Make academics and startups decision makers for their collaborations.
- Make a simple process of communication for when they receive a request from an organization. They have to know what to do, how to make a collaboration and how to manage conflict and decline or accept proposals

How to build resilience in a competitive environment?

Resilience is the capacity to adapt to stressful circumstances. Resilience and resistance will be powerful and fundamental tools to live change in a way that works for us (Paler, 2017). First, you need to manage your own resilience; second, your team's resilience; and third, your organization's resilience. This is a very important concept. You cannot manage business resilience or a collaboration's resilience if you don't know how to be resilient yourself, because your mind is driving your organization's strength. Resilience is accepting competition, managing frustration and looking for solutions and ways of collaborating and strategies for adapting. Your resilience means that you can recover from a "loss of a customer in favor of your competitor", "an angry customer going elsewhere", "a copycat of your features", or "a copycat of your business model, strategy or ideas". The time needed for recovery will depend on how resilient you are and how big the "issue" is from which you are recovering.

Guidelines for building your resilience within competition
- Your feelings need to be managed.
- You need to feel before you think, to know how your feeling is affecting your thoughts.
- The perception of the emotions and the cognitions help us to cope with difficult situations, and resilience in turn helps us to recover quickly.
- Be grateful for what you have accomplished so far and for your journey.
- A positive attitude and optimism are the ability to manage emotions, and the ability to see failure as a form of helpful feedback.
- You need time to recover, understand the issue, conflict or frustration and have a clear mind to find solutions.
- You are not alone. Have a support team around you to help with your recovery and resilience.

As resilience is a skill you can develop, you can learn and improve it! Resilience is a tool within emotional intelligence skills, and resilience is created when you perceive, manage and understand your emotions as information for your personal and professional life. Table 5.2. is showing the emotions for competition and emotions for collaboration. Read the emotions carefully and reflect on which feeling and emotion you are when you are in difficult circumstances in a competition context.

Table 5.2: The different emotions for competition and for collaboration.

Emotions for competition	Emotions for collaboration
Fear	Calm
Dislike	Content
Frustration	Acceptance
Hate	Sharing
Sadness	Resilience
Deprivation	Understanding
Focus on problems	Focus on solutions
Conflict	Caring
Cautious	Generous
Aggressive	Admiration
Anxiety	Compassion
Anger	Engage
Disappointment	Kind

If you want to go from competition to collaboration, it's time to reflect on how you are feeling when you are talking to your competitor or realizing that a competitor is damaging your project or business and understand why you are feeling that emotion. For instance, if you are feeling fear, you need to translate the fear from the dark side (negative emotions and thoughts) to the light side of fear (positive emotions and thoughts). Yes, it's possible! Celia Avila-Rauch in her book, *Dark and Light Side of the Fear in Leadership*, provides guidelines on how to make this transition, such as trusting yourself, building self-confidence and understanding fear as a piece of information to adapt, make decisions, take actions and create solutions, instead of getting paralyzed because you are feeling afraid (Avila-Rauch, 2020).

Table 5.2 clearly shows that you cannot collaborate or innovate if you are afraid, or if you are feeling anxious or aggressive. You have to learn to perceive and understand your emotions before you can manage your fear and translate it into acceptance and resilience. Maybe you are disappointed or frustrated and resilience is the ability to manage frustration and move on. Competition is a distraction, and it's distracting you from your focus on yourself, your team, your organization and your organization's ecosystem.

Ideas for creating a resilient team and organization
Goals
- Generate resilience among individuals, teams and the whole organization.
- Adapt and change from adverse circumstances.

Decision making
- You have to be calm and content to be able to make decisions.
- Bring stakeholders together to analyze the situation and create solutions together.

Influence
- Understand and create space and time for recovery of individuals, teams and your organization.
- Listen, support and be aware of the value of your team and your organization.

Equity
- Train yourself, your team and your organization in emotional intelligence skills.
- Be grateful for your team and organization's achievements and celebrate small milestones.

How to share your knowledge, be open-minded and not crash in the face of your competitor

"I believe in the combined value that academics and corporate leaders can bring to end consumers. We have the solutions and knowledge but not always the time. The customers have the data and the solutions, but not always the knowledge. Professors have the time and knowledge, but not always access to the data or the solutions" Mieke De Ketelaere (De Ketelaere, 2018).

In order to innovate, you have to share your knowledge, exchange information and be open, and not be afraid of sharing. If you imagine a situation where you start a new job as the head of innovation in a company, and you see that the teams and departments are not talking to each other, they are working in silos. Hence, they cannot innovate. Impossible. Instead of feeling panic and working alone at your desk, you have to make a strategy to bring them together to share information across departments and teams as a first step. In this situation, you can start having one-to-one meetings with the managers of the other teams to know how they are working and how innovation can support them (listen, listen, listen). And then, you organize small workshops to mix all of them regarding the topic of their department. For instance, if you are working and doing innovation in IT, you can organize a workshop on "data mining", inviting a professor from a university to come over and share his knowledge with the teams, or you can organize a "Friday Innovation Coffee" every month to talk about innovation where everyone is sharing their ideas and perceptions related to innovation.

The same strategy is applied to competitors – if you want collaboration and innovation, you need to share information, and before that you have to generate trust. And you generate trust when you share information and build a relationship. Maybe you don't know how you will collaborate or work together. Sometimes this can be really complicated if you have two services or products that are very similar. But you can develop trust among your competitors, and one way is to have your collaboration values very clear in your mind, be open, build a relationship with your competitor, and share information. Maybe you can build an alliance, a coalition, or something that could benefit your business or project.

Your competitor cannot copycat your mind, your way of thinking, your strengths. They can only copycat an interface or a product, but not what you are bringing to the table, your own value. You have to remember that there is a strong link between the leader/owner/CEO and the company, project or other type of organization and activity the person is working on. Each person is unique, and when you understand that it is your journey, you are strong against your competitors.

How to collaborate with competitors? It's a very personal decision

"If you can recognize a competitor as a destructive force instead of a sign of value, you are already more sane than most," writes Peter Thiel in the book *Zero to One* (Thiel, 2015).

It's a very personal decision to collaborate with your competitors, but it's also a very strategic decision to make in a company or project. To name some examples: PayPal and X.com merged together to become stronger in the market; in research, academics are collaborating together from the same field to get access to public grants by creating consortiums; with our platform, Collabwith, we are partnering with other open innovation platforms to bring challenges from other platforms to our "marketplace of challenges and technology", bringing extra value to the members of our virtual innovation ecosystem. It's clear that not every person leading an organization, or a project has a mindset suited for collaboration. Every collaboration starts with an open mindset, which is the structure needed to go to the next step.

The "collaboration vs. competition canvas" in Figure 5.1 will help you understand the hidden opportunities of collaboration with your competitors. Of course, you collaborate with organizations which match your values of collaboration, respect, openness, ethics (see Figure 5.1) and have an eye on whether both organizations are following the same mission. The rest of the aspects are pure strategy.

In the personal and soft areas, you have your personal and organization's values and mission, and in the conversation with your competitor you have to be clear, consistent and speak up about your values – what is important for you and your organization, and even your feelings. By talking about the truth (what you think, openly), you are building trust, and you are creating a reputation when you want to collaborate with your competitor.

The first step is to make a list of your direct and indirect competitors, substitutive products or services and other organizations which are doing similar activities, or part of your activities or research. The next step is to analyze each competitor and understand if this competitor could be a customer of yours, a partner, a supplier, etc. You have to be open minded and think about whether you really have a complementary technology, service or product you can build on and bring an extra and new value to your customers and ecosystem. This is the time to be super creative and think outside the box completely. It's your journey, your organization and everything is possible. It's a matter of thinking and talking.

The second part of every chapter in this book follows the "collaboration journey" and applies the subject of the chapter to a phase on your collaboration journey. Here below it's about competition.

There are three questions to reflect on in the "collaboration vs. competition canvas" in Figure 5.1:

LIST OF COMPETITORS	CUSTOMERS	PARTNERS	SUPPLIERS	ECOSYSTEM	OPTIONS TO COLLABORATE	VALUES MATCH	MISSION MATCH
Competitor I							
Competitor II							
Competitor III							
...							
Question to reflect on: How can you collaborate with your competitors?							
Question to reflect on: What is the positive impact of working together?							
Question to reflect on: What is the most uncomfortable aspect about your competition?							
Question to reflect on: Transform your fear of competition into drive and focusing on solutions.							

Figure 5.1: Collaboration vs. competition canvas.

- How can you collaborate with your competitors?
- What is the positive impact of working together?
- What is the most uncomfortable aspect of collaborating with your competitors?
- How can you transform your fear of competition into drive and be ready to take action and create solutions?

These three questions are designed to help you to understand if you are ready to take this step in your organization and to help you in the transition of the feelings and emotions of "competition" to the emotions of "collaboration" (Table 5.2.). If it's not working for you, that is okay. Perhaps you simply don't want to do it or are not ready at this point. That's okay as well. Or if you are getting a cup of tea with your competitor and realize that he is an idiot, obviously you are not going to partner with your competitor in this case, even if he is open for it.

Useful skills for collaborating with competitors
- Focus on yourself, on your organization and on the world around you to know how you see the potential opportunity for collaboration.
- Focus on open-minded competitors to collaborate.
- Values from both sides have to be aligned or negotiated.
- You need to build trust with your competitor to build a relationship with them.
- Build resilience on your side to create self-confidence and focus on the future.
- Accept if it's not working, or there is not a match. Go to the next one.

Difficult conversations with competitors

"Unified team, we were able to ride out the dot.com crash and then build a successful business," says Peter Thiel in the book *Zero to One* on when he asked Elon Musk to merge with X.com, the competing payment system (Thiel, 2015).

The well-known merger between PayPal and X.com involved two of the generational leaders of today. Elon Musk and Peter Thiel had a conversation in a café halfway between both of their headquarters (Thiel, 2015). This was a difficult conversation, but they made it because they had an open-minded and collaborative mindset.

Checklist for a difficult conversation with your competitor
- Be clear, be transparent, be honest and be assertive.
- Have a clear objective in mind with regard to what you need.
- Keep up your confidence and motivation.
- Set clear boundaries.
- Manage expectations.

- It's a transaction-oriented conversation with objective and professionalism, but you have to use the emotional intelligence skills to survive the conversation successfully.
- Keep a nice relationship of appreciation and gratitude.

Now, it's the time to review the "Emotional Intelligence Canvas" (Figure 4.2) because you have to be ready for this conversation, and after the conversation to make the right decision. For further conversations, the "collaboration canvas" (Figure 3.6) is particularly useful too. It's about structure!

Resilience as an answer to accepting competition, resilience as collaboration

Resilience is a useful and highly adaptive trait. As collaborating with competitors is tough, you need to build resilience. And resilience is the opposite of re-working something to the point of exhaustion, it's about how you recover to be ready and full of energy to try again in a different way. Your focus is not on the details of how to do it, but on the mission and on the future. Resilience is expressing gratitude for your learning, your own path or the path of your company. Resilience is having a positive outlook to reduce the anxiety within yourself, your team and your organization. This is possible if you are communicating in an honest, clear and transparent way every time you talk to your team and organization (or even competitor).

Competition is a distraction, a dangerous path to un-focus yourself, and to lose your purpose and misunderstand your organization. Hence, collaboration is about focus and resilience, and collaboration is about innovation. Innovation is the truly open, collaborative, creative way of bringing value to the industry, society and people.

In this chapter on collaboration over competition, I want to share with you cases I admire and professionals who have extensive experience in practical aspects of collaboration. Below, you will learn new perspectives and experiences from thought leaders who are bringing together competitors with a mission.

Conversation with Carlos Lee about "Collaboration Over Competition"

Director General EPIC European Photonics Industry Consortium
@CarlosLeeEPIC

What is the EPIC?

It's a European technology association and a non-profit organization called European Photonics Industry Consortium of 17 years of existence, annual membership funded, European competitiveness oriented. It's a photonics ecosystem.

How do you bring together competitors?

Members of EPIC and the photonics ecosystem are not competing between them, because photonics is high-tech, and their CEOs are PhDs and they are usually a spin-off of universities. These companies are often created because they have a unique technology, hence they are very innovative. It's an ecosystem with 5,000 companies and 1,000 universities which are going to create an industry. It's a vertical consolidation and vertically integrated, which means they are part of the supply chain and value chain.

What do you discuss? How do you cooperate and collaborate?

We are opening the eyes and the mind, because to compete we have to create before a bigger market where you can compete afterwards. Now, the photonics ecosystem is too small to compete, we need to collaborate. The companies are improving their performance, opening their markets and reducing the prices. These kinds of activities are benefiting everyone in the ecosystem. Usually, the company's CEO and owners are passion driven and this factor makes them nice and easy to build relationships with.

How is EPIC organized? How are you creating community?

It's important to share trust and knowledge among the members and of course to determine how much you are willing to share. We need people who are deeply knowledgeable, business-minded, not research-oriented, because we need to solve problems in 6 months, not years. And they have to be nice because they are part of the ecosystem in a voluntary form, they are not sales-oriented. For instance, members are always asking about what others do, how they can help them instead of "we made this, do you want it?" The environment is rather more "I cannot help you, but I know somebody can help you."

We organize technology meetings within a small reach (max. 100 members) where we discuss, in a controlled and reduced environment, members' challenges and their roadmap. In our EPIC ecosystem everyone knows what others are doing. Furthermore, we build trust via networking activities, long lunches and long cafes, with the outcome to share knowledge and collaboration and projects together.

What are the outcomes and results for the ecosystem and the individual companies?

EPIC has the objective of European competitiveness because EPIC has to be part of the game. We are strong, but we have no guarantee to be there in 20 years. And having competitiveness is a way to still be there in the future with no subsidies for research or manufacturing. Our strategy is to build a strong ecosystem where we trust each other and we work together and that we help each other. We are building this network of 1,000 people to save the industry. If we are so strong in collaboration and support, that is difficult to replicate. At the end of the day it's about friendship, helping each other, sharing knowledge and working together. CEOs have to collaborate and work together, let the salespeople compete. We are building respect of each other, and facilitating a better understanding of each other, and appreciating each other. Especially in the case of small companies, we have to collaborate.

Some people like to network and others don't like network, you have to believe in the power of networking, the leader is deciding where to allocate the budget, you can organize more networking events to ensure this relationship building creation and you have to put your heart into it. On the other side, investment is particularly important because we want that photonics companies to remain European because these companies are coming from European universities.

Conversation with Karin Ekberg about "How to Collaborate with Your Competitors"

Former Chair of the Board of Directors at Sustainable Apparel Coalition
    CEO Leadership and Sustainability
    @KarinEkberg10

What is the SAC?

Sustainable Apparel Coalition is a coalition of retailers, manufacturers, service providers, academic institutions, NGOs, etc. it's a ten-year-old organization. And their goal is to develop an index that can measure the entire life cycle performance at the brand level, at the facility level and at product level. And communicate these results to the consumers transparently and focus on apparel and textile industry.

How do you bring together competitors? What is your goal in the SAC?

It has been a long learning journey for many of the brands who are working together, especially at the beginning. The topic has to be very interesting to bring competitors to collaborate. The Sustainable Apparel Coalition really wanted to make a change in the industry, and this change has to be measurable and all companies must work together.

Many brands thought that this idea was great, so they were prepared to come together. Even though I remember many meetings at the beginning, when it was very difficult for us to know how much we can say about what we are doing internally, how much we can share with our competitors. All the time, we learnt that we could share a lot about sustainability, not about market share information, for instance.

What do you discuss? How do you cooperate and collaborate?

You need to create that open room for talking and set up several rules, we talked about these rules a lot, for instance, that you cannot criticize ideas if someone has an idea, or that you need to let people speak out, and you need to listen well, let people speak, that you need to let everyone speak even if there are people that always want to speak much more and others that want to speak less. And you have to respect that some people and some organizations are less aware, or they are not that far from the sustainable journey and so you need to find a common platform and understanding, build your own vocabulary, etc. and just being very open and of course always drive for results. That you can always take your decisions out of your different industries.

How is SAC organized?

The Sustainable Apparel Coalition has a lot of members. But SAC also has a big staff, executive director, and people responsible for many different areas, different responsibilities for different parts of the tool, such as for the facility and environmental module, or for the product module. And there are people responsible for marketing and recruiting new members, etc. At the end, SAC is a not-for-profit organization, it has a board, where brands and manufacturers can become members as well, and then there is a governing body board of SAC that the executive director reports to.

What are the outcomes and results for the ecosystem and the individual companies?

Improving in the environmental area, where all the participants see a lot of improvements, year by year. They improve their own results, they save energy, they save water. The individual companies learn more and learn from each other. Because the index is built in a way that you always have the possibility to move to the next step and improve.

Summary

To sum up this chapter, I will leave you with a number of exercises that entice you to collaborate with your competitors and grow from inside out.

To practice

1. Make your list of potential competitors.
2. Define your values for collaboration.
3. Be resilient yourself first and build resilience within your organization second.
4. Prepare yourself to have difficult conversations.

In the following chapters you will find

– Tips on how to create a successful community and ecosystem.
– Tips on emotional intelligence for communities.
– You will learn that innovation needs a well-established community to grow and make impact!

Notes

(López de Vallejo, 2018) https://collabwith.co/2018/07/irene-lopez-de-vallejo-on-working-with-professors-and-start-ups/
(Baeza-Yates, 2018) https://collabwith.co/2018/10/podcast-prof-miralles-cto-baeza-yates-discuss-how-important-is-change-for-innovation/
(De Ketelaere, 2018) https://collabwith.co/2018/06/mieke-de-ketelaere-on-collaboration-with-academics-and-women-in-tech/
(Piller, 2020) https://collabwith.co/2020/06/podcast-prof-frank-piller-on-avatars-for-collaborative-innovation/

References

Avila-Rauch, C. "Dark and light side of the fear in leadership". 2020.
Darwin, C. "Origin of Species". 1859.
Paler, I. "Power tool: Resistance vs Resilience" 2017.
Thiel, P. "Zero to One: Notes on Start Ups, or How to Build the Future". 2015.

"First step, clearly define your ecosystem, second step, assess how to organize the defined group, third step, check that these groups work well together, and identify what their big challenges are".

Russell O'Brien, CEO at Cognitis Innovation, and former Head of Innovation and Entrepreneurship at City of Auckland in New Zealand where he established a collaborative ecosystem for innovation and entrepreneurship (O'Brien, 2018)

Chapter 6
How to Create Your Own Community
and Ecosystem? Diversity Acceptance and Inclusion

Summary: In this chapter, you will learn the importance of creating an ecosystem in order to foster abundance through innovation and collaboration. Your close net relationships within the ecosystem are known as your community and they are the unit which helps sustain you.

Community and ecosystem are two different concepts, and yet they are often mixed up. To start, let's go first to academic definitions and then to what each one looks like in reality. The Cambridge Dictionary defines community as "the people living in one particular area or people who are considered as a unit because of their common interests, social group or nationality". For instance, Collabwith is a community, because the members who have joined the community hold common interests of innovation and collaboration in the fields of industry and research. The definition of ecosystem varies based on whether one refers to biological ecosystems or social business ecosystems. The Cambridge Dictionary defines an ecosystem as "all the plants, animals, and people living in an area considered together with their environment as a system of relationships" and business ecosystems as "a group of businesses or business activities that affect each other and work well together". Collabwith does not only represent a community, it represents a mix between biological and business ecosystems. Most of the interaction is conducted in a virtual environment that is based on relationships. The interaction of actors in the community happens through sharing of knowledge, collaborations, events and rituals. These activities allow resistance and congruence to be shown and expressed, leading to new insights that work well to drive innovation. Both definitions apply to the Collabwith platform because without creating a community with common interests, it is difficult to build relationships to work together, and for this, you need to create activities, and a common place (in this case, virtually) to "affect each other". At this point, you might think that community and ecosystem are interchangeable terms and in some cases they are. They both have the common denominator of bringing people together to build relationships which leads to knowledge and information sharing and leads to the co-creation of innovation and faster growth.

Why an ecosystem for innovation?

An innovation ecosystem is a community of members who focus on innovation and creating impact by bringing people together to collaborate. Innovation is a way of turning creativity into value, but there is more to it than just coming up with a new idea or concept. Innovation is the act of bringing a new service, product or process to life and

https://doi.org/10.1515/9783110665383-006

putting it into place where people and companies can use and engage with it. A diverse ecosystem of stakeholders, actors or members coming from universities, accelerators, angel investors, corporates, SMEs and other professionals (see Figures 3.1 to 3.3) create a fertile business ecosystem of interaction. The interaction between the members of the ecosystem creates value through the velocity of the sharing of information and resources. The ecosystem is a place for ideators, researchers, entrepreneurs and investors to meet each other, and to bring people together with a common interest leads to new forms of meaning making and value creation. This phenomenon even happens virtually.

Within ecosystems we see the creation of a phenomenon called the network effect, which happens when members of the ecosystem begin helping each other, interacting and sharing knowledge and information among themselves. The sense of trust and belonging empower members to be vulnerable and take risks and explore new ways of being. Time is needed to build a trusted community of people who come together and share an identity and work to do something super creative and interesting together. This is only possible by facilitating the creation and fostering of relationships.

What are the benefits of being part of an innovation ecosystem?

"We should connect one maker lab with other maker labs and bring people together. Because creative outcomes are coming from knowledge diversity. We have to connect local innovation labs with virtual tools" says Prof. Frank Piller, RWTH Aachen (Piller, 2020).

An ecosystem is helping to build relationships among the ecosystem stakeholders and people (Figures 3.1), but an ecosystem is not created alone by itself without support. The ecosystem has to bring value to every member or actor in the ecosystem, and the ecosystem has to make a positive impact on the different industries and society. Figure 6.1 depicts how an ecosystem can create value and impact. For the ecosystem to function, it first needs to be populated with people from different backgrounds and institutions, (Figures 3.1). Secondly, the people have to be engaged; hence, you have to create engagement and pique the interest of the people in the ecosystem. Thirdly, the ecosystem has to support the interaction among the ecosystem members. This interaction, if it's successfully orchestrated, attracts more people and members, which is otherwise known as the "network effect". Fourthly, the interaction needs to bring value to each member, to the industry and to organizations including universities, governments, society, and investors. Generated value supports the growth of the ecosystem and the argumentation for being in the ecosystem. And lastly, the ecosystem needs to generate value and impact in the environment in which it is embedded. When these criteria are met then innovation is actually being created and the ecosystem is being effective.

When you create your own ecosystem for innovation, you have to develop a strategy that encompasses every action and that you are doing for the ecosystem. The creation of a community feeling, or ecosystem motto, is the "glue" and "raison

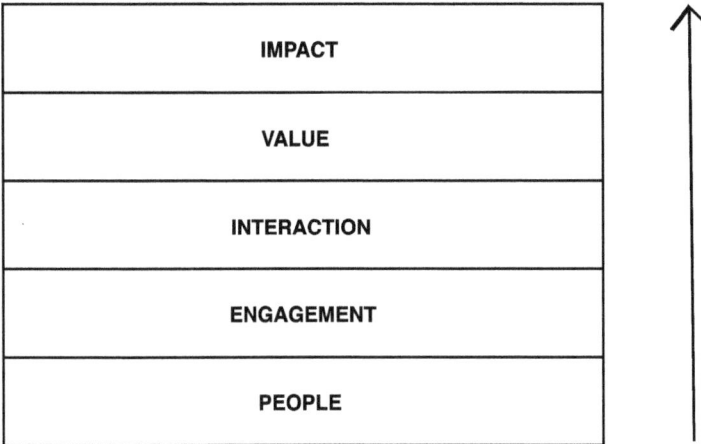

Figure 6.1: Ecosystem strategy.

d'être" that will connect diverse group members within the ecosystem. If you are creating a "virtual innovation ecosystem", the same strategy applies. The only difference will be in the execution. Important things to be considered are the effort needed to bring people together and how to create trust, engagement and interaction in a virtual environment. One of the advantages of a virtual environment is that it is not bound by physical space; this makes the cost of bringing together a diverse group of people from different environments next to nothing. This in turn increases the "knowledge diversity" (Piller, 2020) and the likelihood of matching the right partners to solve the problem at hand.

Benefits of an innovation ecosystem
- Access to resources, people, knowledge and technology.
- Access to public and private investment opportunities.
- Connect the right professionals and ideas for your organization and for your project at the right time and in a shorter amount of time.
- Create value from your ideas, find solutions to your challenges, solve your issues, and create new jobs for innovation, startups and other research projects.
- Connect with other startups, SMEs or organizations that can bring value to your project or organization.
- Create collaborations with universities, academics, policy makers and other institutions to bring value to your innovation projects and strategy.
- Access to knowledge and support for legal, finance, accounting and IT questions.
- Access to knowledge on leadership and innovation management.
- Help others with your knowledge and your connections.

- Help others to grow with your network and grow your network at the same time with the right innovation professionals.
- Increase your network via the networking activities of your innovation ecosystem.

How can an innovation ecosystem help you?

(see Figure 3.1: Collaboration journey opportunities and actors inside the ecosystem)

For Academics:
- Find additional funding for research.
- Help a business or organizations by giving advice or sharing research and knowledge.
- Find case studies for teaching activities and action research.
- Recommend the best students for internships.
- Get access to a database of industry organizations that want to work with academics.
- Promote your research results and technology via ecosystem media activities and social networks.
- Become a board member of a startup.

For Organizations:
- Get easy access to a global database of academics and startups that want to work with industry organizations and other types of businesses.
- Find the knowledge you are missing inside your organization.
- Find a keynote for your next business conference.
- Get an academic to validate and review your project and ideas.
- Get recommendations for exceptional student workers.
- Find startups with the innovative solutions you are looking for.
- Find collaboration partners.
- Find investors to fund new company ventures.

For Startups:
- Find board members from academia or industry.
- Find mentors and coaches that are successful entrepreneurs.
- Find experts from academia and industry to fill your knowledge gaps.
- Contact academics to get advice on your struggles.
- Get visible to industry organizations that want to work with startups as customers.
- Become a case study for academics.
- Get recommended students from professors.

- Generate your legal advice for contracts.
- Get access to global databases of professors and businesses wanting to work with startups.

For Universities:
- Bring research to life, to the industry and society.
- Increase your number of university/industry collaborations.
- Find additional funding for research projects from industry and investors.
- Find partners for research consortiums.
- Get access to industry databases of organizations that want to work with academics.
- Support academic entrepreneurs to go from research results to creating products for the market.
- Support the interaction between researchers and industry partners to find new case studies for their research.
- Promote your research results and technology via ecosystem media activities and social networks.

For Investors and Venture Capitalists:
- Scout interesting startups, SMEs and projects to invest in.
- Understand the industry challenges and opportunities.
- Discover what research projects academics and universities are engaging in.
- Support your startup portfolio to join research consortiums and get extra sources of funding.
- Support your startup portfolio to connect with industry customers.
- Support your startup portfolio with experts from the ecosystem.
- Support your decision making, connecting with experts.
- Promote your startup portfolio to the ecosystem and to industry organizations.

For Governmental Institutions:
- Increase the interaction between industry and academia and startups by facilitating collaboration.
- Increase the impact of research and startups on the industry and on society coming from public and private investment.
- Increase visibility of your country's research results and technology.
- Increase the number of international collaborations from your country's research centers, universities, accelerators and other innovation institutes.
- Support your country's innovation ecosystem in being visible and accessible to other countries.
- Promote the technology and research coming from your country's universities and accelerators.

For Incubators and Accelerators:
- Increase the speed at which startups are funded by investors, venture capital, and corporates.
- Increase the possibilities for funding of your startups.
- Increase the number of industry organizations and corporates who can become customers of your startups.
- Create awareness and visibility of your startups and developed technology.
- Extend your resources to transform ideas into reality.
- Connect with experts who can help you in your decision making regarding your startups.
- Promote your technology and startup alumni to the ecosystem.

How to build an ecosystem?

"People socialization is much more complex than personality – taking care of all senses of a relationship, how to manage the process and how to bring them together is very important," says Prof. Anton Kriz, Associate Professor – ANU – Tsinghua Master of Management, Director at inManagement Consulting (Kriz, 2019).

If you want to create an ecosystem, it is important to consider some of the personal skills that will benefit you during this process. First of all, you need to have strong social intelligence, as this will enable you to understand the social dynamics and the needs of members of the ecosystem. This intelligence gives you insight into how to best support engagement and interaction within the system. Empathy is one of the key aspects of social intelligence for yourself, your team and your ecosystem. At the same time, you need structure to create and successfully orchestrate the ecosystem because the objective is to bring people together from different backgrounds with a common purpose of innovation and collaboration.

Below you will find some basic considerations that need attention before you start creating the ecosystem.
- Self-reflection.
- Self-awareness.
- Act on your ecosystem values.
- Understanding of people, events and environments.
- Re-think and re-do.
- It's all about people.

The second part of every chapter in this book follows the "collaboration journey" and applies the subject of the chapter to a phase on your collaboration journey.

The "ecosystem and community canvas" (Figure 6.2) has been created for individuals, teams and organizations that want to create their own innovation ecosystems. Every phase has three steps related to designing the ecosystem, and all of them are important when following the "ecosystem strategy" (Figure 6.1). This structured approach will help bring people together who want to be engaged and interact with each other to bring value and impact to the ecosystem.

Starting phase

Knowledge: This box is about making the identity of the ecosystem clear. To name some examples: if you want to focus the ecosystem on innovation for sustainability, or innovation across sectors/ regions, or innovation in aerospace, digitalization in Africa, or on innovation in your local area or country. Knowledge is the starting point for creating an identity and purpose from the point of view of sharing knowledge for innovation. Hence, the question for you is: which kind of expert knowledge do you bring to the ecosystem?

Support: Innovation is about helping others and supporting them to innovate and collaborate. It is important to realize that no single person can bring innovation into the market by themselves (which, again, is actually the definition of innovation). When you are doing something innovative for the market, you always need new ways of doing things, new knowledge, and all the support you can get. Hence, the question you should always be asking yourself is: how can you help the ecosystem? And each member of the ecosystem should ask this question of themselves as well.

Actors: Here, you make a list of actors who you want to add to your ecosystem and community. You can see an example in Chapter 3 (Figure 3.3) – for instance, you might bring in corporates, academics, investors, consultants, startups, universities, policy makers, etc.

Preparation phase

Activities: One of the main objectives of the ecosystem is to bring people together and help them build relationships. To do this, you need to plan activities to bring the people together and provide a space for them to connect and to collaborate. Your role is that of a facilitator and your goal is to share knowledge and information to ensure that the innovation succeeds from idea to impact.

Purpose: Now, it's the time to define your purpose. This does not come earlier in the process because you have to first think and reflect on the knowledge you are contributing and then define the structure of the ecosystem. The purpose is the motto mixed with the reason to create the ecosystem. Hence, you have to answer the following questions: What is your ecosystem theme and purpose? What is the value creation you are aiming for within the ecosystem and which problems are you solving?

There is a lot of talk about one's purpose in life – because when you feel you are striving to fulfill this purpose you will live a meaningful life. The quest to define your personal purpose requires self-reflection and the focus to pick out the patterns in your life that have always driven you forward. Defining your purpose and the purpose of your ecosystem gives clarity and sheds light into the future. Once you are able to define it, it will become the foundation for your ecosystem. You will need to answer the questions about what knowledge and experience you are bringing to the table and how this can support the topics being addressed in the ecosystem. What is the value you are creating through your contribution to the ecosystem and what problems are you solving?

Information Flow: I argue that the foundation of innovation is sharing information, which means that if you have people or teams (silos) that are not sharing information between each other, you cannot innovate. Hence, the first order of action is to make sharing information and sharing knowledge a priority. As a result, you can make a list of the information that the ecosystem has to share and in which format to share it: news, events, showcase expertise from ecosystem members, how to collaborate, what ecosystem members need and how ecosystem members can support each other.

Definition phase

Needs: Finance is not the only need from an innovation ecosystem perspective. I will be honest: money is necessary to make an impact, because without money it is impossible to make a change or an impact in the respective industry or in whatever ecosystem you are a part of. That being said, it is not the only need. As a facilitator, you have to make an effort to seek to understand the needs and issues that your ecosystem is facing. These questions can help to guide you to find relevant information about the challenges being faced. Is it a systemic issue? What kind of issues is every ecosystem member facing? Talk to them! Schedule video conference calls and focus on the skill of deep listening as a way to discover hidden needs and issues. Make a huge list, categorize items on the list and then prioritize them as "urgent", "less urgent" and "needs to be addressed at some point".

Solutions: An ecosystem has to be proactive and supportive, not only be there to host a list of professionals in a room (or virtual room). Once you have defined the needs and issues, you can think about potential solutions, but it is highly recommended to use the collective intelligence of the group to generate solutions for possible new futures. This is a time when you can create workshops or brainstorming sessions to co-create ecosystem coherence.

Tools: If you are creating a virtual or local ecosystem for innovation, you need to consider which tools the ecosystem needs to be able to share information. Nowadays, there are options to create groups on social media, WhatsApp, Telegram or community channels like that on the Collabwith platform. The guiding question being, how you are using the tools to create meaning and bring value to each inter-action. The tools you pick will support the facilitation of the ecosystem and its mem-bers to share information and knowledge, which leads to value creation.

Bonding phase
Values: Value is created in an ecosystem through the active engagement of its mem-bers; if they are not engaged, then it's not an ecosystem. An ecosystem is not a group of individuals without a cause – it is a system of relationships that connect people with common interests. The common interests start from shared values. Hence, you have to define the common values for your innovation ecosystem. For instance: open-ness, honesty, transparence, innovation, collaboration, respect and diversity.

Manifesto: You can define the common interests in the form of a manifesto so that the ecosystem members can reflect on their common interests and have some-thing to identify with. The manifesto acts as a physical embodiment of the ecosys-tem's values, mission and vision. One example of aligning your values for the future would be to orient your ecosystem towards the sustainable development goals (SDG) from the United Nations. Integration of these seventeen goals shows that your ecosystem is focused on making an impact by aligning itself with an overarching goal that is higher than just survival itself.

Education: The creation of an ecosystem is more than just bringing people/organi-zations together to help each other get ahead. An ecosystem is grounded in relation-ships which support every member, and the ecosystem as a whole supports every member. I am speaking here of a transcendence of consciousness, moving from an ego-centered to an eco-centered consciousness – in other words an ecosystem mind-set. This is a big step in a world that is so focused on itself and its possessions. Our existence is predicated on our relationship with the social field of the world around us. Moving to an ecosystem awareness is the social innovation that is crucial for our future as a civilization. To make this shift, education is one of the important pillars that supports the sharing of knowledge, information, best practices, guidelines and other important aspects needed to instill the ecosystem mindset as the common way of being in a relationship with each other. Every ecosystem is different; hence, through educating its members to become sensitive to their own needs and the needs of the other members, they become dynamic with the ability to always be able to sense what is needed to support the ecosystem.

The "ecosystem and community canvas" acts as a guide to focus the awareness on all parts of the ecosystem. One's ability to successfully build relationships and navi-gate social environments is a skill which Daniel Goleman calls social intelligence. In order to create a high-performance community of innovators, the focus should be put on educating the members of the ecosystem about innovation, but also about emotional and social intelligence. The difference between both is that the first one

Figure 6.2: Ecosystem and community canvas.

STARTING PHASE

PREPARATION PHASE

DEFINITION PHASE

BONDING PHASE

Knowledge

WHICH KIND OF KNOWLEDGE DO YOU BRING TO THE COMMUNITY AND ECOSYSTEM?

Support

HOW CAN YOU HELP YOUR COMMUNITY AND ECOSYSTEM?

Actors

MAKE A LIST OF ACTORS YOU WANT TO ADD INTO YOUR COMMUNITY AND ECOSYSTEM:

CORPORATES
ACADEMICS
INVESTORS,
CONSULTANTS,
STARTUPS,
UNIVERSITIES,
POLICY MAKERS
...

Activities

YOU NEED TO SCHEDULE ACTIVITIES TO BRING PEOPLE TOGETHER.
THE OBJECTIVE IS TO SHARE INFORMATION AND KNOWLEDGE:

Purpose

WHAT IS YOUR ECOSYSTEM AND COMMUNITY THEME AND PURPOSE?
WHAT IS THE VALUE YOU ARE CREATING WITH YOUR ECOSYSTEM AND COMMUNITY?
WHICH PROBLEMS YOU ARE SOLVING?

Information Flow

LIST THE INFORMATION AND THE FORMAT YOU WANT TO SHARE:

NEWS,
EVENTS,
SHOWCASE EXPERTISE,
CURATE COLLABORATIONS

Needs

DEFINE NEEDS AND ISSUES YOUR ECOSYSTEM AND YOUR COMMUNITY ARE FACING.

Solutions

WHAT KIND OF SOLUTIONS DO YOU NEED TO BRING TO THE ECOSYSTEM AND COMMUNITY?

Tools

CREATE GROUPS IN SOCIAL MEDIA CHANNELS OR COLLAB WITH CHANNELS.

Values

TRANSPARENCY,
INNOVATION
COLLABORATION
RESPECT,
DIVERSITY.

Manifesto

CREATE YOUR OWN MANIFESTO FOR THE ECOSYSTEM, INCLUDING MISSION AND VISION.
CHOOSE YOUR SUSTAINABLE DEVELOPMENT GOALS (SDG) AND COMMUNICATE THEM.

Education

WHAT DO YOU HAVE TO EDUCATE YOUR ECOSYSTEM ON?

INNOVATION,
COLLABORATION,
OPEN-MINDEDNESS.

is the emotional skills of yourself and the capacity to know yourself, and the second one is the capacity to understand and build relationships with others. This may sound paradoxical, but to shift to an ecosystem mindset you need to first increase your self-awareness and emotional intelligence. This increased self-awareness deepens your ability to sense the social field and is the beginning of the embodiment of the eco-system mindset. Your social intelligence will unlock creativity, challenge-based innovation, problem solving, critical thinking and collaboration, and will increase engagement and interaction among the ecosystem members via proper communi-cation. We need to listen to understand others and to learn how to be in relation-ships with each other. We need to develop competencies for our team through attitudes, values, cognitive and emotional skills, and flexibility to adapt to chal-lenges and expectations.

"When you close the mindset gap you can develop a real collaboration where the company and the start-up can take the best from each other," says Luca Emil Abirascid, Founder and Director at Startupbusiness (Abirascid, 2019).

How to help your ecosystem members to be more socially intelligent
- Make people more empathetic, support members to actively listen to each other and to care about what others are saying (i.e., meetings without laptops or smartphones).
- Make an understanding that "focus" means focusing on yourself, focusing on others, and focusing on the rest of the world.
- Help people to be nice, kind and caring to each other.
- Train people's emotional intelligence skills to be able to recognize and under-stand other people's feelings, as well as the team's feelings.
- Help people to stay engaged during difficult conversations.
- Help people to focus on positive interactions to generate positive energy and deal with difficult people.
- Help people to analyze the interactions between people, relationships and conver-sations and encourage them to take space for self-reflection alone or with others.
- Bring in people who have a contagious positivity.
- Help to build relationships among ecosystem members.
- Share the message that positive social connectivity makes you happier and en-sures a longer life.

Social Intelligence according to Ignacio Morgado (Morgado, 2010) is the capacity to know oneself and to know others. Social Intelligence develops from experience with other people and learning from successes and failures in social settings. E.L. Thorndicke, a professor at Columbia University, was the first to name emotional intelligence as a skill in the 1980's. The root of the word "intelligence" relates to your ability to learn (Thorndike, 1920) and being emotional is feeling your feelings. Emo-tional intelligence is your ability to recognize and regulate your reaction to the feelings that you are feeling. It is a flexible skill that you can develop even if you aren't born with it. Personality is the final piece of the puzzle, which is described as intelligence personality (IQ). Both IQ and emotional intelligence skills (EQ) are distinct qualities we all possess. Together they determine how we think and act. Of the three, emotional intelligence is the only quality that is flexible and able to be changed. Social and emotional learning are possible, because our brain is plastic; that is, it can change its internal organization and functioning to store information and reproduce it later. It is important to consider the plasticity of the wax and the neurons to understand how we can better regulate emotions and feelings. The emotional brain works faster than the rational one. Why does reason come later? Because the emotional brain is prepared to prevent dangers by anticipating them and their possible consequences. In fact, reasoning about a situation that causes fear can help eliminate those feelings if we realize that there is no real reason for fear. Reason can modulate our emotional behavior in response to what we are feeling. To explain this from another perspective, emotions communicate what we are feeling, and reason interprets the messages. Our ability to reason promotes our ability to have empathy.

People are prone to react to their emotional impulses and this is often difficult for them to avoid, but it has been demonstrated that people can modify their responses and this skill can actually be used to generate individual and social wellbeing (Morgado, 2010).

How do you deal with fear of collaborating for innovation and adopting innovation?

(This answer has been developed in collaboration with Celia Avila-Rauch.)

Fear appears often among people who are engaging in innovation and relates to the feeling of not having everything under control. However, being prepared to take over responsibility, being clear about the goals of the team and being able to accept mistakes are actions you can take to counter this feeling of loss of control. The most irrational fears will enter our lives when our expectations start to waiver, and we become vulnerable. Fear refers to emotional fears, which have more to do with a defensive attitude towards problems and adversity, rather than seeing opportunities and solutions. Fear in innovation has to do with change and becoming visible. How do the changes influence us? For many people, the changes imply challenges, for others loss of control. We believe that human beings live and experience changes throughout their lives, and each change generates a certain fear or excitement to get out of our comfort zones. It forces us into action and tests our capacity to adapt to the environment. Uncertainty causes a certain fear until we adapt again to the new situation.

To understand people, we need to know something about what moves them, both positively and negatively. We need to know about their wishes, goals, plans, values, and what their fears and dislikes are. The more transparent persons are with their feelings, the easier they are to understand to empathize with. Mature leadership means the ability to manage stress, emotional intelligence skills, communication, ego and resilience. These are the basic principles in the leading process. When we get caught up in the habit of only reacting to our emotions at all times, this is a sign that they are controlling us and not the other way around. We need emotions to function and to stay connected to our human experience. The use of mindfulness helps us to stay connected to the emotions that are arising inside of us, shift away from our reactionary states and develop a deeper sense of self-awareness.

Another common expression of fear in innovation is the inhibition of logical and clear thinking. To counteract this form of fear it is important to keep connected to your purpose. It is important to realize that your goals are probably not the same as your team's, and this can often lead to conflict and fear of failing to meet everyone's expectations. Engaging in dialogue and communication, as well as lowering the demands in terms of what is being expected, can help alleviate this fear. In the end, nobody cares if you are a success or a failure, everything depends on the person.

Checklist for dealing with difficult people
- You cannot change them – don't take it personally!
- Try to understand what context the other person's thoughts, values and feelings are connected to.
- Listen to their opinion and what they have to say.
- Keep a distance from toxic and difficult people and reduce the contact with them to a minimum.

Checklist for dealing with difficult conversations
- Is the person prepared to communicate? Are you ready to talk? Maybe it's better to make a cut and give each other distance for a while.
- Don't take their comments personally.
- Be empathetic (listen and try to understand what the other person is saying) and also be direct (express your point clearly and talk in a professional, objective and calm way).
- Listen to their perspective and put the focus on the context.
- Protect yourself with self-esteem not with ego.
- Look at your needs and their needs, focus on the message, and take some distance and reflect your contribution to the issue in some way.

Checklist for knowledge that needs to be brought into your innovation ecosystem
Innovation
- What is innovation?
- How to innovate?

- Teach the different tools and processes for the front-end innovation.
- How to host a brainstorming session.
- How to do a design thinking workshop.
- How to do user-centered innovation.
- How to network for innovation.

Collaboration
- How to collaborate for innovation.
- How to research together with universities.
- How to apply research results to their organizations.
- How to define a challenge.

Ecosystem
- What is an innovation ecosystem?
- How to build relationships at work (innovation, collaboration, research, projects).
- How to be socially intelligent.
- How to use emotional intelligence skills for innovation, collaboration and entrepreneurship.

Digital transformation
- How to design interfaces and services.
- How to do digital transformation in your business.
- Train in modern technologies and how to apply them to their business.

Remote working
- Best practices for innovation projects done while remotely working.
- Building remote organizations.
- How to create a psychologically safe environment for your team and organization.
- How to build relationships with online tools while working remotely.

Entrepreneurship
- Understanding accounting, finance, investment and IT tools!
- How to make an investment deck.
- How to write public grant proposals.
- How to make sales and deal with customer management.
- How to be a marketer and a social media manager!

How to be digital savvy in virtual ecosystems
- The goal is to facilitate sharing information and transferring knowledge.
- Create a space for informal conversations and for networking.

- Create an open list of ecosystem members such as startups, academics, research results, research projects, partners, including challenges and interests.
- Create a space for online training, webinars and online workshops that take advantage of the expertise and knowledge being shared for the common good by its members. Create a regular newsletter or email to share valuable information and inspire members through storytelling.
- Create multimedia content with inspiring and real stories from outside and inside of the ecosystem (podcasts, videos, interviews or other media).
- Create multimedia content with best practices, guidelines and tips to support the ecosystem with the previously defined necessary knowledge.
- Communicate the ecosystem's progress to its members via reports to increase the sense of belonging.
- Create an online ecosystem support space that enables members to ask questions and where you can request help from and for other members.

How to build a community?

"Building a community of interest, that becomes alive on its own and is able to maintain itself. Then we can focus on supporting them in different areas" says Russell O'Brien (O'Brien, 2018).

A community is a group of people who are socially connected and actively engaged in dealing with each other and the world around them. There is a velocity of movement and action between these people and thanks to the internet, communities are no longer constrained by the need for shared physical space. To become a community builder, it is important that you create a structure that is consistent and that invites a diverse segment of individuals to come and interact together. The structure should give you the ability to measure the impact of the interactions that are taking place. Consider this: the community should be open for collaboration and open-minded toward different ways of doing business and/or research together. The community is like a meta-team that helps each other to grow and work together. If you have a strong community, you can do whatever you want with your business, product, service or organization. The level of trust, passion, engagement and interaction is a way to measure that they care about you as an ecosystem, and the community as a whole. A community shares a purpose, a sense of belonging, and it creates high quality outcomes for the community and its members.

The existence of an ecosystem does not preclude the presence of community within its borders. For an ecosystem to thrive, it needs active communities of actors interacting, creating culture and co-creating through collaboration. As an innovation ecosystem leader, you are responsible for building a community for the ecosystem, you need to make tools available, create rituals and feed energy into the group, while also allowing the community to self-organize and be a part of the co-creation process.

This book introduces a number of tools to support community builders. One of the key tools introduced is the "collaboration journey" (Figure 3.4) which provides a meta-view of the collaboration which acts as a roadmap for the journey. It is an effective tool that educates the community about how the process of collaboration works. It not only describes the process of collaboration, it helps members identify which phase of the collaboration journey they are in. This insight gives them contextual and relational awareness to move forward. Another tool that is being put forward in this work is the "collaboration canvas" (Figure 3.6) which compliments the "collaboration journey" well. It is designed to help users by giving structure and transparency to the collaboration. Some of the benefits come from helping users to manage their expectations, increase understanding between collaborators and improve their communication. The "emotional intelligence canvas" (Figure 4.2) is a tool that supports collaborators and community builders at the level of the individual, as well as at the level of inter-relational interactions. This canvas is based on the principles of personal growth through improving the skills of emotional intelligence. Emotional intelligence plays a crucial role in humanizing and improving the interactions of heterogeneous, diverse groups of individuals who face the challenges of coming from different organizations and often do not have the advantage of being able to physically inhabit the same space.

The canvases can be used in combination or individually and are meant to cultivate fertile ground to support the organic growth of communities and collaborations. They are not meant to be used as step-by-step recipes for creating cookie-cutter communities. Social groups are conceived through interrelation and interactions, and therefore are complex in nature. It is important to remember innovation is the creation of something new. So please use them as tools in your toolkit to help bring out that which is individual, special and emergent in your community, which in turn results in the whole being more powerful than the sum of its individual parts.

How can you create a community for your ecosystem?

- Make visible: the rules for the community, such as respect, listening and being open to other people's opinions.
- Make visible: a code of conduct and best practices guidelines to manage expectations and demonstrate how they can support each other.
- Make visible: how the community is structured to increase the value of participation for its members and the impact of the community as a whole.
- Create an open list of ecosystem members with profiles and make them easy to find and to contact them.
- Make it easy to search ecosystem members, ecosystem knowledge, and ecosystem technology, including filters by industry, topic, areas of interest, startups, academia, research, professionals and organizations (members around Figure 3.1).

- Create a communication channel and bring members together virtually to share news, information, events.
- Facilitate informal and formal conversations about the ecosystem areas and fields you want to create the community around.
- Create virtual networking events to allow people to meet and talk.
- Create webinars, online training seminars and workshops based on the needs and challenges facing the ecosystem and community.
- Create an environment where community members can share information and knowledge among each other.
- Consciously create opportunities to work together and facilitate collaboration among members.
- Create and facilitate investment opportunities for innovation projects, research projects and startups.
- Facilitate the information flow between individuals and organizations.
- Empower the group and individuals to make a positive impact within the community while following the purpose.
- Keep actively listening to the community about their opinions, their experiences, motivations with random one-on-one conversations and through official feedback channels.
- Empower self-organized autonomous community leaders who work to facilitate relationships among community members, who provide inspiration and support, and who are adept at identifying the needs and motivations of the ecosystem community members.
- The community has to be able to evolve together with its members; it's alive with the environment, the expectations, the happenings at local, national and international levels.
- Invest in emotional intelligence training for community leaders and members.
- Train the community members on how to create high-performing communities and ecosystems.

How can you create a virtual innovation ecosystem?

"Don't forget to bring online and offline experiences to engage people," says Prof. Anton Kriz Associate Professor MBA-IBPC at The Australian National University Associate Professor – ANU – Tsinghua Master of Management, Director at inManagement Consulting (Kriz, 2019).

A virtual innovation ecosystem is per definition spatially remotely based and relies on decentralized knowledge and producing decentralized innovation. Table 6.1 displays the "ecosystem strategy" (Figure 6.1) together with the description and actions necessary to shift the ecosystem to the virtual realm. The objective is that the ecosystem you are creating understands the "collaboration journey" (Figure 3.4) and they use the "collaboration canvas" daily (Figure 3.6) to be able to increase the interaction and the engagement within the ecosystem. Your ecosystem becomes a community when the interactions between members increase and they are mostly intrinsically motivated with a focus on the purpose of business. The increased interaction focused on business helps collaboration become an essential part of the business model. This means you have created an ecosystem which is enhancing growth among its members through collaboration. One method that spurs the success of collaboration is creating a map of your ecosystem, your value and supply chains. Then ask yourself how every member can bring added value, and how you could create cross collaborations through knowledge sharing and enhancing creativity among the members.

Table 6.1: Ecosystem and community dynamics framework.

	Description	Actions	Tools
People	Your ecosystem or community has to be full of people, not empty.	Create awareness via social media networks. Participate, sponsor virtual events. Partner with relevant ecosystem members.	Social media Partnerships
Engagement	Your community has to read your emails, comment on your messages and follow you in different social networks.	Structure communication (avoid spam). Bring value to every action. Bring people together with purpose.	Newsletter Social media Online events
Interaction	Your community has to network among members and create collaborations and activities together.	Curate relationships. Curate networking. Facilitate collaboration.	Online workshops Networking events Messaging tools
Value	Your community has to share their knowledge, share news and support each other.	Empower members to work together. Visualize cases of collaboration. Marketplace for opportunities and challenges.	Groups Social media Messaging tools
Impact	Your community needs to create innovations through collaborations and bring ideas to the market.	Make reports and measure progress. Visualize cases of market success. Train in entrepreneurship and resilience. Create a peer-mentoring program.	Social media Online workshops Coaching

It is important at the level of policy makers that leaders understand how innovation is created and how to bring this new innovation to the market. It would be advised that policy makers take a meta view of how ecosystem and community creation and the adoption of innovation policies can benefit the orchestration of innovation ecosystems at a government level. The strength of the innovation communities of a country will be determined by how strong the collaboration between its members is. A well-functioning ecosystem of heterogeneous actors who collaborate in synchronization is exceedingly difficult to replicate and would give it an exceedingly large competitive advantage over other countries.

"People socialization is much more complex than personality, taking care of all senses of a relationship, how to manage the process and how to bring them together is very important," says Prof. Anton Kriz Associate Professor MBA-IBPC at The Australian National University Associate Professor – ANU – Tsinghua Master of Management, Director at Management Consulting (Kriz, 2019).

The mood we are in influences our thinking and our decision making. When we talk about fear, we are referring to several aspects, but mainly we are referring to uncertainty, social skills and changes, where our ego and our self-esteem are at stake. Of course, our skills in emotional intelligence and tolerance of frustration will help us to overcome this fear. The fear in these cases is not a fear of a real threat, but of situations that can be frustrating for us. Fear is a sensor that warns of vital risk. It is activated every time it detects the presence of a stimulus or situation that threatens vital integrity or its balance. It allows us to become aware of the difficulty of the situation, of what we can lose, and consequently, we must decide to escape or face it.

Nowadays, the topics of happiness and being worthy are considered to be desirable business competencies, but what about resilience and wellbeing? Nobody is perfect, and for this reason we need to learn to develop strategies for communication, compassion, empathy and emotional intelligence to develop a new work and innovative culture. Emotions are not only a means to achieve a certain goal, they also help us to decide which goals we want to achieve at all.

Checklist for making people visible virtually
- Every member has to have the opportunity to present themselves.
- Create a consistent content of webinars, videos, podcasts, articles and interviews created by the ecosystem members.
- Design a communication strategy to display every member of the ecosystem.
- Train your ecosystem and community members how search engine optimization (SEO) works and how to use social networks.
- Create public and virtual debates with your ecosystem members.
- Create a directory of ecosystem members, publicly accessible.

- Every ecosystem member is an ambassador for the ecosystem. You have to provide them with the guidelines and materials so that they can create their own visibility within the ecosystem.

Relationships are important in innovation. And the question is how we include inclusiveness of people thinking in knowledge to upstage science technology (Ruckstuhl, 2019).

How to create an inclusive and diverse ecosystem for innovation?

"It is about giving everybody an opportunity and about expanding knowledge" says Prof. Katharina Ruckstuhl, Associate Dean Māori at the University of Otago's Business School and Senior Management Team Research Lead and Kahui Maori at Science for Technical Innovation (Ruckstuhl, 2019).

Diversity refers to characteristics that make people different, while inclusion refers to the behaviors and social norms that ensure people feel welcome. An ecosystem for innovation has to have both: inclusion and diversity. Diversity is needed to bring in "knowledge diversity" (Piller, 2020) and a diversity of perspectives, ways of working and opinions. Inclusion is when you are not discriminating against any person or any member because of their background, social status, culture, religion, race, gender, sexual orientation or color. Every person should feel welcome to be a part of the ecosystem and community. The power of inclusion and diversity is effective, and its benefits are visible when you allow for these differences in the ecosystem and every ecosystem member learns to respect and value each other regardless of their different backgrounds.

On a personal note, I would like to share a thought that has come to my mind several times already from my perspective of user experience (UX) and the perspective of marketing and how to target communication. From the marketing perspective, you create a "persona", an imaginary individual to target the communication, and the best practices say that the more accurate the persona is the better. The issue here is that this concept from marketing supports a less inclusive and less diverse focus group, because they use only one persona. This is the problem you can have when designing messages, websites, as well as in the promotion of accelerators, funding campaigns, and events for new entrepreneurs only. Focusing on just the startup entrepreneurs excludes academics, corporates, professionals and women! The diversity issue is coming from marketing. If there is a picture of a young white man, and every communication uses masculine colors and a masculine font type, you will only get customers that represent this one persona. This could be seen as a very controversial perspective, but it's true: branding design and marketing communication need to be inclusive, neutral and diverse. Even if you have "one customer" you want to target, this customer could be a woman or a man with a different religion, sexual orientation, race and other differences that you don't want to exclude. This is one of the powers of UX design and engineering – when you design the information architecture of a website, interface or a system (where the information is located, which features to add, navigation system, etc.) to make it "easy to use" you have to find the "common information architecture" that will work for everyone, for every brain. Although every person has a different way of thinking, or a different way of looking at information, there are not millions of different brain structures, you can see ten people and already have a good idea if your interface will work for everyone. Adapting this approach from user interface (UI) to other applications besides just software, for example, to marketing and communications, will lead to much more inclusive and diverse approaches. For instance, at Collabwith our interface, colors and fonts are gender neutral, and our communication and marketing are focused on entrepreneurs, academics and innovation professionals as the target group. Our interviews, podcasts, articles, vocabulary and web content are diverse and inclusive because we are showcasing it, for instance, to a membership of 50% women and 50% men with different backgrounds. As a consequence, the Collabwith community has 44% women and 56% men, and that is in the domain of innovation and technology which are fields historically dominated by men. Organizations, ecosystems and technology systems can be designed per default as inclusive and diverse, and it's an option that can be taken in the early phases of design.

Communities, by definition, have to be inclusive because inclusion means having a sense of belonging and an inclusive community respects and values every member or group from any type of organization. Every community member is essential to the success of the ecosystem. As you learned in the emotional intelligence chapter, motivation is linked to self-esteem; hence, when you authentically value people, they are motivated, which leads to high-performing and engaged communities.

If you lack diversity in an ecosystem for innovation, you will only see a mono-perspective impact on our society and industry. In the case of gender diversity, you are missing the vast majority of different perspectives if you have only white men as members of the ecosystem. To have an inclusive ecosystem means to design different processes to be flexible and inclusive with different ways of working and looking at issues and ways of finding solutions. If your ecosystem's values include "respect", this means respect for opinions, respect for every person, respect for different cultures, and respect for the society that you innovate with and for.

Inclusive innovation is about how we can change the nature of science and include other ways of thinking and the science itself will be more diverse (Ruckstuhl, 2019).

Checklist for creating a diverse and inclusive ecosystem
- Actively communicate stories and mention role models to a diverse set of community and ecosystem members.
- Recognize that relationships are important for innovation.
- Accept other people's different ways of thinking, opinions, ideas, perspectives and ways of working.

- Acknowledge differences and actively seek out opportunities to work together.
- Be open to sharing knowledge – everybody has the right to learn from various sources about research, science and technology.
- Include people who are not usually included in the innovation ecosystem and listen to them.
- Value and respect every member as a person from the ecosystem.
- Allow participation without critiquing anyone and provide access to information to everyone in the ecosystem.
- Actively bring new members to the ecosystem from diverse backgrounds and cultures, and with different genders, ethnicities, social statuses, ages, religions, races and sexual orientations.

In this chapter on innovation ecosystems, I am talking with professionals who are creating a highly effective ecosystem and community. In the following conversations, they are explaining how they are doing it and why.

Conversation with Carol Tarr on "Diversity for Ecosystems"

President and Chair of the Board at Harvard Club of the Netherlands
Fellow IncludedVC
Lecture Nyenrode Business University
Founder Atomic Spices
@CarolTarr

What is the #poweryourplusone concept?

Women need to be pushed into engagement and we have to tell them that, for example, they have to be in this meeting, because women find a lot of excuses such as "I am not ready, I don't have a degree, etc." Hence, you should compel women to show up and it is important to i0ntroduce them around. You have to be active and an activist in the introduction of women into the "clubs". If you have the power to make it happen, use your power of plus one. #poweryourplusone, which means if you can bring one person from outside into your meetings then do it and nowadays in a digital environment you can bring as many people as possible into these meetings. There is something powerful about being present and experiencing the dynamic of a high-level meeting that will change these women.

At a conceptual level, digital is creating spaces with infinite amounts of rooms and they are not locked rooms. You only need warm referrals and now "digitally" they can magically be there. This line of thinking is about how you can strategically break the barriers and open up the space and allow the conversations to happen and this will naturally lead to a new kind of richness in the interaction and lead to innovation.

How to bring more diversity and inclusion into venture capital decision making?

The way in which venture capital is invested will forever be changed as a more diverse community of people are brought into the fold. One definition of a diverse group means including individuals who didn't grow up eating at dinner tables with a grandfather talking about investment, loans and financial forecast. These individuals don't have the vocabulary and no clue how to do deals. However, this vocabulary can be learned, and this responsibility is on the individual. Learning the financial terms and pitching is very important. American style pitches are about 30 seconds long, and this is very effective. Work on your pitch deck!

Communication is very important to be influential. Another issue is the "meritocracy" – this means that you have to be familiar with the person who makes the decisions, hence you are awarded for being familiar, right accent, right texture, right hair style and voice tone. Whether you like you or not, this is based on beauty, it's not just about business.

One way of thinking does not represent diversity, even if the people are from different cultures, races, genders. You have to make sure that you can reflect other ways of thinking with different values, and that there is a balance. Educational background really matters, you have to go further and deeper, you have to value diversity.

How can we bring more awareness about diversity into the finance and investment ecosystem?

Awareness is not enough, it's not only about doing and organizing webinars on bias and diversity, but you also have to be an activist. Because it takes more than five years to know if you are right in your investment, it takes long to know if you have made a good investment.

Conversation with Martijn Leinweber on "How to Build a Space Innovation Community"

COO at SBIC Noordwijk www.sbicnoordwijk.nl
   @MA_Leinweber

What is the SBIC Noordwijk?

The Space Business Innovation Centre Noordwijk is the place to be for all things "space" and "entrepreneurship". SBIC Noordwijk supports space business-related startups by offering access to an international network, tools, knowledge and finance.

The goal of the SBIC Noordwijk ecosystem is literally become the Space to Be.

How do you bring together the community? Which type of activities are you doing to create a community?

We have a co-working space where people can meet, host events, organize master classes, competitions and hackathons.

How is the community and space tech ecosystem organized?

It is a very international community where upstream companies know each other very well. While space technology and data can be used for so many different applications, this community is much bigger and also less connected to each other. Therefore, we try to connect and bring them together in the Netherlands.

How do you support the space tech ecosystem to cooperate and collaborate?

Making introductions, bringing them together via events and online tools as well as sharing opportunities within the network.

What are the outcomes and results for the ecosystem?

Companies are supporting each other and collaborating more. They learn from each other and are able to start new and bigger projects and they are now forming international consortia for European calls.

Conversation with Juan Maldonado on "Creating an Effective and Self-Maintaining Community of Mentors"

Manager RSM Alumni Network MentorME
@RSMalumni

What is the RSM MentorME Community?

One of the biggest lessons I had in the last decade was when I caught myself binging YouTube videos on my mobile. Years ago, I worked in a Telecom company and I sincerely thought that cell phones weren't destined to be such a central part of our lives. "Who would like to use a phone to browse the internet?" I thought "It's such an uncomfortable experience compared to my kickass desktop!" Understanding that technology is a human-centric enabler is the key element of taking a service mainstream and building meaningful communities. When I was tasked to revitalize a dying mentoring community in one of the top business schools in Europe, that approach was the foundation of turning the program into the most successful mentoring community in the Netherlands. RSM MentorME is an online platform that enables alumni and students to take the hassle out of networking, but to make it work you need to nudge users in the right direction.

What is your goal in the RSM MentorME Community?

RSM MentorME has three main goals
1. Create a sense of belonging to a community where people are expected to help each other. This is incredibly powerful, because students that see the impact a mentor had on them during their school years go on to become multiplicators of this good will with the community.
2. It aids the employability of our graduates and carries forward our mission of positive change. Alumni can find relevant talent for their organizations when they talk to an enthusiastic student that wants to be part of their teams and shares the school's philosophy.
3. It helps us identify and nurture super connectors. The platform allows us to identify volunteers that are doing exceptional contributions and making sure that they're recognized for their value. This in turn improves the presence of RSM internationally.

How do you bring together the community? Which type of activities are you doing to create a community?

At the core of every user experience there needs to be a designer that gives the right nudges to encourage their audience to engage in positive behavior. One example of this is that we make students have a first compulsory consultation with a mentor. They're free to choose any mentor they want, but they need to have at least one mentoring call. This helps students realize that mentoring is valuable and over 60% of them go on to have further calls with other mentors.

We also train students and mentors beforehand with simple materials to make the interaction as seamless and fruitful as possible.

How is the community organized?

The community is divided in 3 different user types: students, young alumni, and alumni. Students are only able to request mentoring calls, young alumni get a hybrid profile to request and give advice in the community, and senior alumni are able to give advice unless they specifically request a hybrid profile for networking purposes.

How do you support the community to cooperate and collaborate?

The big word to use is "nudge". One of the ways to do this is realizing that people usually take the path of least resistance. The way that we encourage this is by creating functionalities in the platform that are comfortable for the majority of our audience. For example, a mentor's availability is set outside of office hours by default. Students get an assignment to complete a first mentoring call in class and we mention the existence and benefits of the program with every student even before classes start.

Graduating students get an email to remind them that they're now mentors and mentees, and that they can update their credentials (which allows us to keep in touch with them for events and other opportunities). They even get alerts on their mobile whenever they receive a request, or to confirm their appointments. This community is always one click away and it is available where they're already looking. This means that we're never pushing the platform on them and encouraging its use, we are actively pulling them by making the use of the platform the path of least resistance.

What are the outcomes and results for the community?

– MentorME is now a success case study for universities internationally – it was awarded the Circle of Excellence Award 2020 and is one of the few European programs that achieved the distinction.
– We have a thriving community with almost 6,000 users worldwide (1,000+ mentors volunteer their time!)
– We have scheduled almost 4,000 mentoring sessions in 2 years.

Conversation with Steffen Conn on "How to Manage an Innovation Community at ISPIM"

Operations Director ISPIM
   @ispim

What is the ISPIM Community?

ISPIM is a community of 1,500 professionals from around the world with a common interest in innovation management.

What is your goal in the ISPIM Community?

The goal of the community is that its members share ideas, insights, knowledge and opportunities and contribute to the field of innovation management.

How do you bring together the community? Which type of activities are you doing to create a community?

Communities are bound together by the actions that their members take. ISPIM Community members participate in our regular conferences, research and knowledge exchange projects, journal and professional publications and special interest group (SIG) activities. Long-term members form their own friendships and professional initiatives outside of ISPIM's official agenda.

How is the community organized?

The community's actions are conceived and developed by a core set of employed staff. Support is provided by the board of directors and many members in various capacities such as SIG and project leaders.

What are the outcomes and results for the community?

ISPIM has 1,500 members and an annual conference with 600–700 people from 50 countries. The outcomes for members are the benefits of being part of the community such as professional opportunities, access to the latest research and thinking, partnerships and publication opportunities.

Conversation with Lana Jelenjev on "How to Create a Community"

Author book "Community Builder, Designing Communities for Change"
    @LanaJelenjev

How can we create a community for transformational change?

When we look at change, we need to look at systemic and generational levels. Looking through these lenses helps us to understand and appreciate the complexity of the change process. In planning actions, I suggest going through the engagement spiral, a model I am developing:

- Awareness: What is there? What is the current status quo? What is surfacing? Who are the people involved?
- Attunement: What work/activities/initiatives needs to be done? Why are these important and urgent?
- Alignment: Who needs to be engaged? Who drives the engagement? What agreements do we need to have? What level of participation is needed? What are our metrics of success?
- Activation: How can we pursue these activities now? How can we plan for the rest of the work? What barriers do we need to plan for? How are we assessing where we are?

And then the cycle continues, but this time it broadens the field. As you go through the engagement cycle you also widen your breadth, depth and focus of impact.

Conversation with Robbert Fisher on "Policies and Innovation"

Chair of the Board Forum Knowledge4Innovation at the European Parliament
　　Former Managing Director Joint Institute for Innovation Policy
　　@robbertfisher

What are policies for innovation?

When talking about innovation and innovation policy, I think it always good to start with what you mean with innovation. For me it is both the process and the result of developing a new product or service and bringing it to the market (either new to the market or new to the company) or implementing a new process or business model. It is important to understand that the invention does not equal innovation but is part of it. The second important aspect is the fact that the innovation process is not linear or a single instance. The process is complex, with multiple feedback loops, often involving combinations of other technologies and innovations. Thirdly, although scientific and technological advancements are at the origins of innovation, there is much more to it to be able to successfully innovate. Regulation, acceptance, finance are all factors that play a major role in the process.

In a large study for the European Commission called "Major Innovations" (Fisher, 2015) we backtracked 10 so-called major innovations (such as GSM, LED and in-car navigation systems) to understand what made these innovations major. In nearly all cases, the R&I policies had helped to create and diffuse knowledge, but the real trigger was regulation or higher-level policy decisions not aimed at scientific or technological goals (i.e., it was driven by the telecom liberalization directive or the dual use of GPS decision). In all cases the innovations were a family of innovations, combinations of several technologies and innovations.

To better understand the complexity of innovation processes, innovation systems and the role of policies, we have often deployed an assessment tool called technology innovation system (TIS) (Hekkert et al., 2007) that provides an innovation system analysis at the level of several functions associated with the development of specific technologies and innovations (knowledge development, entrepreneurial activities, knowledge diffusion, legitimacy, search guidance, resource mobilization and market formation). The analysis shows the strengths and weaknesses of the system but also allows the identification of specific functions where policy has a role and which role it is or should be. As an example, we have applied this to complex innovation systems in sustainable development (Fischer et al., 2017).

A final point I would like to make is that not all innovation has to be based on breakthrough technologies. It is sexy to talk and dream about it, but, in reality, much of the most relevant developments are innovations new to the company, incremental innovations allowing them to grow, be more productive and strengthen their position in value chains. A good innovation ecosystem allows for the development of more radical innovations as well as the uptake of incremental innovations.

Summary

To sum up this chapter, I will leave you with a number of exercises that help ground you in your journey toward creating an ecosystem, community and ecosystem mindset.

To practice

1. Make a community out of your ecosystem.
2. Define your ecosystem online and offline.
3. Train the ecosystem members in social intelligence and emotional intelligence.
4. Curate relationships among ecosystem members.

In the following chapters you will find

- Tips for understanding the monetary value of knowledge.
- Tips on innovation leadership to bring people together.
- Tips for creating an effective impact machine for innovation at your organization.

Notes

(O'Brien, 2018) https://collabwith.co/2018/11/podcast-ispim-fukuoka-ceo-russell-obrien-discuss-how-to-create-a-large-scale-innovation-ecosystems/
(Piller, 2020) https://collabwith.co/2020/06/podcast-prof-frank-piller-on-avatars-for-collaborative-innovation/
(Kriz, 2019) https://collabwith.co/2019/06/podcast-ispim-florence-prof-kriz-on-innovation-leadership-manage-people-carefully-and-differently/
(Abirascid, 2019) https://collabwith.co/2019/01/luca-emil-abirascid-on-entrepreneurship-the-first-thing-to-look-at-is-the-team-because-if-you-have-a-good-idea-with-a-bad-team-you-do-not-go-anywhere/
(Ruckstuhl, 2019) https://collabwith.co/2019/03/podcast-ispim-ottawa-prof-katharina-ruckstuhl-on-inclusive-innovation-being-closest-to-each-other-thinking-and-understand-each-other/
(Fisher, 2015) https://op.europa.eu/en/publication-detail/-/publication/3fdc6ddc-0528-11e6-b713-01aa75ed71a1
(Hekkert et al, 2007) https://www.sciencedirect.com/science/article/pii/S0040162506000564
(Fischer et al, 2017) http://www.recreate-net.eu/dweb/system/files/files/PublicDeliverables/RECREATE_D4.4.pdf

References

Morgado, I. "Emociones e inteligencia social". Ed. Ariel. 2010. Pag 152.
Thorndike, E. L. "Intelligence and its use". Harpers, 140, 227–235. 1920.

"Innovation has two components, it has an invention part as a discovery of new knowledge, and it has the commercialization part, where you bring this knowledge to the market"

Prof. Henry Chesbrough, Faculty Director, Garwood Center for Corporate Innovation, UC Berkeley-Haas School of Business (Chesbrough, 2020)

Chapter 7
What is the Cost of Knowledge for Innovation?
Behavioral Economics for Innovation
and Knowledge Sharing

Summary: In this chapter, you will learn the importance of behavioral economics and behavioral science in the role of knowledge sharing and innovation and how to calculate your rate per hour. It will further discuss the value of knowledge sharing within your innovation project and how to analyze your finances for entrepreneurship.

Do you know people who have a problem talking about money? How many collaboration projects are canceled because one party was not able to invest financially in the project? Does this sound familiar, when one party waits until months of meetings have been conducted before they address the costs of the collaboration? This "avoidance" of talking about money makes the "collaboration journey" longer, and some collaboration opportunities break away because the collaboration takes too long to "negotiate". This chapter is about knowledge sharing from the perspective of collaborations between academia and the industry. It focuses on knowledge coming from startups, academics and knowledge from business professionals from organizations. It will discuss the inherent cost and value that is created through the knowledge transfer between industry (startups and business professionals from organizations) and academics (professors and researchers).

Knowledge is abstract, intangible and non-material, and for this reason it is difficult for the mind to understand the value of "having" or "sharing" knowledge. Knowledge is everywhere, and knowledge is inside every brain. Your knowledge is a part of you and who you are; in fact, it is a culmination of your experiences and the information you have learned through education, study and practice. In most cases it is easy to share your knowledge to help others. Hence, it is difficult to understand the value and the difficulty of putting a price on your knowledge. Nowadays, everyone is sharing information on the internet "for free", including in forums, blogs, podcasts and on social media networks (on your favorite social network). Even brands and companies are sharing best practices and guidelines for free to create engagement, cross-selling and increase communication with their customers. This makes the "cost of knowledge" more complex to understand, and the competition is so great that unless you are a consulting company there is pressure to give your knowledge away. As well, knowledge is super easy to share with everyone, as opposed to a material good that you cannot share with an infinite number of people because it is limited. This "infinite sharing opportunities" characteristic of knowledge is making "knowledge" less valuable somehow. In this context, I find it important to mention again the current situation of "free knowledge" on the internet, where highly valuable knowledge with a

https://doi.org/10.1515/9783110665383-007

high production cost is given away for free in the format of newspapers, magazines, optimized stories (just calculate the video production cost for 15 seconds, for instance, and set it against its zero price), webinars, online workshops, videos, podcasts, online conferences and other sources. As you can imagine now, the "value of knowledge" and the "cost of knowledge" have been diminished in the digital era.

On the other side, if you are looking at the innovation perspective, IP and patents are tangible assets, and they have a tangible value which is recorded on the accounting sheets of organizations. An invention which is processed, framed, structured, recorded and translated into a "stencil" has value. However, if the idea or invention is not patented then it remains only an idea or product that anyone can copy and gain monetary gains from. In this sense, you can create added value with your knowledge after you have processed, framed, structured, recorded, and translated it into a stencil. This process makes the value of knowledge more "tangible".

Despite all of the facts given above, there still exist many opportunities for academics, startups and organizations to create added value with their specialized knowledge and receive payment for it. The "cost of knowledge" is given by the level of interest of the person who needs that specific knowledge, and in the field of academia and other experts, the knowledge is very specific. But it has to be "framed" and "structured" as specific knowledge. If it is very specific knowledge, the interest is higher, and the value is higher for that particular knowledge.

The other way to frame knowledge is to create a technology with this knowledge, or to create a service or a product. This is the way to apply structure to knowledge and materialize it, facilitate its visualization and understand the "cost of knowledge". Another way that knowledge could be structured is into a process or a service. The more structured and framed the knowledge is, the more value the knowledge has.

What is behavioral economics?

Behavioral economics is a theory based on how our psychology, judgment and decision making affect our economic decisions and was created by Prof. Richard Thaler from the University of Chicago. He won the Nobel Prize in Economic Sciences in 2017 for the introduction of this theory (Thaler, 2005).

Behavioral economics is rooted in the concepts of behavioral sciences and focuses on how economic behavior is influenced by different actions or impulses. In the behavioral sciences, researchers set impulses using generic tools and record how the behavior of the participants is modified. Maybe you remember from high school classical conditioning theory (McSweeney, 2014) which uses rewards to influence student behaviors. This technique is used very successfully in video games and gamification techniques to keep players engaged in the game. The incorporation of this technique in digital interfaces has become commonplace, because it is very effective when you do not have a direct interaction with the person to explain why this one behavior is better than the other for them. If you are looking at how to apply behavioral economics in digital interfaces, for instance, Uber has created an interface to influence drivers to work more hours and get more "rides" even in difficult locations. This manipulation of the behavior has been created with a nice and easy-to-use interface with video game features and other rewards.

The same logic applies to influence the decision making by framing knowledge to increase "knowledge value" through the materialization of knowledge. Behavioral economics is framing knowledge and information to influence decision making and behavior. Research on behaviors explains that setting goals, the combination of target and feedback, or checklists are helpful tools to influence behaviors. At the same time, these tools have to be visible and transparent to the person who needs to see the benefit and get rewarded during the process of reaching their goals and marking checklists.

Behavioral economics has other decision-making insights such as individual factors, social factors and contextual factors which influence the decision of every person. In the next sections, I will reveal which of these factors are relevant for the encouragement of knowledge sharing during innovation and collaboration processes.

What is behavioral economics for knowledge sharing?

In the theory of behavioral economics, the three main factors of the individual, the social body and context are used to give insight into how the decision-making process can be influenced (Thaler, 2005). Below I will show how the incorporation of these concepts can be used to encourage knowledge sharing and create action to facilitate the flow of information in your organization and ecosystem.

Temporal distance

One of the contextual factors that influences the perception of knowledge sharing is the time and distance between the action of sharing knowledge and the benefit acquired through this new knowledge. There is usually a large amount of time between the action and the reward. This is because the benefit from acquiring new knowledge depends on many other external and internal factors, not only the action of acquiring knowledge. Now, the question arises: How is it possible to reduce the temporal distance between the act of knowledge sharing and the value delivered to the customer (receiver of knowledge) so that the results are almost immediate? If you want to influence people in the ecosystem to share their knowledge within the community, the incentive to deliver knowledge needs to be tangible and it should have immediate results for both parties. For instance, in the case of a consulting activity, it is required that the consultancy provide value for a specific project within a specific timeframe. This is already a framework or a way to materialize the knowledge you share, but also you can create small digital rewards. For example, once you add the consulting activity to your calendar, your customer immediately receives an email with the agenda or with a list of best practices related to the consulting you will provide. If you are selling a training seminar or workshop, as soon as the client has subscribed online you can program it so that automatically a "thank you" message including a sneak peak of content, or a tool, be sent out. This gives the customer something they can already relate to, and practice before the actual workshop happens. Those activities are very important to reduce the temporal distance between the benefit and the action of sharing knowledge.

Pleasure vs. pain: prospect theory of motivation

As an individual factor, the pleasure vs. pain theory of motivation relies on the human behavior of seeking pleasure and avoiding pain. Figure 7.1 looks at the graph from Amos Tversky and Daniel Kahneman included in prospect theory (Kahneman and Tversky, 1979). This theory describes how the feeling of losing money is more painful than gaining the same amount of money, it has less pleasure in comparison with pain. In the case of knowledge sharing, the loss aversion of paying for knowledge is higher than the action of gaining this new knowledge.

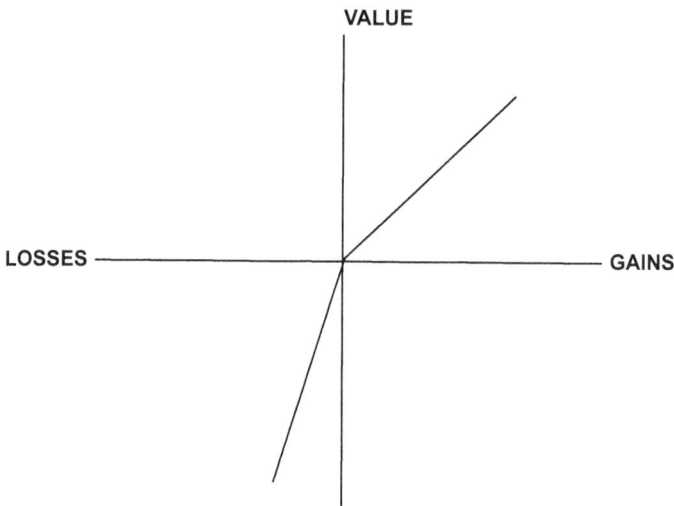

Figure 7.1: "Pleasure vs. pain graph" by Amos Tversky and Daniel Kahneman (Kahneman and Tversky, 1979).

In the case of sharing your knowledge, it is essential to reframe the value proposition to reduce the loss perception and increase the gain perception. Figure 7.1 depicts an appropriate proportion for the maximum impact. It is also important to recognize that human beings give more value to things they already own. This fact has to be part of the equation to reframe the value proposition in order to positively influence the willingness of others to share their knowledge. This means action on one side and reducing the pain of paying for knowledge on the other. One of the potential solutions is to talk about the loss before the action of paying has taken place. For instance, "Don't risk losing market share, get an expert's advice!" In this case, you focus on the loss aversion of the market, instead of the pain of paying for knowledge. Another possible approach is to talk about the gain before the action of paying takes place. For instance, "Get a 20% discount if you sign up now for the workshop" or "Create value from your ideas, talk to an expert." If there is a membership payment for knowledge sharing, then this creates double the pain: the loss of time and money to pay to share knowledge. As a result, the construction of a "gain" has to be higher to incentivize this payment. The other option is to create a paid membership for acquiring knowledge. In this sense, your customers pay double as well, once to have access to potential knowledge they need, plus the payment for the actual knowledge when they need it. In addition, you have to add in the "temporal distance" factor to reduce the time between paying for the membership and receiving the knowledge needed. This double loss and double pain have to be mitigated. The actions to be taken, based on behavioral psychology, could be:

- Setting up immediate small rewards to release feel-good dopamine.
- Creating a novelty environment to incentivize people to share their knowledge.
- Creating a charity-impact effect between the supplier and receiver of knowledge. This means that if they share knowledge it's to have a positive impact. This will increase the feel-good effect related to sharing knowledge and will increase people's level of endorphins.
- Creating a high-luxury environment. This means that you reach a high social status when you pay to share and receive knowledge, which leads to social gratification.

Trust

As a social factor, trust is a very important part of the decision-making process, especially in regard to decisions dealing with paying money. You can find in Chapter 2 a discussion on how to create trust in a digital environment; here it's the trust related to decision making and how the digital environment is impacting the risk aversion of the decision. The researchers Katarzyna Samson and Patrycjusz Kostyszyn describe this phenomenon in their paper by saying, "the decline of trust has been linked to the rapid rise of materialistic value orientation that undermines views about the trustworthiness of others" (Samson, 2015). This means that when you focus your attention more on material goods, you tend to trust people less. On the contrary, if you focus on non-material goods, such as knowledge, you can increase your trust in people.

Behavioral science describes the effect of cognitive overload caused in many digital environments as an overload of information and the attempt to multitask, which can cause people to be less analytic and feel a loss of self-control. This fact raises the question: How can you in the digital environment create trust which supports your decision to commit to acquiring or sharing your knowledge? The answer is that you have to increase strategic thinking to increase trust:

- Simplify processes.
- Make the process clear and well explained.
- Simplification of the environment with UX and usability techniques.
- Offer a welcome package with clear options and small rewards to congratulate people on being able to share their knowledge.
- Add small rewards such as discounts for next events when they share knowledge.

Consistency fallacy

Consistency fallacy is said to be committed when data is treated as informative simply because some theory is consistent with it (Loosemore and Harley, 2010; Coltheart, 2013). The individual factor of consistency is quite interesting, because it's related to the sunk costs or transactional costs. People often believe that consistency is an intellectual and personal strength to be cultivated which brings stability and honesty and is related to a trusted person. However, when you are looking at the consistency fallacy for knowledge sharing, you can create a digital environment with the following insights to increase knowledge sharing among people:

- Create structure and reduce the effort required to think.
- Enhance intellectual messages with stability, for instance: "You network as always, but you can do it right from your desk." The first part of the message "you network as always" brings consistency to mind, and the second part of the message – "you can do it right from your desk" – is where you bring the "new behavior" into the conversation with your user.

Reciprocity

The social factor of reciprocity can be well explained in the context of peer mentoring where you and your peer exchange experience, knowledge and information. Usually, reciprocity describes equivalent actions, and is connected to goodwill and kindness. In social psychology it is described as paying back what you received from others. In the digital environment, this can look like receiving free content in order to make an action for the community. But focusing too much on reciprocity can lead to there not being clear win-win transactions for both parties. If you pay to share your knowledge as in a peer-mentoring format, you pay for the platform to share your knowledge, and then you share your knowledge for free to make an impact and get knowledge back. Getting a positive feeling means releasing dopamine, and this is the immediate reward. This is the reason why the peer-mentoring platforms are successful as a knowledge-sharing framework, because they focus on doing good and getting good back (usually, they are free platforms).

The design architectural choice

As a contextual factor, the choice of design plays an important role in the interaction and promoting sharing. One example of how to apply this is when you make one choice more attractive than the others and stay within the maximum of 3 options to avoid information overload. This attractiveness of one particular choice is to give a feeling of satisfaction (dopamine) and make the users feel smarter. In the context of sharing and acquiring knowledge, when a person has 1,000 options from which to select the best "knowledge supplier", the person can feel overwhelmed and less analytic. Hence, it's better to structure the information in blocks and create labels such as "trusted", "recommended" and other labels relevant to the topic to help guide the choice.

What is behavioral economics for innovation?

One of the basics of innovation management is to facilitate knowledge sharing and information flow between the teams, organization and ecosystem. If there are silos across an ecosystem or organization, outside of which people are not talking to each other, then it will be impossible for innovation and collaboration to happen. This holds true, no matter if you are in a digital or in a physical environment. The fundamental action to do first is to analyze the relationships and see if there is an exchange of information and knowledge and see what the root issues are. The definitions above on what behavioral economics is for knowledge sharing can help guide the analysis. After the initial analysis, the next step is to question how you can influence the collaboration via behavioral science and behavioral economics. One of the best places to start is where the monetary transaction for the innovation process takes place. Collaboration is crucial for creating innovation and bringing it to the market, but the economic factors and how companies understand the value of innovation are both factors that have the ability to stop innovation before the innovation makes it to the market. That means the innovation gets killed before it can deliver its promised impact to the industry and society. The temporal distance factor of innovation is very lengthy – in general, the benefits are not seen until months or years later!

How much does knowledge cost?

Knowledge is intangible and non-material, and for this reason it's difficult to assess its cost or its value. In the context of innovation, knowledge is often coming from research centers or from researchers at universities. There is a cost for transferring this knowledge into a new technology or another knowledge framework such as papers, publications, books, classrooms, workshops, etc. Additionally, there are other costs associated with bringing this knowledge to the market.

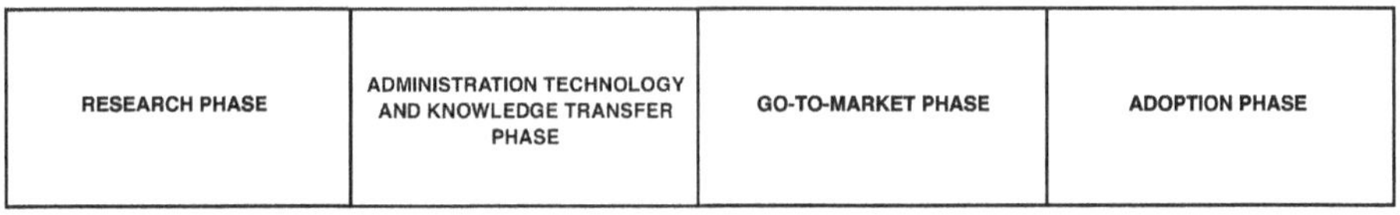

RESEARCH PHASE	ADMINISTRATION TECHNOLOGY AND KNOWLEDGE TRANSFER PHASE	GO-TO-MARKET PHASE	ADOPTION PHASE

Figure 7.2: Knowledge and innovation investment.

Figure 7.2 depicts the cost of knowledge from an investment perspective, and this is only a very simple overview of the production and operation costs of knowledge in our society. Universities are not the only ones investing in research. Research centers, startups, SMEs, corporations and even individuals are all entities that are doing knowledge research on their own.

This section looks at the cost of generating knowledge sharing. Governments, public institutions and grants provide public funding to universities and other organizations to create knowledge transfer offices. It is important to note most of the public funding is set aside merely for the administration and support part. This support mechanism is essential for the innovation ecosystem, as it creates a single point of contact per university to better transfer knowledge and technology from research to the industry. The next step after the knowledge transfer is gaining investment money needed to "go to market", or in innovation you can say to adapt and transfer research into a commercial product, feature or a commercial service. Currently, most investment money comes from private funding outside of the industry, from individuals such as angel investors or venture capitals who are investing in a company to bring their innovation to the market. Last year, the European Commission created a new way of funding of "go-to-market" public grants called the "European Innovation Council" based on the need for the investment required to bring innovation to the market and make an impact. Ten years ago, the European Commission created the European Institutes of Innovation and Technology (EIT) with the objective of promoting innovation in European countries in different areas such as digitalization, sustainability, raw materials, health, energy, food and manufacturing and to support education, research and businesses to work together to create innovation through collaboration and bring impact to the industry and society.

How to calculate the cost of "knowledge"?

If you are an academic, startup, or professional, and you have expert knowledge and want to share it, Table 7.1 will help you to calculate the value of your knowledge. It will give you a reference as to how much you can ask per hour, based on shorter engagements. However, if you are doing a project or an activity of longer duration, you will find another table later in this book that will help you to assess the cost and value of your knowledge. Table 7.1 is a calculator to help you to calculate the value of sharing your knowledge expertise per hour.

The ratio shown below equals the maximum price per hour and helps you to calculate the maximum you should charge for one hour of consulting or one hour of technical assessment. If you are doing a one-day activity, you have to adapt the cost to reflect a reduction of your ratio per hour when you are sending a proposal, or when you are in price negotiations. The same is applicable when you are doing a research project. For instance, academics could be providing advice and sharing their knowledge to startups for free, but they could charge 800 EUR to corporates. A Nobel Prize winner could theoretically ask for 50K euros per hour, or an astronaut 10K euros per hour. This is an interesting approach, and that can change how value for expert knowledge in an innovation ecosystem is calculated.

Table 7.1: Knowledge value calculator per hour.

Category	Formula Calculator
Number of years of experience*	+7 EUR per year of work experience or research experience
Social Media followers	+50 EUR per 10K followers
Number of voluntary activities	+5 EUR per voluntary activity
Last salary received*	Last salary/500
Number of positions as board member	+10 EUR per position
Number of years of entrepreneurship experience	+3 EUR per year into entrepreneurship
Number of recognitions and awards	+10 EUR per recognition or award
Number of academia/industry collaborations	+20 EUR per collaboration
Number of publications	+10 EUR per publication
Number of patents	+30 EUR per patent
Number of books written	+20 EUR per book

Table 7.1 (continued)

Category	Formula Calculator
Customer's country	Take into consideration your customer's country of origin to balance your cost per hour
Customer's type	0 → Startup, non-profit X 0.5 → SME, research center, innovation institute X 3 → Corporate

In the ecosystem perspective for innovation, the cost per hour can be related to the type of customer you are sharing the knowledge with, and this decision is always up to you. The platform Thumbtack, which offers freelance jobs in the USA for a variety of sectors, from wellness to construction, provides a calculator for each sector with an average price per hour. This helps both sides of the knowledge or activity transaction – the seeker of knowledge knows the cost in advance and can make decisions based on her financials, and the provider of knowledge can assess how much she can ask for.

Different types of knowledge sharing

The calculation of the value of knowledge sharing is always relative to the supply and demand and the ability to answer a need with the right solution. Do you remember this story – or a similar story but with the same moral? There was once a factory owner who had a broken machine which was very important for the factory operations and essential for the business. He requested an expert to repair the machine, and many different experts came and went without success. Finally, one man came to the factory and repaired the broken machine in five minutes with a small trick and asked for 10K EUR for his services. The factory owner complained about the high cost in relation to the time required to repair the machine. The expert answered that the repair took only five minutes of work because he had twenty years of experience and knowledge of those machines. This story relates to the different ways of sharing your knowledge and experience and the value you can bring to your customer. Every case is different, but one thing is clear, you can share your knowledge in different ways, and you have to be open minded to the variety in value you can generate with your knowledge and that your knowledge has value! Below you can find examples of activities that you can engage in to share your knowledge:

- Conference call.
- Speaker.
- Workshop.
- Brainstorming.

- Presentation.
- Strategy check.
- Technology transfer.
- Whitepaper.
- Feasibility study.
- Testing products.
- Innovation project.
- Research project.
- Internship.
- Student thesis.
- Board member.
- Coaching.
- Research consortium.
- Case study.
- Consulting.

How much does the collaboration for innovation cost?

"Innovation Management is something complex, it's applying new knowledge, a new product, a new service, a new process, a new idea but it has to be commercialized, innovation is not only something new, but it has to have an application," says Prof. Christopher Tucci, Professor at Imperial College London (Tucci, 2019).

If you have money available, you can make creative things and you can make an impact. It is very important to think about the basics of finance when doing innovation, because innovation makes an impact. One thought experiment when sharing knowledge is on the potential profitability of innovation in bringing value to the market – in the end, where there is no money and no new ideas there is no impact in the case of collaboration. The budget is for you and your fellow collaborators, but the impact will be not only for your collaborators but also for the industry and society around the innovation ecosystem. See the "collaboration canvas" in Figure 3.6 on how to collaborate and talk about impact.

The UK universities have created an annual report called "Higher Education Research in Facts and Figures" (UK Universities, 2018). This report records the research and innovation collaboration costs, together with knowledge transfer activities. The report states that the 166 UK universities organize 115,000 collaborations per year. This means an average of 700 collaborations per year per university and more than half of UK research is produced through international collaborations (UK Universities, 2018). Let's continue to calculate the amount of energy invested in collaboration by each university in the UK. On average, every university needs 6 months minimum to close a deal for a collaboration, and a minimum of four teams are involved from the university including: the legal department, the tech transfer office, and international relations and communications (of course, this depends on how the university is organized). Hence, you have 4 people (legal, tech transfer office, communications, innovation) minimum involved per collaboration, which corresponds to 120 hours per person on average during those six months. Tasks that need to get accomplished for the collaboration to be set into place include searching for opportunities, collaboration negotiations, managing expectations, legal negotiations, and the financials. This translates into an average investment per university of 480 hours spent per collaboration, assuming that 4 persons contribute 336,000 hours on average per university to manage 700 collaborations per year. This easy calculation is the cost per hour of the personnel involved (using the lowest possible wage of around 30 euros per hour for personnel costs. This amounts to 10 million euros in total costs per university for managing university/industry collaborations distributed among academic and administrative departments. And here you can see some benefits of this investment only for managing knowledge and technology transfer activities (Figure 7.2):

– UK higher education institutions received £4.2 billion from knowledge exchange activities in 2015–16 (UK Universities, 2018)
– Total income from contract research was £1.245 billion in 2015–16 (UK Universities, 2018)
– Income from consultancy was £455 million (UK Universities, 2018)
– The total reported income for collaborative research in the UK was £1.292 billion in 2015–16 (UK Universities, 2018)

If you are involved in leading these types of collaboration projects, it is important to understand the value and need for your expert knowledge. It is also important to be able to calculate the cost and value of those activities. Table 7.2 is a table you can use as a calculator to guide you; and if you are doing a research or innovation project, Table 7.3 is the guide for the project cost calculation.

Table 7.2 and Figure 4.5 are examples of the type of costs you have to think of to be able to make an accurate calculation of the value you are providing in the form of an activity, or in the form of a project, and the costs around the transfer and impact. Some of the costs listed in the tables will be more relevant than other costs depending on your particular case. You have to be aware of what costs are relevant for you and calculate accordingly.

Let's calculate the value of entrepreneurship and "going-to-market"

"Innovation has two components, it has an invention part as a discovery of new knowledge, and it has the commercialization part, where you bring this knowledge to the market," says Prof. Henry Chesbrough (Chesbrough, 2020).

Table 7.2: Calculator for an innovative activity (knowledge transfer).

Category	Formula Calculator
Preparation costs	Preparation costs could be materials or software development needed to perform the activity, etc.
Time to prepare and to host the activity	Cost per hour: x number of hours and x number of people involved (your own and team hours, salary in hours and prototype hours).
Overheads	+20% in case they apply, and it could vary from university to university.
Extra error and risk buffer	+20%
Cost of sales	Pre-sales activities (+10%) Or direct-to-customer (+10%) Or intermediates (+20%) Or fair trades (+30%)
Cost of marketing	+10% (to include and cover your costs for website, social media, events, online advertisement, etc.)
Cost of travel and accommodation	If you need to travel to perform the activity, include travel, accommodation, or public transport.
Extra costs	Online subscriptions, books, papers, computers, and other hardware, or materials needed to perform the activity.

Table 7.3: Calculator for innovation project cost.

Category	Formula Calculator
Material costs per unit	Physical materials needed.
Production costs per unit	Production costs could be UX design, graphic design, industrial design, software development, manufacturing, etc.
Time to produce or prototype per unit	Cost per hour: x number of hours x number of people involved (your own and team hours, salary in hours and prototype hours).
Overheads	+20% – these overheads will vary from university to university.
Extra error and risk buffer	+20%
Cost of sales	Pre-sales activities (+10%) Or direct-to-customer (+10%) Or intermediates (+20%) Or fair trades (+30%)
Cost of marketing	Project website, social media costs, events, campaigns, online advertisement, etc.
Extra costs	Online subscriptions, logistics, books, papers, travels, public transport, computers, other hardware or materials needed to perform the project.

As Prof. Chesbrough said very well, innovation is about commercialization, which means innovation is about business and doing business with knowledge. You will learn the lesson that innovation means business when you are making the transition between innovation management and entrepreneurship, to really bring creativity, ideas and innovation to the market!

Table 7.4 is a calculator guide to help you to understand the cost of doing business, and you can use this calculator guide as well for your financials and accounting for your startup and for your business if you want. Private investment is one of the enablers that help bring innovation to the market, and some investors are business angels, venture capitalists, family offices or corporate ventures. When one angel investor only offers to invest 20K euros in your startup, he is not taking into account the real cost of creating a new business, or bringing innovation to the market, which is different and more expensive. When one startup begins the entrepreneurship journey, they are attempting to bring an innovation to the market; at this point it is not yet a business, product or service that everyone knows – it's new. Hence, they are creating their own market, and this means changing the current market. Entrepreneurship implies that you need to triple the effort invested, because there is a need to educate the consumers, partners, supply chain actors or value chain actors to bring awareness and to support the adoption of the new "thing" that has been created. Investing in startups and working with them is an action of exchanging knowledge, technology and money to create impact together.

To be able to get a feel for the startup journey we will use the pretend example of you, the reader, creating a startup. Of course, there is a cost for your website and marketing is mandatory. These might not be investments that lead directly to sales, but if you are not doing them, you will lose customers. In order to calculate your forecast, you can start step by step, and day by day. You can start with your sales during the first month, and forecast this every month, and you can optimistically increase them by 10%. The estimation of sales is based on your history. And if you look at the costs vs. sales, you can see which activities are related directly to your growth, and which activities are relevant for your company's economic growth. Finance for startups is applying common sense from the beginning and is about properly balancing sales and costs. In some cases, such as manufacturing or other heavyweight deep technology, you might need a high investment to create a product or service, but the same rules apply to a small company when it comes to finances and accounting. These factors equate to your cost of bringing innovation to the market, and are very important to measure each week, month, quarter and annually. Besides this, you and your team (including investors, if you have them) have to be trained in what is innovation, and how to bring your product to the market, which means training in entrepreneurship, leadership, finance and doing business.

It requires commercialization of road maps. We work on the industry side by helping companies with their scale-up challenges and help those companies connect with academics and researchers (Laurin, 2019).

Table 7.4: Calculator for entrepreneurship (innovation – going to market).

Category	Formula Calculator
INNOVATIVE PRODUCT OR SERVICE COST	
Material costs per unit	Physical materials needed.
Production costs per unit	Production costs could be UX design, graphic design, industrial design, software development, manufacturing, expert consulting, etc.
Time to produce or prototype per unit (product or service)	Cost per hour x number of hours x number of people involved (your own and team hours, salary in hours and prototype hours).
Extra error and risk buffer	+20%
Cost of sales	Pre-sales activities (+10%) Or direct-to-customer (+10%) Or intermediates (+20%) Or fair trades (+30%)
GENERAL COSTS	
Cost of marketing	Branding, company website, social media costs, campaigns, online advertisement, post-sales services, activities to generate sales, activities to generate awareness, including partner and client's lunches, etc.
Salaries	Your own salary, your team's salaries.
Infrastructure	Office rent, electricity, phone, internet, water, city taxes, office supplies.
Other operational costs	Accountant, banking commissions and fees, online subscriptions, packaging, books, papers, office material, postal costs, travel, public transport, logistics, or material needed to perform the company processes.
OTHER COST	
Material and Hardware	Computers and other hardware.
IP and patents protection	IP, company name protection, patents, and copyright.
Expertise	Agencies, consulting, financial advice, notary, legal advice and legal contracts.
Savings to pay in the future	VAT, TAX, emergencies, crisis buffer, new investments.

Table 7.4 (continued)

Category	Formula Calculator
HR	Team-building activities, paid holidays, office food, sports, books and training.
Others	Company merchandising, parking tickets, taxi invoices, others.
INCOME FORECAST WITH BUSINESS SENSITIVITY	
Sales	Different sales channel and different product or service's sales. Ensure payment from your customers.
Forecast: scenarios	Create scenarios for no-sales, reduction or increase of 20–50% sales. This is helping you to make decisions and take actions for your business. Use the first month to forecast your finances step by step.
Monthly and weekly account review: cost/income overview	Review and write down costs and income invoices per week and per month. Create a weekly and monthly overview of costs/income. Include spreadsheet and bank account overviews. Separated bank accounts for personal and business.
What is your most important "category" for your business?	Understand which part of your business is producing more income and which one you have to stop and give more attention to.
What are your highest costs?	Understand which "cost" is higher and how you want to reduce it and if this cost is important for your business or not. You need to spend money to grow your business, while at the same time reducing costs to a minimum.

We are looking for commercial outcomes that create prosperity for the company and community and the province (Laurin, 2019).

How to talk about money?

- Be the first! You have to open up about how much money your knowledge costs.
- Learn the language of money, investment, tax, finance and accounting.
- If you don't know, ask questions openly about budget or costs.
- Learn how to manage your own finances (as a small scale), and then go for your own business projects.
- Do your calculations first, so you know your value.

- Talk about your purpose and mission for your project, activity and business, because to make this impact you need money. Be intentional with your budget, investment and costs.
- You are supporting them to create more value and impact to everyone.
- Understand your priorities, your costs and your incomes.
- Think about abundance, not deprivation.
- You have to have a plan for the money. Frame it! What do you want to do with it? Make that clear to everyone.
- Send financial updates to your team and collaborators!
- If they don't want to pay your value, then they don't respect you, that means stop talking to them.

When to talk about money in the collaboration journey?

Building a footprint in the town where your business was founded in partnership with the academic institutions that are there, not only helps drive talent acquisition, but also helps create opportunities for collaborative research necessary to put through your ideas and your concepts to leaders and it helps, to give you different perspectives and different alternatives to consider (Laurin, 2019).

Experience has shown that the clearer you are on defining all aspects of the collaboration in the initial phases, the smoother and faster the collaboration will function. On the Collabwith platform, you have to add your rate per hour already in your profile! This is very important for supporting you in talking about money and creating transparent conversations from day one. Another feature on the Collabwith platform that supports transparency about finances happens when you "make a request" within a structured framework: you can set your estimated hours for the activity you want to do together, and the cost per hour you are willing to pay or receive. You can explain in the comments box your budget constraints. This helps tremendously in speeding up the progress, increasing clarity and managing the expectations of the other party. Talking about money is difficult, and it is difficult to ask for an amount of money that takes into consideration your value, your knowledge and your technology. It's easier to give it for free, rather than making the effort to overcome the fear of talking about costs, economic benefits and income. And there are many excuses for avoiding talking about money and budgets, such as "I want to have neutral results for research, so I don't pay academics", or "I am doing it only with passion, not only for money". If you are looking at the behavioral economics factor, "doing it for free" as a voluntary activity generates immediate endorphins, a positive effect and feel-good emotions for everyone; hence you do not have to wait to have the benefits of the knowledge transfer and it's a way to reduce the temporal distance of action-to-benefit, because you are getting the endorphins of satisfaction immediately as self-gratification. This feeling is important to motivate people to share knowledge during the collaboration and innovation activities but should not take the place of receiving payment for delivering your expert knowledge.

The fear and ethics of making money within research

"Innovation is for me personally a journey of discovery in which I learn from and together with others to create effective solutions that solve real-life problems," says Maik Fuellmann, CEO and Co-Founder of QUIZZBIZZ Ltd. and Consultant at The Institute for Knowledge and Innovation – South-East Asia (IKI-SEA) (Fuellmann, 2020).

Have you heard about the case of beverage companies paying for research studies saying that sugar is not bad for health and instead blaming fat to be bad for our bodies? Companies and researchers have created these statements to help sell products and services and this is unethical.

There have also been other cases of companies buying out research results and technology (IP and patents) and closing them down, so they don't have to compete with these technologies on the market. When a company is not using the technology or research results, they acquired the knowledge because of anti-competitive behavior which is just as unethical, and these are bad practices! This, however, does not mean that all collaboration between industry and academics is like this. These are exceptions.

It's important to understand the fear related to ethics and money in order to take action instead of being paralyzed by the fear. You can improve your legal contracts and negotiations knowing that you want to avoid unethical usage or actions with your IP, technology or knowledge. Some academics prefer to make zero money to feel good and avoid all legal negotiations and processes. They prefer to refer to themselves with statements like "I am not bought" to prove that "I am a good academic, because I don't commercialize research because I am doing it only as my passion."

If there are an internal process and a legal contract that say that the outcome of all activities of academics are owned by the university, then academics cannot co-create freely with the industry. Every university, country and culture is different. It is important to realize that the same dynamic is happening on the other side of the conversation when professionals, startups and other organizations are experiencing a fear of talking to academics or they don't respect the value of academic knowledge and technology.

The real ethical issue here is when research is stored away without any use of it, despite its societal benefit. Universities are pushed to commercialize their research and turn their research into proprietary knowledge, as claimed by the OECD (OECD, 2006). Of course, this results in knowledge not being disseminated. Such behavior restraints competition in innovation markets and wastes talents of the researchers (Samovica, 2020).

The solution is to apply emotional intelligence to understand the fear and overcome the fear with action. Below are guidelines to take action from an individual perspective, social perspective and legal perspective.

How to deal with the fear of making money with research results and from academia/industry collaborations?

(Avila-Rauch, 2020)

– Understand that in the academic world, the intellect is valued, but it is not measured with financial compensation. The industry on the other hand establishes its value based on economic remuneration where intellect is valued, but knowledge is required to be financially rewarded.
– This is associated with knowing how to value yourself as a professional and how to take yourself seriously and take your responsibilities seriously.
– Receiving money for your services or for your intellect is a way of taking responsibility for your tasks, and as a person.
– When we carry out a task or a job, we are dedicating time, knowledge, experience and effort to it. This must first be taken into account by the person who provides the knowledge or service, and second by the person who has contracted the service.
– In a competitive world you will decide how to negotiate according to your personality – how you negotiate your value involves good self-esteem and self-respect.
– The clearer your self-esteem is, and your goals, the easier it will be to negotiate and not resign.
– Dialogue with a good attitude and objective assessment of the situation, as well as the quality of the negotiation, will say more about your value.
– It is important to assess what you will achieve, the problems that you will solve and the impact that your solutions will have.
– If the client is not willing to pay, it means that you have not been able to negotiate well, or that this is obviously not your client.

Checklist of legal tips to avoid unethical usage of research results

(Samovica, 2020)

– Handling personal data is essential to protect the identification of individuals. In the case that the research involves individuals and their identity, one must obtain consent from the individual in question to publish their information or engage in pseudonymization.

– Confidentiality in research must be strictly adhered to. The parties working on research together should have a clear understanding of which aspects of their research are covered by confidentiality clauses because each partner must be able to distinguish the information from their own knowledge.
– Ownership, royalties, decision rights, legal authority and the continuation of said research are just a few aspects that need to be legally determined when collaborating with others.
– The authorship should reflect contribution, and therefore it is best to establish the sections of research each author would be responsible for.
– Establishing a collaboration agreement is necessary to determine what intellectual property belongs to whom and should be standard.
– The fair use doctrine should be established to provide the rights to the creator of work and the benefit to society, while protecting both and stating in which manner and for which objective.
– Having a patent does not necessarily give anyone the right to use or exploit said research. An ethical issue arises when a patent is being used for harmful or negatively competitive reasons.
– Researchers have the possibility to choose whether they patent their research or not. Patented research acts as a tool for competition, rather than a means of exploring collaboration.
– In case of publicly-funded research, there is a need to give back to society and expose the results to members of society that could benefit from the findings of the research.
– Engage in data sharing agreements that ensure that the data shared is not misused.
– Sharing intellectual property is when shared IP enables parties to need to be consulted agreeing on further use and commercial exploitation. By these means, all parties would be aware and could decide on the future of the research.

In this chapter, I interviewed different professionals and academics dealing with budgets for innovation at European, national and organizational levels. I want to highlight their stories to create a dialogue at the end of this chapter about the cost of innovation, the value of knowledge and the importance of finance in innovation creation.

Conversation with Lina Gálvez Muñoz on "How to Calculate Budget for Innovation Ecosystems"

MEP European Parliament
   Economic History and Institutions Full Professor at the Economics Department at Pablo Olavide University
      @linagalvezmunoz

How do you calculate the benefits of knowledge sharing for innovation and for the innovation ecosystem in Europe?

The benefits of research and innovations are seen in the long term, but they are there, as the innovation performance of the EU has increased by 8.9% since 2012, surpassing the United States for the second year.

How to talk about the European budget for research and innovation activities?

We need to talk clearly about the impact of R&I funding in the EU to increase the awareness of public opinion and engage citizens, as science has to work for the benefit of society. The European budget for R&I is fundamental to advance in the European project, we are knowledge.

How to calculate the value of entrepreneurship of "going-to-market" for innovation and research in Europe?

The value is positive when they are game-changing innovations with a potential to support the recovery and the EU ambitions on digitalization and climate. R&I is critical to ensure a sustainable and inclusive recovery, the competitiveness of our economies and the transformation of our socio-economic systems.

How can European organizations share their knowledge to increase innovation and impact with innovation and research?

Reinforcing the knowledge triangle approach, the collaboration between research, education and innovation is key to share knowledge and experiences between relevant innovation actors and to increase the impact of innovation and research.

Why is it important to make an impact by sharing knowledge for innovation in Europe?

Because the comparative advantage of Europe in a global world lies in knowledge and knowledge-based innovation. We need to reinforce knowledge and excellence to achieve a resilient, ecological and digital future, without leaving anyone behind.

Conversation with Yannick Legré on "The Cost of Research Transfer"
Former Managing Director EGI
    https://www.egi.eu

How do you manage the knowledge transfer process and activities?

EGI is a foundation that coordinates, at the European level, the activities of National Computing and Data Centers publicly funded. EGI in itself has barely any self-knowledge to transfer beside its know-how, which constitutes the core of its business model. Most of the knowledge transfer activities related to EGI knowledge target its own members. However, EGI also acts as a catalyzer to stimulate and optimize the knowledge transfer processes and activities of its members. Both mainly take place as ad-hoc processes and activities in EU-funded projects while a few are part of the Foundation's recurrent activities.

How do you calculate the value and cost of the research project for knowledge and technology transfer purposes?

The cost calculation is fairly straightforward we usually took the cost of each of the activities that contributed to the Key Exploitable Results (KER) identified within the project and combined them. When one activity contributed to multiple KER, we had to allocate a fraction of the cost to each KER. The calculation of the value is trickier though, because the value of knowledge and technology transfer does not reside in its financial income only. For EGI, as a European coordination body, it was more important, under my direction, to generate new opportunities for its members, stimulate their knowledge and technology transfer, as well as advancing the strategic objectives of the foundation as defined by its members in the multi-annual strategy map.

What are the budget challenges you are facing in the framework academia/ industry collaboration?

Despite being a trendy activity for the past decades, knowledge and technology transfer is still not fully integrated within the academic world's activities. Although there are some very noticeable differences depending on the countries. However, most of the European academic institutions still consider it as a "dirty" activity staining the purity of the research. As a consequence, planned activities and sustained budget are rarely programmed and these activities required opportunistic and ad-hoc budgets. Those budgets mainly come from EU or national grants.

Another challenge is that there is still a fundamental dichotomy and lack of trust between academic and industry actors, which culminates in the budget discussion between the two worlds. As the proverb goes, "the devil lies in details" and many collaboration opportunities have failed, or taken so long that the collaboration necessity disappeared, solving the investment ratio or the royalties distribution matrix.

Conversation with Dominik Kufner on "The Cost of Innovation"

CEO KC Wearable Technologies
  www.kc-textil.com

What is the cost of Innovation?

I have trouble with the generic term of "innovation costs". There are three main types of costs.
(1) Fixed overheads, like rent or salaries are there whether an existing staff is allowed to innovate or not. Innovations do not add to these overheads.
(2) Variable costs like materials are put into a product calculation and are therefore covered by the revenue. Therefore, they are not real costs.
(3) Extraordinary investments like IT systems or your example (digitalization) are usually capitalized and then depreciated. So, they are investments, not costs.

The only real costs that produce real losses are unutilized fixed overheads. Technicians, which are there anyway, but get their projects cancelled by their managers – in the ill-conceived notion that this will reduce costs – these overheads become net losses. That is the cost of not innovating.

Is there a cost of not doing innovation?

The risk of not innovating is far more serious. In outerwear for example, there is a global reduction in sales volume of around 50% and next year a further reduction of 50% is expected. The only way to combat this trend is by giving consumers "a reason to buy" again. Example: We recently developed a silver textile range. These products have been proven to destroy coronaviruses on contact. They are now used in clothing to make sanitizing pockets – for facemasks or smartphones. It is garment features like this which will entice reluctant consumers to buy again. There are no real costs produced by putting such pockets into garments; only variable costs which are added to the garment price.

Additional sales will contribute to profit. Missing out on additional sales will add to losses. That is one risk of not innovating. Another risk is the response of creditors. Some companies seem "shell-shocked" and have turned inward. Creditors get extremely worried when they see losses and no innovations or other actions to turn things around. We will see a wave of bankruptcies and many of these will be such companies that are unwilling to embrace new product or sales initiatives. The whole industry needs to quickly wake up from the lockdowns and work on product innovations wherever possible.

Conversation with Kimberly Cornfield and Martin Scott about "Calculate the Value and Cost of the Research Project for Knowledge and Technology Transfer"

Kimberly Cornfield, University College London, European Research and Innovation Office (ERIO), Head of Proposal Management
Martin Scott, University College London, European Research and Innovation Office (ERIO), Head of Innovation Management
https://www.ucl.ac.uk/research/europe
@ucl

What is your role at University College London?

We support our academic and clinical colleagues at UCL in developing international, interdisciplinary and cross-sector research and innovation collaborations. We focus on supporting our colleagues and their international collaborators in applying for, and subsequently managing, funding from the European Union's (EU) Framework Programs for Research and Innovation (R&I). These funding programs run over seven-year periods, and the current program ("Horizon 2020") will conclude at the end of 2020. Horizon 2020 has made ca. €80 billion available to support R&I carried out by both public and private sector organizations and aimed to ensure that Europe continued to develop excellent science, industrial leadership and tackle global challenges with its international partners (European Commission, 2020b). The next program, "Horizon Europe", is to commence in 2021, and will again make ca. €80 billion of funding available over the next seven years (Zubașcu, 2020).

UCL remains one of the top beneficiaries of the Horizon 2020 program worldwide, having secured ca. €350 million since the start of the program in 2014 (European Commission, 2020a).

How do you manage the knowledge transfer process and activities?

We have seen an increased emphasis from the EU for research collaborations to focus on developing groundbreaking innovations, as well as to achieve real-world impact through R&I collaborations with industry. In order to remain competitive in applying for Horizon 2020 funding, and to achieve project success as well as post-project impact, UCL's knowledge and technology transfer processes have become increasingly important throughout the entire project lifecycle, as well as increasingly complex to manage.

To successfully manage the complexities around the knowledge and technology transfer process in multi-partner collaborations ERIO has, over the past seven years, developed and implemented specialist proposal development, project management and contract management services, underpinned by an innovation management service.

ERIO's services are founded upon deep and current understanding of the specific EU contractual requirements, and impact expectations, for work conducted under these types of collaborations. The ERIO team works closely with our Principal Investigators at UCL by advising them and their consortia on these requirements and facilitating the technology transfer process for their projects' outputs.

At the early concept stage, we work with our academic colleagues in establishing what the EU is looking to fund, and to assess the Intellectual Property and know-how that is anticipated to arise from the subsequent project. We identify who else should be involved internally and externally, to improve the chances of success in both receiving funding and successfully progressing the state of the art. Internally, we link in the relevant technology transfer departments and advise the same for our consortium partners. Externally, we look for the organizations with which we can collaborate to support the technology transfer process, such as companies that can directly take the technologies to market, as well as consultants, networks and incubators that can advise on the technology transfer process during the implementation of the research. Integrating a comprehensive technology transfer process and ensuring the right technology transfer stakeholders are involved from the early stages of a research project, prepares the project and the team to enter each subsequent stage of development, or to commence commercialization following the end of the research project.

How do you calculate the value and cost of the research project for knowledge and technology transfer purposes?

Developing research and innovation collaborations and leading an EU framework program proposal is time-consuming and therefore costly. Proposal preparation, which includes developing the technology transfer plans, typically takes between two to six months, and involves on average eight to twelve organizations across Europe and internationally. If the proposal is successful and is subsequently awarded funding, the costs related to the implementation of the project are included in the budget and reimbursed through the contractual mechanisms. However, the process up to the start date of the project is always carried out at the cost of each of the partner organizations, with the coordinating institution responsible for by far the largest portion of work, and therefore the biggest share of the upfront costs.

When considering the value and cost of such projects, we first consider the success rate of project proposals submitted to EU framework programs, as the average success rate across the Horizon 2020 program is 12.6% (.European Commission, 2017.). We therefore assess each R&I proposal and collaboration against the criteria set out in the funding call, with special attention given to the innovation and potential impact dimensions. If the concept is truly novel, and the proposal can be further developed to increase its competitiveness within the available timeframe, ERIO offers its full support services to UCL academic colleagues. We do not carry out a detailed costing of this process for our academic and support teams.

We calculate all costs from the implementation, which in most cases will be 125% of direct (i.e., identifiable) costs reimbursed. While the reimbursement will not typically cover all of UCL's (significant) overhead costs, it is still an attractive research-funding rate.

However, the financial costs of participating in an EU framework program proposal are greatly exceeded by the intrinsic value of participation, both to our organization and UK organizations more broadly, in particular the continued partnership and engagement with our European partners. Since the EU membership ("Brexit") referendum in the UK, the value of participation in these collaborations has become ever more important as a means to maintain and increase UCL's global engagement and visibility as an excellent academic research institution across the EU science and industry landscape.

How do you calculate the ratio per hour of academics?

The EU framework program has specific requirements and guidelines on how to budget and report the costs associated with the implementation of the R&I projects its funds. Personnel costs are budgeted based on the full month cost of each employee, academic or administrative, and how many full-time months are planned for each employee's contribution to a project. However, during the implementation phase of these projects, the reporting and reimbursement is based on the hourly rate of each individual working on the project. The hourly rate includes all the direct costs the employee's organization incurs, including national insurance, and pension contribution etc., any overhead costs are accounted for separately, based on a flat rate set by the EU.

Aside from the implementation phase of such projects, ERIO does not typically use an hourly rate as a method to manage and monitor the work associated with planning these large-scale R&I collaborations. Given the scale of the work and the team that is coming together across organizations and countries, and the flexible approach required to bring the team together and collate the contributions to meet the EU's non-negotiable deadlines, recording costs by hour would not be a feasible monitoring method. The amount of time that is invested into developing such proposals is often as much time as is possible within the timeframe and is therefore immeasurable. It is understood that the upfront costs are high, and that is where ERIO works with our academic colleagues to establish if the proposed project would be sufficiently competitive to justify the resources required, including their own time.

ERIO's proposal development services were initially funded through success fees, based on a percentage of the overall budget of each project supported by ERIO. This fee would be paid separately from the awarded grant and was usually shared among project partner organizations. This is also how proposal development services are costed in the private sector. Time is not the direct factor used to cost the value of work; instead, the cost of the work is associated with the value of the award. This approach enables all those involved to invest as much time as needed, with a set costing based on the value of the award.

What are the challenges you are facing in the framework academia/industry collaboration?

The academic environment operates more slowly than industry, which traditionally conducts its activities at a much faster pace. However, following the recent successful acceleration of Covid-19 medical devices and therapies developed at UCL (UCL, 2020), we expect that there will be a further transition and strategic drive towards a more fast-paced and business cycle-sensitive approach within academia, better enabling open innovation and European/global research and innovation collaboration with industry (Dahlander and Wallin, 2020; UCL, 2020).

The Intellectual Property regime applicable to Horizon 2020 projects enjoys broad acceptance across both the academic and industry sectors. At its core is a simple mechanism, under which the project partner that develops Intellectual Property ("IP") within a project owns that IP but is also obliged to grant access to the other partners if they need it. The partner must also grant similar access to their "background" (IP developed before the project began), again if needed by other partners. The reasons for which such access is needed include both the requirement to carry out project tasks as well as to exploit a partner's own IP derived from the project's results.

Issues arise, however, when a larger corporate partner wishes to ensure they have maximum "freedom to operate" across what can sometimes be an overly complicated corporate structure spanning multiple jurisdictions. The corporate partner is usually participating in an EU project with a particular commercial aim in mind, such as developing a new product or service, or improving upon an existing one.

However, the corporate entity participating in such a project is not usually one that directly commercializes any IP, instead tending to be a research lab or development studio. To ensure the smooth functioning of the corporation's overall R&D portfolio, and to avoid potentially messy situations where a piece of IP with "strings" attached (in the form of access rights, or even joint ownership with an EU project partner) is inadvertently amalgamated with other proprietary IP, corporate partners tend to approach negotiations with a view to maximizing their freedom to operate, and minimizing the internal friction arising from the exploitation of a project's IP.

This approach tends to manifest itself as requests for the IP to be easily assigned to an exceedingly long list of subsidiaries and parent companies, or even any company worldwide fitting certain ownership criteria. Similar requests also tend to arise in relation to access rights to other project partners' IP, to ensure that the corporate entity that will eventually commercialize the project IP will have the necessary access, even if the project partners have never dealt with (or in some cases even heard of) the corporate entity in question. Corporate partners may also wish to place restrictions upon the dissemination of project IP (e.g., in the form of academic publications) until, for example, a patent can be filed to ensure the viability of exploitation plans.

In broad terms, this approach therefore sets the academic partners' desire for contractual transparency, ease of compliance, and (to an extent) academic publishing, against corporate partners' desire for freedom to operate, to minimal internal friction, and to ensure IP is protected so as to facilitate exploitation. Horizon 2020 contracts already involve seven- or eight-figure budgets, but in some cases the potential downstream risk to a corporate partner arising from developing and implementing IP that may be subject to onerous conditions can exceed these amounts. As such, sensitively and rapidly negotiating IP rights and IP ownership regimes within the frame of a Horizon 2020 project can occasionally become a high-stake balancing act. Taking great care to understand and then correctly resolve the various, and sometimes competing, requirements of partners spanning different sectors is therefore a vital component in the successful management of a Horizon 2020 project.

What kind of ethical issues when orchestrating an academia/industry collaboration?

Conflicts between the project and organization(s). If a partner organization, for example a small business, change their priorities, this can result in a conflict within the project where capacity is lost and must be obtained elsewhere. For example, if an area of development is considered to be scientifically promising but not immediately marketable, key commercial partners can become less interested in continuing the work and therefore their participation and general level of engagement may dwindle. Another outcome is that the partner who intended to commercialize the results is no longer interested in doing so, due to changing priorities or team within their organization.

Lack of clarity on exploiting project results. When this is not addressed and clearly planned from the early stages of proposal development, issues can arise during later phases of the project, and put at risk the exploitation and potential commercialization of results. As post-project impact is an element of the initial award, this can put at risk the planned objectives we contractually agreed to achieve with the funder.

Summary

To sum up this chapter, I will leave you with a number of exercises that help ground you in your journey to create a financial mindset for innovation.

To practice

1. Be aware of the factors that hold you for sharing your knowledge and pay for knowledge.
2. Calculate your own ratio per hour!
3. Train yourself in financial vocabulary and rules!
4. Deal with the fear of industry/academia collaboration.

In the following chapters you will find

– Tips to adapt your organization processes to collaborate.
– Tips on innovation best practices for collaboration.
– Tips to acquire new technology effectively for your organization.

Notes

(Chesbrough, 2020) https://collabwith.co/2020/05/podcast-prof-henry-chesbrough-on-the-role-of-the-open-innovation-in-the-recovery-plan/
(Tucci, 2019) https://collabwith.co/2019/05/podcast-ispim-florence-prof-tucci-on-innovation-management-if-you-are-not-interested-enough-it-is-hard-to-convince-others-to-support-you/
(UK Universities, 2018) https://www.universitiesuk.ac.uk/facts-and-stats/data-and-analysis/Documents/higher-education-research-in-facts-and-figures.pdf
(Laurin, 2019) https://collabwith.co/2019/04/podcast-ispim-ottawa-jeremy-laurin-on-scaling-start-ups-as-entrepreneurs-that-need-to-learn-that-your-very-first-customer-might-not-be-from-your-backyard

(Fuellmann, 2020) https://collabwith.co/2020/03/maik-fuellmann-on-online-learning-and-fight-COVID-19/
(Avila-Rauch, 2020) https://collabwith.co/2020/09/fear-to-ask-about-your-fee-doing-business-and-innovation/
(Samovica, 2020) https://collabwith.co/2020/08/tips-to-avoid-unethical-usage-of-research-results/
(OECD, 2006) https://www.oecd.org/science/inno/36311146.pdf

References

Coltheart, M. How can functional neuroimaging inform cognitive theories? Perspect.Psychol.Sci. 8, 98–103. doi: 10.1177/1745691612469208. 2013.
Dahlander, L. and Wallin, Martin. 2020. Why Now Is the Time for "Open Innovation". [online]. Boston: Harvard Business Review. Available at: https://hbr.org/2020/06/why-now-is-the-time-for-open-innovation
European Commission, Directorate-General for Research and Innovation and Directorate A Policy Development and Coordination. (2017) *HORIZON 2020 IN FULL SWING – Three Years On – Key facts and figures 2014-2016.* [online]. Brussels: EC. Available at: https://ec.europa.eu/programmes/horizon2020/sites/horizon2020/files/h2020_threeyearson_a4_horizontal_2018_web.pdf
European Commission, Horizon 2020 Framework Programme (H2020). (2020a) *H2020 Dashboard.* [online]. Brussels: EC. Available at: https://webgate.ec.europa.eu/dashboard/sense/app/93297a69-09fd-4ef5-889f-b83c4e21d33e/sheet/a879124b-bfc3-493f-93a9-34f0e7fba124/state/analysis
European Commission, Horizon 2020. (2020b) *What is Horizon 2020?* [online]. Brussels: EC. Available at: https://ec.europa.eu/programmes/horizon2020/what-horizon-2020
Kahneman, D. and Tversky, A. Prospect Theory: An Analysis of Decision under Risk. Econometrica, Vol. 47, No. 2. (Mar. 1979), pp. 263–292. 1979.
Loosemore, R., and Harley, T. "17 brains and minds: on the usefulness of localization data to cognitive psychology" 2010.
McSweeney, F.K., Murphy, E. S. The Wiley-Blackwell Handbook of Operant and Classical Conditioning. 2014.
Samson, K. and Kostyszyn, P. Effects of Cognitive Load on Trusting Behavior – An Experiment Using the Trust Game. 2015. https://doi.org/10.1371/journal.pone.0127680
Thaler, R.H. Advances in Behavioral Finance, Volume II. 2005.
(UCL, 2020) University College London (UCL), UCL Institute of Healthcare Engineering. (2020) About UCL-Ventura. [online]. London: UCL. Available at: https://www.ucl.ac.uk/healthcare-engineering/Covid-19/ucl-ventura-breathing-aids-COVID-19-patients/about-ucl-ventura
Zubaşcu, F. 2020. Leaders agree on slimmed-down €80.9B for Horizon Europe. [online]. Brussels: Science Business. Available at: https://sciencebusiness.net/framework-programmes/news/leaders-agree-slimmed-down-eu809b-horizon-europe

―――――――

"We have to disseminate and absorb innovation before generating new innovations"

Prof. Henry Chesbrough, Faculty Director, Garwood Center for Corporate Innovation, UC Berkeley-Haas School of Business (Chesbrough, 2020)

Chapter 8
Getting Real and Making Impact – Procurement Innovation and Corporate Venturing

Summary: In this chapter, you will learn how innovation procurement works, and how your organization can adapt innovation procurement best practices to contract innovative solutions. Furthermore, you will find out about the psychology of the "sales innovation process" and how selling innovation is about increasing trust, reducing fear and looking for matching needs.

Impact is happening when adoption of innovation takes place. On the path leading up to this, the hard work going into the front end of the innovation will be wasted if effort is not being spent as well on the adoption of the innovation. You can see that all the media and industry are focused on startup investments from venture capital firms on the one side and generating ideas on the other side. The procurement processes regarding innovation are maybe not as attractive to communicate as the investment in startups or talking about great ideas. However, it is important to adopt innovation procurement processes as well in the private sector and in public institutions.

What is innovation procurement?

Innovation procurement is the process that supports buying innovation goods by organizations. The official definition coming from the European project Procure2Innovate website is: "The public authorities who support the process of innovation or purchase innovative goods and services are often directly awarded with improved services at optimized costs and help to stimulate future markets and address key societal challenges" (Procure2Innovate, 2020). This definition describes only the innovation procurement for public institutions, but it is applicable to private organizations which have the objective of purchasing and contracting innovative goods or services as well. The European Parliament adopted in 2014 the new "public procurement directives" (EU Public Procurement, 2020) to facilitate innovation partnerships, increase flexibility and simplification, have better conditions to collaborate, support the calculation of life-cycle costing and include research activities such as pre-procurement. This is a well-designed process and supports activities for public institutions which can be adopted by any other kind of organization as well.

Innovation procurement occurs in the adoption phase (Figure 8.2) of the innovation process, where organizations take on innovative services and products. This is where impact caused by innovation occurs, when organizations can create jobs

https://doi.org/10.1515/9783110665383-008

and when you can drive change in processes and in people. One of the ways to measure impact is to measure how many purchases of innovative services have been executed by public administrations and by private organizations and monitor their outcomes.

How can your organization adopt innovation procurement?

It might be the case that your organization is small, and you can "buy" innovative products and services directly, or your company may have a complex purchase and procurement system in place. In both cases, you can follow the innovation procurement guidelines. As Prof. Bueso indicates, the first thing is to be open-minded towards innovation and willing to change a little bit how your organization is dealing with internal procurement processes, as well as to be comfortable with taking risks (Bueso, 2020). In this context, risk is when you are ready to adapt your way of communicating and your way of accepting proposals to not only work with established organizations and proposals. The innovation procurement process shares similarities with our "collaboration journey" (Figure 3.4). Both start with looking at your needs first (Figure 1.4), then you start your phase of discovery (Figure 1.5) and do an analysis of your needs and options you have discovered (Figure 1.6). The innovation brokerage is a key element in both processes (Figure 2.4) and naturally it follows with how you can cluster your partners (Figure 3.5).

Innovation procurement-related activities

- Look at your needs first (Chapter 1).
- Use as many tools as you can to broker new innovation products and services matching your needs. Have open eyes and open ears to scout newcomers to the market.
- Create relationships with super innovators, understand them and help them evade the complexity of procurement.
- Be a visionary and ask yourself this question: How can you use this innovative product or service?
- Contact experts if you need to know how to use a specific technology or if you need to understand a new trend.
- Create once-a-month events to meet super innovators and informally discuss your needs, listen to their projects and explain your processes. Everything is about bringing people together and talking!
- Look at the product cycle cost to assess companies – the lower priced bidder is not always less expensive in the long term.

- Look at the positive effects such as sustainability impact, ecosystem benefits, ethical ways of working, professionalism, understanding of innovation and passion for their product and company. In what ways does this company care about the sustainable development goals (SDG)?
- A well-explained process helps to create trust and a common understanding of the objective of acquiring innovative solutions.
- Help the super innovators to understand the procurement process and help them to be associated with established industry actors to learn from them and apply together on the proposal. Make it part of your process; create a small team to help small companies to understand how to work with you.

The following best practices come from a report created by the European Commission in 2007 called "Guide on dealing with innovative solutions in public procurement: 10 elements of good practice" (EU Guide for Innovation Procurement, 2007). This report is a must-read and all the report itself is highly relevant and so well thought through that it is applicable now and in future. You can find a summary below with updates for today's available technology and including the psychology of innovation from prior chapters in this book.

Innovation procurement best practices

(EU Guide for Innovation Procurement, 2007)

- Create a professional procurement team with innovation understanding.
- Communicate your needs and your forecast to the market years in advance if it's possible.
- Identify innovative services and products on the market. Use available digital platforms and other tools, such as the Collabwith platform.
- Inform the super innovators which you have identified and share your needs with them.
- Create a group of key end users to understand their needs and work with them as a reference for feedback and decision making on the innovative solutions.
- Bring together experts from your organization and the decision makers, show them the new products and services and ensure their involvement and active participation during the procurement process.
- Ask for solutions because you bring the needs and the challenges.
- Listen and analyze ideas coming from the super innovators, be open to their proposals.
- Define the selection criteria after having a new perspective of the market including the super innovators' products and services. Cost, quality and impact should be taken into account.

- Identify and cluster the risks before and after the selection of the innovative so-lution together with the decision makers inside your organization.
- Be open-minded to pilots, co-innovate pilots, co-research during the pre-procurement phase.
- Be open-minded to receive incentives, to receive equity and a part of intellectual property in case of co-creation, and as a benefit of doing pilots with super innovators.
- Monitor and follow up the pilot and the implementation by creating clear milestones, performance indicators and satisfaction surveys of the key end user group, including quantitative and qualitative feedback.
- Be open-minded to learn together inside your organization every time you are doing innovation within your procurement process and adapt an innovative solution.
- The innovation definition has to be adapted to your organization, but everyone has to be aware of what is innovation and how to innovate. Innovation is a journey.

On a personal note, one of my first jobs during my university time was an internship for 2 years in a purchase department at a national telecoms operator in Spain. I spent 20 hours per week there, on top of my university classes at the technical university. It was an amazing experience, because I had the luck to work with the best managers I've ever worked with since and I learned how to negotiate budgets, contracts, deal with relationships, and how to support people from other functions who want to "buy" things and, of course, deal with the internal politics. At the same time, I learned how important a purchase department is, and how decision making works, and it is not about price! The EU commission's guidelines from 2007 are best practices not only for innovation procurement but also for procurement in general. Later on, when I was managing innovation and driving green IT at an international fashion brand, one of the critical points for me to influence was the "purchase decision making" as it was a critical factor (the entry point) of innovative services and products. This was, of course, not the first course of action, rather a natural step to take after the second year – after exchanging with the current vendors about how to do "things" in a different way and after having won over the whole department to innovation. As a practical case from that time, we had to buy a new "collaboration tool", and yes, innovation was there with a "usability" approach. Usability means that in the procurement process you take the user feedback and user experience into account for the request for information (RFI), request for proposals (RFP) and for the selection process, including a testing period with users. If you need to add another buzzword to be accepted you can add "agile methodology for procurement", driven by the innovation team who is helping to take care of innovation, and user requirements. This is a very smart move, because the technical team is not alone in collecting requirements from an isolated desk or system tickets (in this case); you help them, and you open the question from a real user perspective with real needs. You can do this properly with ethnographic and observation techniques or with one-to-one interviews with proper open questions to discover needs. The same group of "key users" from your organization is the group with whom you will discover needs, test the different solutions and create an insightful report for the procurement team, including the innovation score, the green score, the impact of the solution in your organization, the impact on the satisfaction of the key users (you can use net promoter score [NPS] to make things easy to calculate in a spreadsheet for the procurement team) and future employees. And of course, you are participating in all the meetings with the different vendors, and you can advise innovative solutions to be taken into account from your "scouting efforts". Hence, your innovation team will support the procurement process to select more meaningful and impactful solutions which will increase employee satisfaction (end user, customer, citizen, etc.) and increase the cohesion between procurement teams with other departments. Adding another personal note, I remember that in our innovation team, we listened to the procurement team and other employees and we discovered that the approval process of the purchase orders was one of bottlenecks for approving projects and services. Therefore, together with the system integration team and the procurement team, we created a new web-based interface on top of the SAP system for approvals to make it easy to approve, where the decision makers were able to receive an email with the purchase order (PO), click to approve, or click to decline, go to the new web-app, look at a list with all POs and approve or decline much more easily. The team won the SAP innovation award that year. In conclusion, innovation is always a clever idea to improve processes and to acquire innovative solutions to make life easier for everyone!

The best moment to start a startup-corporate collaboration is in the 'middle', not too early and not too late. When a startup is at a very early stage, it is hard for a company to help it to grow up, there are some cases but not many, and when a startup has become a scale-up it is hard too because the scale-up is already launched on its own path. I personally consider the best time when the startup already received its first investment, has an MVP (minimum viable product) or a POC (proof of concept) or is already on the market but needs a partner to boost its business. If the company is also interested in investing in the startup, the scale-up phase can be very expensive, while the 'just after early-stage' phase can be the best one (Abirascid, 2019).

Checklist for adopting innovation procurement in your organization

- Open mindset about innovation, every public and private institution has to be ready for the future.
- There is a new social status of being an innovative organization.

- Be an active partner in the innovation ecosystem.
- Continuously train in how to manage partnerships, build meaningful relationships with super innovators and monitor the progress of the adoption of innovation.
- Continuously train in how to create a positive impact within your organization.
- Continuously train and educate in entrepreneurship and emotional intelligence.
- You know you can do things in a different way, maximize the impact of your decisions!
- Innovation is a lot about finance; hence, empower your ecosystem to economically grow by adopting innovation.
- You have the power to innovate your organization, your market, your industry and your region by selecting innovative solutions.
- You are making the final decision to remain an old timer or to become a Tesla.
- You have this power to change the market towards a more innovative market. Use this power to make a positive impact.

Prof. Bueso (Bueso, 2020) from the University of Zaragoza mentions two other main factors to take into account to evaluate innovative solutions from a procurement perspective. One of the factors is that the metrics to evaluate "usual" vendors may not be applicable to startups or to the innovative solutions usually contributed by SMEs. For example, it is neither possible to ask for an ISO140001 certification for a startup or SME, nor for specific capital, nor for a detailed documentation of 20 years of business performance. Nevertheless, Prof. Bueso (Bueso, 2020) clarifies that it's possible to ask for other forms of proof: pilots with other organizations, the team structure, a risk mitigation report, an impact report or letters of intent from other customers or references. The second factor that Prof. Bueso (Bueso, 2020) has written about is the monitoring of the execution and performance by the procurement department after the selection of the organization with the innovative solution. One team (max. 5 people) has to define the performance indicators for the execution and for satisfaction. They should meet regularly with the selected provider to ask if they need support from the administration or from the organization and take action to help. You can use here the "emotional intelligence canvas" (Figure 4.2) to facilitate communication and increase trust – besides being an active listener, kind, respectful and open to new ways of working and thinking. Equally important: creating a performance plan, including a technical support system during the execution, and with lessons learned at the end from both sides.

The mindset is that "we are all together to make this happen"; it's not "us" and "them", it's the organization and innovative solution provider "together" – you are all a collaboration team to drive change and to bring this innovative solution successfully to the market or into the organization. This means that the responsibility is on both sides, because now the two sides become one.

Checklist for changing your procurement process to buy innovative solutions:

- Bring your innovation team into the process to support you.
- Think agile for procurement to add user-centered innovation and ensure satisfaction in your organization.
- Adapt your "purchase criteria" to facilitate SMEs and organizations with innovative solutions to apply to your request for information (RFI) and request for proposals (RFP) and other calls.
- Add the "sustainability factor" and "innovation factor" to your selection criteria.
- Become a member of digital platforms that you can use to scout innovations and startups to see what is going on in the market and to scout your future solutions.
- Create a small team to promote your procurement and organization's needs, and to technically support SMEs and super innovators in the end-to-end process.

The psychology of the first meeting

There is another important aspect when a startup and a super innovator are approaching an established organization (public or private) and there is an incredible fear which both sides are experiencing. For instance, an innovation manager inside one organization has the power to make a decision on whether he prefers a Microsoft solution or a startup solution. If the innovation manager chooses the Microsoft solution, and the solution does not work, the responsibility is Microsoft's. However, if the innovation manager selects the startup solution, and it doesn't work, the responsibility is the innovation manager's, and it could have consequences for his reputation, his performance review and his position. It is very important to understand and be aware of implications like these and foresee the emotions on each side. The startup and the innovation manager will need to adapt their decision making, their communication and their attention accordingly when they are meeting during the procurement or sales process. Other emotions involved in this process are fear, trust and self-confidence. For innovation procurement, trust is very important. Trust concerning service delivery, performance and how confident you are in the innovative solution being the solution to your needs and challenges. It is crucial to be aware of these emotions during the process and build communication to mitigate fear, and to enhance trust and confidence in the innovative solution and in the startup. The technology offices at university and procurement teams always mention that it is very important to build relationships to establish collaborations for innovation. Relationships are not created from one day to another, and it is imperative to differentiate relationships vs. friendship. A professional relationship for collaborative innovation is based on having a common objective and mission that are shared, along with a well-defined need and solution. The collaboration is happening because the relationship is a process that both parties understand. Trust is related to self-confidence and related to confidence in the solution and into your need, the clearer you are with your needs and the more confident in innovation, the easier it will be to adopt an innovation. The "collaboration canvas" (Figure 3.6) and the "emotional intelligence canvas" (Figure 4.2) are tools to help you with communication, managing expectations, dealing with communication and creating trust. Organizations have to be ready to innovate together with small companies, such as startups and SMEs, who are the source of innovative solutions. Usually their products are cheaper than the market leader's products, and they are more passionate when working to apply an innovative solution. It is better to try out sooner rather than later and to be a pioneer in your industry and a reference for other companies and organizations.

The company and the start-up speaking the same language is the first step. Then, of course, there must be some industrial, commercial or financial common interest but for example, I'm seeing that more and more start-ups are preferring investments from an industrial partner than purely financial ones because they know the industrial partner can bring them more than just money. That's why even the smartest venture capitalists are working closely with companies in order to facilitate the growth process of the start-ups where they are investing, and of course create more options also for the exits (Abirascid, 2019).

Another perspective to take into account is the startup journey and the emotional journey of a super innovator or entrepreneur. The startup journey is one of self-discovery and is a business learning journey with hard years of hustling until the startup starts to have its first customers, and then until the business starts to have a regular turnover and starts growing. Usually, startups are bringing a new product to the market which means they have to create the market for this new product or service. Startups face an industry transformation journey which, as you can imagine, is hard. One of the best books on entrepreneurship which mentions briefly the psychology of entrepreneurship is *The Hockey Stick Principles: The 4 Key Stages to Entrepreneurial Success* by Bobby Martin where the 4 stages are tinkering, the blade years, the growth inflection point and surging growth (Martin, 2016). The first two phases are about trying to figure out how the business works and adapting to customer acceptance and feedback. Booby Martin said, "It's an interesting stage, because it's the hardest type psychologically and physically, and it's also when the most important work is being done for the business" (Martin, 2016) for the blade years phase, which could be years and years. Figure 8.1 shows the classical "iceberg illusion" drawing of what is visible from an entrepreneur and what is not visible from the entrepreneurship journey. The visible part is about the success (actual or fake), and the invisible part is the emotional journey of persistence, resilience, sacrifice, failure, bad days, disappointment, discipline, hard work and dedication. If the entrepreneur is not trained or aware of emotional intelligence skills, he may come to the first meeting at a time when he is feeling disappointment; therefore, he will not explain his business or innovative solution properly. If the entrepreneur is trained and aware of emotional intelligence skills, he can move from a feeling of disappointment to a feeling of calmness and performance when explaining his solution. This will lead to a completely different performance of the startup at the meeting. Ideally, the organization and the decision-making team should be aware of the emotional journey of a startup to understand how difficult and hard it can be to bring a new solution to the market.

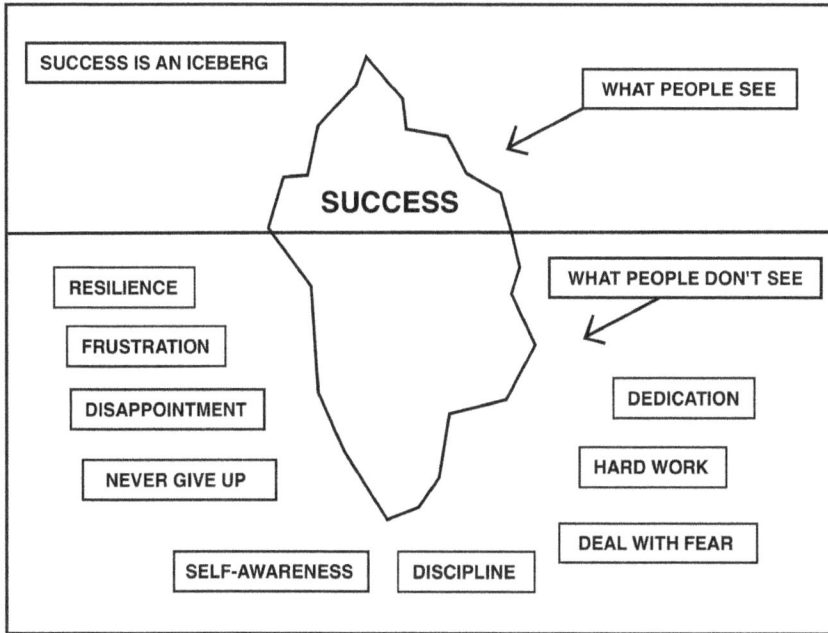

Figure 8.1: Emotional stages during the startup journey.

Because during phase 2 of the hockey stick growth of the business, according to Bobby Martin, "It's also a time when the founder him or herself is doing a lot of the heavy lifting and handling important aspects of the business – selling, product development, customer service – and they're also learning like crazy" (Martin, 2016). Figure 8.1 shows the emotional stages, and not the daily tasks of running a new business with an innovative solution (which is unlike opening a bakery in your city). Usually you are meeting with a founder who is dealing with fear, incertitude, frustration, resilience, motivation, priorities and struggling with self-esteem. And this emotional and learning journey is about himself and also present within his team.

How to build relationships? Before, during and after the innovation procurement

Relationships are one of the criteria that every report on innovation procurement or knowledge transfer mentions and became a topic in almost every meeting and interview I have been doing or reading. Relationships as key for collaboration and for innovation are built based on trust, needs of each other, respect, assertiveness, kindness and acceptance. Of course, the relationship gets stronger if both parties manage their emotional intelligence skills. You can see the values for the collaboration in Figure 4.2 where you find a guide on how to use the emotional intelligence skills depending on the situation and on moods at that particular moment.

As it is very important to build relationships to close a "deal" for an innovative solution, you can imagine how to have this new relationship virtually and how to close the "deal" for your innovative solution virtually. In the end, it is all about matching needs, offer and supplier, and trust regarding yourself, the collaboration and the activity you both will do together. At the same time, it is a mix of empathy regarding the entrepreneurship process in the innovative organization, and the innovative organization has to send a structure proposal for the collaboration for innovation. Meaningful interactions are the key, and trust is generated by "learning together by doing it together". Use the virtual environment to become much more efficient, and the offline (or non-administrative online environment) to know each other. And remember that trust for business is not the same as trust for friendship. You are doing business; you are not making friends because being kind is not being a friend.

Here is one of the last canvases for the "collaboration journey" – where and how the innovation is sold to corporates and other organizations.

Selling canvas for an innovative collaboration

Startup – academia – organization (public or private)

We are paying attention to new things and new trends, but we need to focus more on how to get business results from these past and current innovations (Chesbrough, 2020).

You have to know how to deal with your emotions and how to communicate when you are selling your innovative solution to an organization. The canvas in Figure 8.2 helps you drive this process of creating a professional relationship, translate fear into trusted action and deal with the process of learning together to innovate. On a personal note, the fastest deal I made was on two remote meetings, because it was clear what to offer, what the customers were looking for, and what the other party needed. It was clear for everyone, and we built trust during the process. You

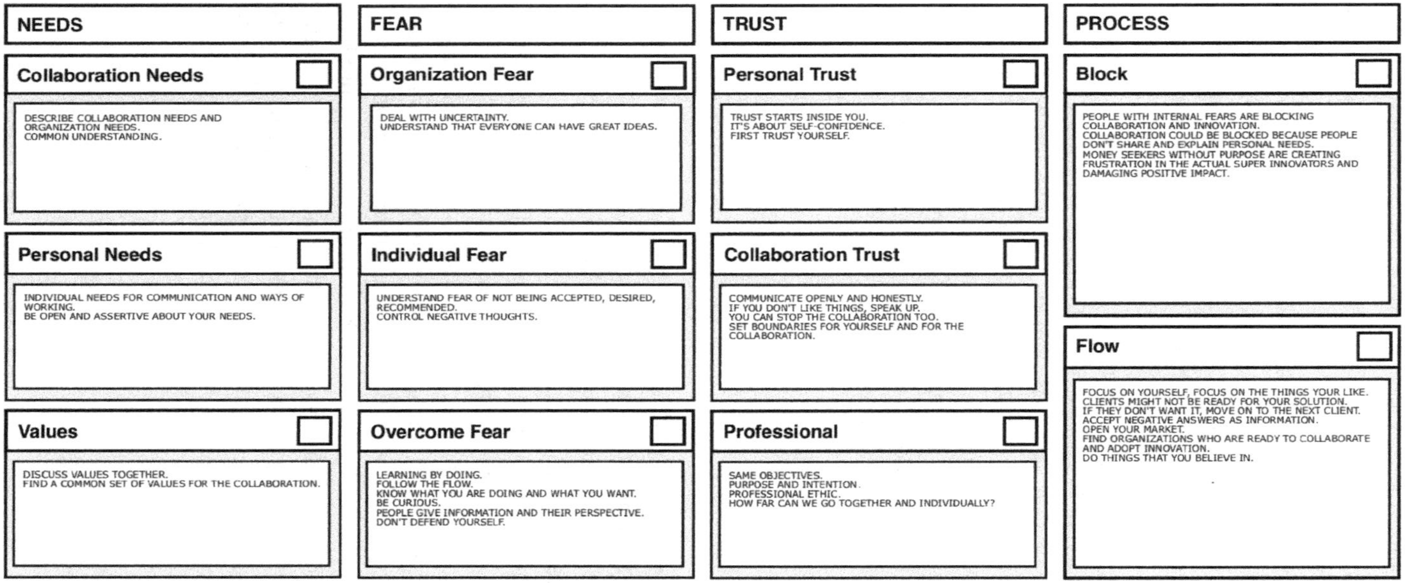

NEEDS	FEAR	TRUST	PROCESS
Collaboration Needs	**Organization Fear**	**Personal Trust**	**Block**
DESCRIBE COLLABORATION NEEDS AND ORGANIZATION NEEDS. COMMON UNDERSTANDING.	DEAL WITH UNCERTAINTY. UNDERSTAND THAT EVERYONE CAN HAVE GREAT IDEAS.	TRUST STARTS INSIDE YOU. IT'S ABOUT SELF-CONFIDENCE. FIRST TRUST YOURSELF.	PEOPLE WITH INTERNAL FEARS ARE BLOCKING COLLABORATION AND INNOVATION. COLLABORATION COULD BE BLOCKED BECAUSE PEOPLE DON'T SHARE AND EXPLAIN PERSONAL NEEDS. MONEY SEEKERS WITHOUT PURPOSE ARE CREATING FRUSTRATION IN THE ACTUAL SUPER INNOVATORS AND DAMAGING POSITIVE IMPACT.
Personal Needs	**Individual Fear**	**Collaboration Trust**	**Flow**
INDIVIDUAL NEEDS FOR COMMUNICATION AND WAYS OF WORKING. BE OPEN AND ASSERTIVE ABOUT YOUR NEEDS.	UNDERSTAND FEAR OF NOT BEING ACCEPTED, DESIRED, RECOMMENDED. CONTROL NEGATIVE THOUGHTS.	COMMUNICATE OPENLY AND HONESTLY. IF YOU DON'T LIKE THINGS, SPEAK UP. YOU CAN STOP THE COLLABORATION TOO. SET BOUNDARIES FOR YOURSELF AND FOR THE COLLABORATION.	FOCUS ON YOURSELF. FOCUS ON THE THINGS YOUR LIKE. CLIENTS MIGHT NOT BE READY FOR YOUR SOLUTION. IF THEY DON'T WANT IT, MOVE ON TO THE NEXT CLIENT. ACCEPT NEGATIVE ANSWERS AS INFORMATION. OPEN YOUR MARKET. FIND ORGANIZATIONS WHO ARE READY TO COLLABORATE AND ADOPT INNOVATION. DO THINGS THAT YOU BELIEVE IN.
Values	**Overcome Fear**	**Professional**	
DISCUSS VALUES TOGETHER. FIND A COMMON SET OF VALUES FOR THE COLLABORATION.	LEARNING BY DOING. FOLLOW THE FLOW. KNOW WHAT YOU ARE DOING AND WHAT YOU WANT. BE CURIOUS. PEOPLE GIVE INFORMATION AND THEIR PERSPECTIVE. DON'T DEFEND YOURSELF.	SAME OBJECTIVES. PURPOSE AND INTENTION. PROFESSIONAL ETHIC. HOW FAR CAN WE GO TOGETHER AND INDIVIDUALLY?	

Figure 8.2: Selling innovation canvas for an innovative collaboration.

can argue that there are many different cases, but all of them, given that they are successful, are based on matching needs, having a common understanding and open and honest communication.

There are a lot of issues with how-to books on selling and all the marketing around entrepreneurship, innovation and digital tools. Marketing and all the social messages of selling are there to get clicks. They are playing with your emotions and your fears to force you to buy and to create frustration. They are creating a distortion of your reality and preventing you from thinking of what exactly you need. The first step is to talk with potential partners in an open and honest way and start a conversation about your needs, their needs and how to work together. Communication is the action of sharing needs, values, listening, understanding and finding a common ground to make it happen together. If the other organization or person is afraid for whatever reason, this means that they are not ready for innovation or for the collaboration. You should understand that it's better to accept that if a collaboration is not working you have to move on to the next partnership. You have to find the right organization which is ready to innovate and accept innovative solutions.

What is corporate venturing?

"Manage uncertainty (unknown), instead of risk management (well-known)" says Joanne Hyland, Founder and President of the rInnovation Group, Member ISO 56002 STANDARD Innovation Management and Former Vice President, New Venture Development at Nortel Networks (Hyland, 2019).

Corporate venturing is when a corporate organization creates a venture capital internal fund to invest in startups and innovative solutions. It is a way to acquire new technology and new knowledge related to the company vision and a complement to the research and development teams. Corporate venturing can be an externalization of the innovation procurement process, when the procurement process invests in pilots, proof of concepts or doing research together with innovative startups or SMEs, and where the company invests in their innovative solutions and can receive equity or licenses and other advantages for being the first customer or groups of first customers. The term "corporate venturing" is a little bit misleading because it could be any kind of organization, corporate, university, research center or SME that is actively investing in novel solutions.

Corporate venturing best practices

–   Establish mechanisms and processes to share and transfer knowledge and technology between your startup portfolio and your organization leadership. Because

you are investing in startups and innovative solutions to gather their knowledge and technology.
- Corporate venturing should work like independent venture capital because you invest in startups with a long-term view and strategy.
- Design an independent group of experts from the organization for the investment decision-making process.
- Mission and vision of the corporate venturing should be the same as the startups, organization and fund investors.
- Corporate venturing is another way to innovate your organization and create a competitive advantage in the market.
- As an innovation process, your organization has to manage the front end of innovation for corporate venturing by selecting startups (technology and knowledge driven) which match your criteria and going through the funnel of ideas to implementation.
- Focus on seeding other innovative solutions from startups to help your industry, market and technology to grow as an innovation ecosystem for your organization to gather strategic benefits and collaborate to innovate.
- Corporate venturing is bringing funding, reputation, expertise, resources and a playground for the startups and innovative solutions.

Joanne Hyland, who was VP New Venture Development at Nortel Networks, said that Nortel helped startups to grow organically over a 3–4 year timeline, and 200 employees were involved to manage the startup portfolio. In the end, Nortel went from startup investment to merge and acquisitions and maintained their discovery and scouting work of innovative solutions (Hyland, 2019).

Driving change to adopt innovation

Startups and innovative suppliers need somebody to connect them (InnoBrokers, 2020).

The figure of the innovation broker is well known and sometimes called a technology broker, knowledge broker or business developer. An innovation broker can be in the form of a personal service, or it could be a virtual platform such as Collabwith. The innovation broker, or other digital platforms dedicated to connecting startups or technology with organizations, also have the function of an innovation adviser. Martin McGurk, a Senior Innovation Lead at Innovate UK has said that "the innovation adviser must be a relationship builder and trust-worthy with an ability to listen. They open the eyes of the business to new possibilities while allowing the business to make the decision on where to go next" (McGurk, 2019).

How to measure the impact of innovation?

We have to disseminate and absorb innovation before generating new innovations (Chesbrough, 2020).

As observed in Chapter 6 about innovation ecosystems, it is important that the ecosystem and brokers are helping the industry and other organizations adopt innovative solutions. The goal is to increase the success and impact within industry and society for super innovative projects inside SMEs or corporates and startups. The issue is that currently we are measuring the investment but not the customers' acquisition and technology adoption of innovation.

To measure the impact of innovation, establishing key performance indicators (KPIs) to adopt new technology and innovation for established companies and industry leaders is the first step:

- Unify the KPIs across universities, nationally and on European level to measure knowledge and technology transfer.
- Number of collaborations on innovation projects, on research projects where the co-creation of a new product or new service, but also the adoption or modification of existing products and services to adapt to the new needs and market takes place.
- Number of collaborations – startups with academia.
- Number of collaborations – startups with industry.
- Number of collaborations – academia/industry.

First of all, the facilitation of finding European technology and innovation for industry and academia, not only on visualization but to enable and to facilitate collaboration and knowledge and technology transfer by reducing the legal documents across borders and by reducing the administrative bureaucracy. Adding tax benefits for corporate venturing will facilitate the sharing of risk when adopting new technology from startups, universities or research institutions.

The impact of innovation stems directly from the benefit of a collaboration for innovation or adopting innovative solutions. The amount of impact is not only measured through job creation or economic growth. As a basis, setting your project side-by-side with the UN's sustainable development goals provides a clear way to understand the impact of a specific innovation or a collaboration for innovation. If your collaboration has an impact on one or many sustainable development goals, this is a good start for defining your impact. The subsequent step is to define the impact inside your industry, inside your supply chain and your value chain. For instance, it is worth it to identify and define which organizations or people are enjoying a direct and indirect benefit from your innovation. On top of this, you can identify the benefits for your "collaborator" or partner when doing a collaboration for innovation together, plus your own benefits. You have to assess the impact and benefits by going beyond the normal and traditional thinking about impact.

In this chapter, I interviewed high-level experts with hands-on experience with the topic of innovation procurement and corporate venturing to explain and clarify the concepts and remove all confusion possible between those terms.

Conversation with Joanne Hyland about "Corporate Venturing"

Founder and President of the rInnovation Group
    Member ISO 56002 STANDARD Innovation Management
    Former Vice President, New Venture Development at Nortel Networks

What is the role of corporate venturing inside an organization?

It depends on how an organization defines corporate venturing. In some organizations, it can be about nurturing internal startups, others about investing in external startups and, in others, it can be about both. Therefore, the role of a corporate venture is tied to an organization's strategic objectives for the purposes of growth and organizational transformation.

How has the evolution of corporate venturing been throughout the years?

Corporate venturing was a term and model popular in the 1990's and 2000's yet it lacked strategic relevance or a link with an organization's innovation intent. Since then, models have emerged that ensure innovation initiatives are more tightly coupled with an organization's future ambition. The corporate venturing model is now more commonly known to be about investing in external startups to get a window on technology and access to new markets. It is only one part of an organization's innovation strategy. Internal pursuits have evolved to be more embedded in the organization around strategic innovation focus or as an innovation function that leverages research activities, collaborates with corporate venturing arms and seeks out strategic partnerships to fill competency gaps.

How do you see the usage of digital platforms in the corporate venturing process?

If we consider corporate venturing to be about the external-in view, then digital platforms enable collaboration, help to build networks within the innovation ecosystem and facilitate innovation challenges as an open call or with incubators and accelerators. For the internal-out strategic innovation view, these platforms aid with idea and opportunity portfolio and process management and enable the pursuit of new business models.

How do you see the position of corporate venturing in the innovation ecosystem? And within innovation procurement activities?

Per above, we have tended to move away from the term "corporate venturing" because it is a model that is most often not managed within an integrated innovation management system. As a result, it lacks the right strategic linkages and governance to truly be successful in growing and transforming the organization. For a strategic innovation or new business creation model, there is a very critical orchestration role that takes place to connect various internal and external stakeholders with an innovation strategy that spans organizational entities and the innovation ecosystem. The term innovation procurement is not used within industry. In fact, procurement and innovation functions or roles are oxymorons. If the "procurement" is about finding ideas and opportunities and progressing them to market, then depending on how loosely or more specifically the term corporate venturing is used, it can be about managing the innovation process or as a complement to an integrated innovation management system approach.

What is the role of corporate venturing in the adoption of innovation vs. the go-to-market phase?

Corporate venturing can aid with innovation adoption by using external startups and other stakeholders in the innovation ecosystem to help internal stakeholders see the value of a given opportunity for the organization. This would be about seeding early investments with experimentation partners to reduce uncertainty and make the case, compared with development and market access partners during the go-to-market phase.

Conversation with Ivo Locatelli about "Public Innovation Procurement"

Senior Expert – Team Leader Public Innovation Procurement at European Commission

What is innovation procurement?

It's buying the process of innovation which can include research and development services with some partial outcomes or buying the outcome of innovation which can be created by others. In this case, the buyer buys research and procurement services of products or services or process which don't exist. First, the public buyer will describe their needs and describe what they need, and the suppliers will come out with innovative products and services or process that meet the specific needs set by the buyer. The second case, the public buyer, instead of buying out the shelf access as early adopter and buys the new product, service or process which is new to the market, and contains some substantial innovation characteristics. Of course, this brings value to the stakeholders, and you will intervene in the different steps of the innovation chain.

It's very important how you manage the internal process, if you set up a team, someone who knows the project, you have to include the lawyers, who have to be flexible, and you have to include the supplier itself. Innovation partnership is a new innovation procurement, which exactly aims to create a partnership between buyers and suppliers to come to innovative solutions.

How does the innovation partnership work for innovation procurement?

Innovation partnership is split into different phases, substantial market consultation, and technological trends and new things coming up, and you go to the selection phase and you go up, and you go to execution phase and then contact management. It's split up into different phases, and you can drop certain partners in each phase, and to be absolutely transparent, you have to be extremely clear with the conditions for the selection. And the partners are not delivering or meeting the requirements which are set up by the public buyers.

How do you see the digital platforms for innovation brokerage?

I think digital platforms could be a brilliant idea to help the process for innovation brokerage, and a very useful tool to different sides of the ecosystem. It's extremely modern and efficient; of course, the role of the broker is a role of intermediation, with the platform being the starting point. But the broker work requires to have a lot of contacts, consists of building relationships, developing trust, understanding the needs of the buyer, and the understanding of full the new technologies of emerging and knowing the supplier side.

What are the criteria for selecting innovation or to know when something is an innovative solution?

We do not have criteria. You have to start with a proper market analysis, a proper benchmarking and figure out market engagement. As a buyer you have to identify the technological possibilities in advance before drafting the tenders because by doing so you avoid referencing outdated technology. You can identify specific needs, more than specific technology. For instance, you can define your needs in a functional way, so the buyer defines the outcome instead of defining a specific technology. Look at the needs, not at the solutions you need.

How do you see the position of innovation procurement in the innovation ecosystem where you can find technology transfer and corporate venturing?

Innovation procurement is just one of the elements of the innovation ecosystem. Corporate venturing is about financing the startups while technology transfer is part of the procurement of innovation. An important dimension and truly relevant aspect from a contractor's point of view of discussion with the supplier are the intellectual property (IP) rights. Traditionally, the public buyer keeps the IP, and this is not good, as the buyer has less interest to develop it further. Now we push towards a position where the IP should be kept on the supplier side, or towards some other type of the agreement as there are different types of situations. One value is that the public buyer could be the first customer for the startups and of course, this aspect is an enormous strategic buy.

What are the first steps if an organization wants to adopt innovation procurement?

It's a cultural change, in the sense that you do not need to buy any longer in the way you have usually done, but you can buy something new, and you set up a procedure, an open-minded approach, that you can buy in a different way. Engaging with the market is the first starting point.

Conversation with Prof. Dr. Pedro José Bueso Guillén on "Innovation Procurement"

Professor TU Law at University of Zaragoza

What is public procurement innovation?

It is a way to procure products and services which are not available in the market at the present time, but the public buyer's strategy determines that it is going to procure in a next future to satisfy its own needs. The public buyer pushes the demand forward and ask companies to develop the required product or service participating in an R+D+I process. Companies are expected to become more competitive after participating in such a process.

What are the best practices for applying innovation procurement?

The public buyer shall design a public procurement strategy and identify its future needs to be satisfied by innovative products and services; the public buyer shall communicate to the market such needs, establishing a dialogue by means, i.e., of public market consultation; depending on the results of state-of-the-art analysis and the market consultation, the accurate procedure shall be launched; functional specifications based on KPI are a key issue for a successful public procurement of innovation; risk management and IPRs management are an important part of the tender, and shall be faced by the public buyer taking into account its business model and the business model of the companies.

What are the main challenges for applying innovation procurement in public organizations and companies?

To be aware of the advantages of such a way to procure, to accept that it is a better way to procure, to change internal workflows, to improve competencies and skills of the staff to develop it.

Summary

To sum up this chapter, I will leave you with a number of exercises that start you off on your journey to increase innovation in your organization with innovation procurement practices and corporate venturing.

To practice

1. You can buy innovative solutions by adapting your procurement process.
2. Be aware of the emotional journey of startups and super innovators!
3. Invest in startups from your area of expertise to increase the performance of your ecosystem.
4. Be ready to make impact with innovation.

In the following chapters you will find

- – Tips for understanding innovation leadership.
- – Tips on leading transformation change for innovation.
- – Tips for adopting digitalization to outperform on collaboration for innovation.

Notes

(Chesbrough, 2020) https://collabwith.co/2020/05/podcast-prof-henry-chesbrough-on-the-role-of-the-open-innovation-in-the-recovery-plan/
(Bueso, 2020) https://collabwith.co/2020/09/prof-bueso-on-innovation-procurement-or-innovation-adoption/
(Hyland, 2019) https://collabwith.co/2019/06/podcast-ispim-florence-joanne-hyland-on-innovation-management-ist-about-transforming-the-organization/
(McGurk, 2019) https://collabwith.co/2019/11/standards-innovation-management/
(Abirascid, 2019) https://collabwith.co/2019/01/luca-emil-abirascid-on-entrepreneurship-the-first-thing-to-look-at-is-the-team-because-if-you-have-a-good-idea-with-a-bad-team-you-do-not-go-anywhere/
(Procure2Innovate, 2020) https://innovation-procurement.org/why-buy-innovation/
(EU Public Procurement, 2020) https://ec.europa.eu/growth/single-market/public-procurement/rules-implementation_nn

References

Guide on dealing with innovative solutions in public procurement 10 elements of good practice by European Commission. Luxembourg: Office for Official Publications of the European Communities 2007 – 26 pp. – 14.8 x 21 cm ISBN 92- 79-03471-5.
Martin, B. The Hockey Stick Principles: The 4 Key Stages to Entrepreneurial Success. 2016.
Raagaard Ernst, C., Díaz Martín, L., McGrath, M., Pöcklhofer, H. Catalogue of Best practices on PPI. Innovation Procurement Brokers. 2020.

———

"Innovation leadership is as if you are a CEO without having the power of a CEO"

Jara Pascual

Chapter 9
Innovation Leadership – Make it Happen!

Summary: In this chapter you will learn about the importance of leadership to drive innovation and that for leading innovation you need specific leadership skills, including emotional intelligence, to make effective impact and change.

Innovation leadership is using innovation as a transformative tool to make impact. For many years this was called only innovation or innovation management. But innovation management is when you focus on managing your innovation process, and your team.

When there were conversations about organization and innovation then the predominant term used to be "innovation culture". This can be a mistake, because it creates tension and friction between the "innovation team's" and the "senior management's" responsibilities and effectiveness. When innovation is making an organizational and business transformation, that is because the rules of leadership are applied, and the correct term to be used is "innovation leadership".

There are different ways to apply your leadership skills for innovation at the team level, at the organization level, when doing entrepreneurship (which means bringing an innovation to the market, not starting a normal business), at the level of society and industry. In all cases, you make a change, and the greater the change you make, the greater your leadership skills have to be. A leader for innovation is a transformational leader with kindness, with active-listening skills, with elevated levels of emotional intelligence and social intelligence. A leader who is making a change without having the power or authority to make the change happen. It is in this particular situation when the highest levels of leadership become necessary and when what exactly leadership means becomes clear.

Becoming a good leader for innovation has a natural part ("natural leader"), but it's also a natural evolution of learning, growing as a person, experiencing, knowing about yourself, and growing with your cases, experiences and responsibilities. If you are a good leader for your team, then, when it comes to driving innovation for the organization, you can start using the same techniques and apply them or translate and adapt them for managing innovation at the organizational level. The same translation is applicable to becoming an entrepreneur if you have an innovation leadership background. Which leadership skills from innovation can you apply to transform your market? Which leadership skills do you have to learn? A good transformational leader is capable of adapting the skills required to the new circumstances with a clear mission related to the change, and a strategy for how to execute the change.

In the previous chapters, we talked about the importance of bringing people together, and how to enable collaboration for innovation. This chapter is on how a

https://doi.org/10.1515/9783110665383-009

person and their leadership style can really make a difference in how the innovation is conceptualized, prototyped, implemented, created, brought to market, and adopted.

On a personal note, when I was doing an MBA at RSM Erasmus University in Rotterdam, and we had a class in change management, the professor said that change is very difficult to make. Only 30% of change management projects are successful. This was surprising for me because I had a good track record in doing transformations, so I started to analyze what I was doing differently from others, and the professor recommended reading the book *The Heart of Change* by John Kotter (Kotter, 2012). Again, I was surprised to see the importance of emotions and psychology for change and for being a transformational leader. When I was working as a senior manager in IT innovation, the first point I realized was that the departments and teams were working in silos, and "almost" hated each other. And for me, the most important step to innovate is to share knowledge, and that was not the case. The second problem was that people were untrusting vis-à-vis innovation and thinking that it was a joke or not important at all. The next issue was that there were no processes in place, or information about innovation – or any strategy at all. After six months (transforming people takes time) and after four years in the role, people in the department were collaborating with other teams, with business departments, sharing tons of ideas in our internal idea forum, collaborating with professors from universities, contacting startups, including innovation in their "performance review" and as an official key performance indicator (KPI). Innovation was trusted because I was trusted. I was people-oriented, with a focus on mission, strategy and strong emphasis on values and what is important.

One of the key messages I shared about innovation was that everyone is creative (Katz, 2003). This sentence helped me to make a statement with the IT colleagues who were reticent when it came to finding new ideas. On top of the conversations, I started working within the teams, meeting team members randomly to have informal coffee breaks with them and talking about their thoughts. The goal was to change the negative attitude towards innovation to a positive one. "The right people, the right attitudes" (Chan Kim, et al., 2001). My IT colleagues were the right people (Chan Kim, et al., 2001) – experts in their domains, full of knowledge and information for making new products for their employees, IT departments or other business units, but with no motivation and the wrong sentiment. It was particularly important to change their mindset because the IT teams were focused on "keeping systems running" and did their own daily work. They were tied up with their own tasks, working at full capacity, and they didn't want to add extra time for innovation. One of the essential jobs was to change this mindset to a future-oriented mindset. Further, I introduced workshops, calls and small presentations from universities and other consulting companies where the conversation was about other ways of doing the same things, and future insights and trends from industry actors. At the beginning, people from different teams didn't want to share the same workshop or room. So, I was receiving calls from the heads asking me why the other "colleagues" are invited. In order to avoid conflict at the first stage of change, I accepted the advice, and I did separate workshops for each team. Being a huge fan of Swedish startups and universities in the field of research, I knew about the power of an innovation café, and wanted to apply this technique to help people come together. The issue of a fragmented culture (Goffee, 1996) was impeding innovation. If the colleagues were not able to talk to each other or even share information cross teams, there was no chance to create a product together. For this reason, I created the "Freitag, Kaffee, Kuchen" (Fridays, Coffee, Cake) event in order to make people talk cross-team, cross-department and across business units. I organized an event every month the first year, and then every two weeks, inviting different people every time. I also baked a cake the day before. The setup was quite simple: an Outlook invitation, a normal meeting room, one hour, one cake, and pots of coffee and tea with cups. People were joining without a schedule or time pressure, and they were talking about project issues and other matters.

These events became more popular and complex when there was a topic to brainstorm on how to find ideas to solve an issue. This is an example of empathetic design (Katz, 2003), where "innovators" empathize with the users for whom they have to innovate and with whom they work. The idea was if the IT colleagues met the business and IT partners with their issues, they were more likely to create new products which will work for them and determine the trends to support disruptive innovation. Another outcome of these events was that if they have to work together, they have to be a good team. In order to force this success factor (Bohmer, 2004) in the potential teams (new teams were created to do a new project), they have to trust each other, be identified as a team and feel that they are working together efficiently towards the new idea. In this case, the goal was to make a prototype from an idea they generated together. The "Freitag, Kaffee, Kuchen" event was an incubator for crowdsourcing inside the company (Li, 2010). I saw how the business units were happier to create a separate budget for the new projects and ideas. IT teams were strongly focused on their KPIs based on the "keep systems running" approach. I talked directly with the SVP about how important it was to create a new KPI for innovation. Only one was needed – "be innovative by generating three ideas per team and one prototype." Usually the research KPIs (Samsonowa, 2012) are more complex, and they could involve areas of communicating, profitability and value creation. But there was a need to have an innovation performance measurement to strengthen the trust in the process and make it serious for the teams. The KPIs were the official measurement, but an informal performance measurement was needed. I created the innovation awards to congratulate teams for their efforts in innovation. The prize was a diploma signed by the SVP, and they were handed out during the Christmas party in a meeting room. Diplomas were framed and related to "fastest prototype ever", "green innovation", "most popular idea", "most voted-for idea", "best innovator", etc.

This is an example of the degree to which you cannot separate a department from a person. The leader has an incredible impact on the performance of the team and the performance of the organization, and this is including the innovation department and any type of innovation activities related to transformation. An important note to add is that innovation always has leaders above and below, and you can find good and bad leaders in both directions. So, if your leaders above are toxic and not good for the organization or for innovation (even though they are "in theory" leading innovation), it's up to you to make the decision to leave the organization or to focus on the energy you have to commit to maneuver in the toxic environment. If you are looking at the positive impact, you see how a leader can impact the emotions and behavior of one team and organization in a positive way. This can create lasting impact, because when you change a mindset and perspective from the heart, the change will remain because it's part of the people, it's not only a process to adapt, you make a change inside them. Innovation leadership is when you can listen and understand, and you adapt your leadership skills to make people transform and make a positive impact.

> Leadership is a process of social influence which maximizes efforts of others towards achievement of a goal.
> (Kruse, 2019)

Typically, innovation management has focused for a long time only on processes, and it seems like the importance of people and leadership was forgotten along the way to creating impact with innovation. The importance of social intelligence was introduced in Chapter 6 ("How to Create your own Community and Ecosystem?") and I have stated that emotional intelligence is key to becoming an effective leader to create high-performing teams and drive innovation. The base here is to understand your values for leadership, be it in a personal or professional environment, because the same principles apply to your personal and professional life. The question to answer is about what is important for you, what the values you have acquired during your life are, and what kind of values you need to drive innovation and see which values are matching your personal values and the values for innovation. You need to focus on this intersection of values to grow your leadership style for innovation. As an example, you can find a list below of leadership values for innovation:

Leadership values for innovation
– Authenticity
– Respect
– Openness
– Transparency
– Communication
– Creativity

- Collaboration
- Integrity
- Courage
- Learning
- Innovation
- Curiosity

This list of leadership values for innovation, again, is only a starting point to help you find your own values, or where to start to understand which values are important for driving innovation. The next step is understanding the difference between innovation, ideation, invention and creativity to be able to help your organization and your team to understand innovation and to really innovate, because there is a misunderstanding of each concept, and it's important to learn from the differences and apply each concept correctly when you are talking about innovation leadership.

"Innovation is delivering value, to the corporate, to the customers or end users. Innovation is always experimentation as well, but at certain point you have to bring it to the market," says David Grundy, Group Head of Blockchain/DLT at Danske Bank (Grundy, 2020).

Innovation
Generating value from creativity, using any kind of value, and any kind of creativity.

Ideation
A process to generate more ideas with or without a theme.

Invention
Creating a new "thing" that did not exist before.

Creativity
A quality to generate ideas or ways of doing things in different ways.

Emotional intelligence for innovation and collaboration has been introduced in this book several times. If you look at Figure 9.1 you can understand the impact of your emotions on innovation leadership and how to deal with your emotions as a leader, and your team's and organization's emotions to manage innovation as a baseline.

The mood meter is a measurement tool for emotional intelligence skills. And the first question to answer is: How are you feeling? The first dimension of the mood meter is divided between two axis dimensions: pleasantness and energy.

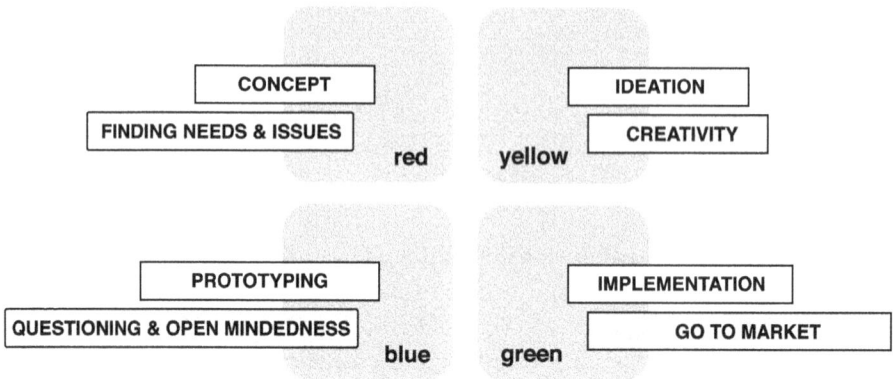

Figure 9.1: Innovation leadership with emotional intelligence using the mood meter.

Pleasantness is your internal psychological state which you can rate from minus five to plus five, and the second axis (energy) is to pay attention to your body – what is your energy like right now?

When combining these two dimensions, you create the mood meter. It has four colors, yellow, red, blue, and green. You need a couple of seconds to feel which emotion you are feeling right now. It may be difficult to find the right word, as probably you do not have access to the needed emotional vocabulary, or you were not aware of your emotional state. The goal of the mood meter is to better understand your inner self. There are underlying reasons why you feel the way you do. The following section explains the colors of the mood meter with the meaning for innovation leadership.

If you look at Figure 9.1, the first **quadrant in red** is the emotion of anger, disappointment, rage, annoyance and frustration. It might seem negative, but these emotions are very useful for creating new concepts based on finding new needs and issues. When you are disappointed because a process has an issue, the user experience is terrible, or there is no product or service for what you do need, or when you see a new solution but it's not yet in your country, or when you have frustration, you are located here. This is perfect for starting a new concept, a new project, or a new organization if you have the feeling that you are the one who will fix it. It's the time when you might recognize your emotion of anger or frustration and your will to make it.

The second **quadrant in the color yellow** is the quadrant for the emotions of happiness, joy, serenity, ecstasy, optimism and interest. These emotions are needed in order to be creative and to ideate. These emotions are effective in brainstorming sessions on how to solve an issue, how to improve a process, how to improve the user experience, how to design a service or a new product, how to create new solutions, how to write a business model, etc. The yellow quadrant is ideal for enhancing creativity and positive thinking related to the new solutions you are creating, because in this ideation phase you should never criticize ideas, you have to be open, accept new ideas, accept whatever creativity comes from your team members and other experts.

The third **quadrant in blue** corresponds to the emotions of sadness, grief, pensiveness, disapproval and empathy. These emotions are useful for error checking, questioning the solutions, being critical in a productive manner, and learning from feedback, understanding the issues with a critical eye, and starting a debate with experts on the potential solutions, concepts and ideas. These emotions are practical for prototyping, mockups, paper prototypes, and building physical models, to see if they are working or not, because it's important to have several iterations until you can get the final product, service or innovative solution. There is no perfect one-time-prototype, it's all about testing, gathering feedback, accepting errors, co-working with a multidisciplinary team with different opinions, expertise and backgrounds, and maybe starting over again if necessary. So, the negativity and a realistic view of the pessimistic emotion in the blue quadrant will help you to be critical enough to iterate and improve your innovative solution.

The fourth **quadrant in the color green** is where the emotions of contentedness, calm, acceptance, trust, adoration, building consensus and satisfaction are. These emotions prompt you to relax and get ready to do business, to be resilient, to be positively objective, to be realistic with your financial and your legal part of work. In this quadrant, you are covered when dealing with the setbacks you are experiencing when you are bringing an innovative solution to the market. With these emotions, you are ready to go to market and implement your innovative solution with resilience, learning, commitment and confidence. The innovation leadership side is to understand the four quadrants of Figure 9.1 to be able to drive your team, your senior management and your organization through these quadrants to make innovation happen. Even if you are an entrepreneur, you have to drive your customers, your partners, your board members and your employees into those quadrants from Figure 9.1 to ensure innovation and to drive change in the market you are innovating. Every emotion is information and an opportunity to take action. It's up to you to profit from the information that each emotion is providing to you.

Emotions and cognitions are information. All emotions are an important source of information about what is going on inside you. Neuroscientists, psychologists, and intelligence researchers agree that emotion and cognition work hand-in-hand to perform sophisticated information processing. Based on Brackett (Brackett, 2019), your emotional state determines where you direct your attention, what you remember, and what you learn. How you make decisions when you are in the grip of strong emotions – such as anger or sadness, but also elation or joy, which make you perceive the world differently – and the choices you make at that moment are influenced for better or for worse. Your social relations and how you interpret other people's feelings provide you signals about whether to approach someone or avoid them, whether to associate with someone or distance yourself, to reward or punish. Emotions even influence our health.

In his book, *Emotional Intelligence at Work*, (Weisinger, 2008), Dr. Hendrie Weisinger describes that you can see that three prevalent emotions play a role in a working day. These are frustration, anxiety, and enthusiasm. Negative emotions stay longer than positive emotions. How can you know that your perceptions of life correspond to reality? Many people are not aware that all data they have on emotions depends on perceptions, and that it is easy to misinterpret their own emotions. How do you pick up the emotions of another person? You need to be aware that sounds, but also facial expressions carry emotions. You need to find out what the emotional state of your environment is.

Dr. Hendrie Weisinger proposes five key concepts based on the application of the theory of emotional intelligence skills of the group at Yale University as a good reference tool for applying your emotional intelligence skills:

– High self-awareness: the ability to tune in to information about yourself and to use it to help you navigate through life successfully. If you are not aware, you lose your boundaries.
– Mood management: this involves controlling your emotions and impulses and adapting to changing circumstances. It is the difference between what you see and your interpretation of it.
– Self-motivation: the ability to get yourself to do necessary tasks, to bounce back quickly from setbacks, to "psych" yourself up. How good are you doing things that you cannot stand?
– Interpersonal expertise: the ability to relate well to others, workout conflicts, give and take criticism, build consensus, enhance team communication.
– Emotional mentoring: the ability to help others manage their emotions, to help others learn to motivate themselves, to help others work out conflicts.

The first three points are all about the person. He called these "interpersonal emotional intelligence" – nobody can know how frustrated or happy you are, nobody is deciding how motivated you can be. The last two points involve other people. How good you are at building consensus, how good are you at working out conflicts and dealing with team communication, or criticism?

Innovation leadership canvas

"Open Innovation is helping us to break the silos inside the organization and bring people together," says Steve Rader, Deputy Director of NASA's Center of Excellence for Collaborative Innovation (Rader, 2020).

Innovation leadership needs specific guidelines to make the organization or the industry ready for the future, and ready to adapt new innovative solutions and embrace innovation as a normal way of doing and operating the business. The "keep systems running" approach is not sufficient for an organization's survival, and not favorable for the mental health of the employees or team. Innovation is a way to bring wellbeing to your organization, to become more productive on the central operational goal while providing mental breaks with innovation and new projects for thinking about the future of the teams, the future of the organization and the future of the industry.

An objective of innovation leadership, as Steve Rader said during the interview in the podcast "Business of Collaboration", is breaking the silos inside the organization and introducing the power of innovation inside an organization.

Figure 9.2 presents the "Innovation Leadership Canvas" including the part of emotions you have to take care of when leading innovation. The boxes included in this canvas are the important points to think, reflect and execute when you are leading innovation. Of course, you need processes, values (you really believe in and match with your organization), budget (knowledge has a cost, as you saw in Chapter 7), strategy for effective transformation, how you manage teams and people, how you think about the future, and how you look for hidden needs to be able to innovate.

These boxes composing the "Innovation Leadership Canvas" are the most important elements on which you have to base the conversation as a leader for innovation.

Processes

Make a list of processes and tools that your organization might need for the innovation management process and innovation.
- Front-end innovation management.
- Design thinking.
- User-centered innovation.
- Innovation culture.
- Idea forum.
- Open innovation external platform.
- Knowledge management platforms.
- Collaboration for innovation platforms.

Culture

There is always a feeling attached to the subject of innovation, and feelings attached to the leaders who are driving innovation, and also there are emotions around the phases and processes of innovation (see Figure 9.1). Watch out and take care of your organization's mood when working on innovation and innovative solutions, and help your team and your organization to manage their emotions:

Processes

FRONT-END INNOVATION MANAGEMENT.
DESIGN THINKING.
USER-CENTERED INNOVATION.
INNOVATION CULTURE.
...

Values

CREATIVITY.
OPEN-MINDEDNESS.
TRANSPARENCY.
LISTENING.
UNDERSTANDING.
COLLABORATION.
COURAGE.

Strategy

CREATE AN INNOVATION MANIFESTO.
CREATE A STRUCTURE TO BRING PEOPLE TOGETHER.
ADD KPIs FOR INNOVATION INSIDE YOUR ORGANIZATION.
MAKE A COMMUNICATION PLAN FOR PROJECTS' PROGRESS
AND TRENDS.

Future

YOUR TEAM AND ORGANIZATION HAVE TO BE PREPARED
FOR THE FUTURE:

WHAT IS DAMAGING YOUR COMPANY?
WHAT COULD DAMAGE YOUR BUSINESS IN THE FUTURE?
HOW WOULD YOU BUILD YOUR COMPANY AGAIN?

Culture

MANAGE EXPECTATIONS.
CLEAR OBJECTIVES AND GOALS.
REMOVE CONFUSION.
INCREASE EMPATHY.
FACILITATE MEANINGFUL RELATIONSHIPS
SUPPORT IDEATORS IN DEALING WITH FRUSTRATION, ANXIETY
AND ENTHUSIASM.
BE MINDFUL OF SETTING THE EMOTIONAL TONE.
BRING INSPIRATION AND KNOWLEDGE
ENHANCE COMMITMENT.

Budget

YOU NEED SEPARATED BUDGETS FOR:

CONCEPTS.
PROTOTYPES.
MARKETING.
GO-TO-MARKET.
PERSONNEL.
INVESTMENT.
INCOME.

Team

YOUR ORGANIZATION HAS TO BE PSYCHOLOGICALLY
SAFE.
TRAIN YOUR EMPLOYEES I1
INNOVATION AND EMOTIONAL
INTELLIGENCE.
MATCH IDEAS WITH YOUR NEEDS.

Needs

LOOK FOR NEEDS INSIDE:

CUSTOMER FEEDBACK.
ISSUES ON COMPANY PROCESSES.
SERVICE DESK TICKETS.
USER OBSERVATION DATA.
BRAINSTORMING SESSIONS.
CONSORTIUM PARTNERS.
PROBLEMS TO SOLVE.
CHALLENGES TO OVERCOME.

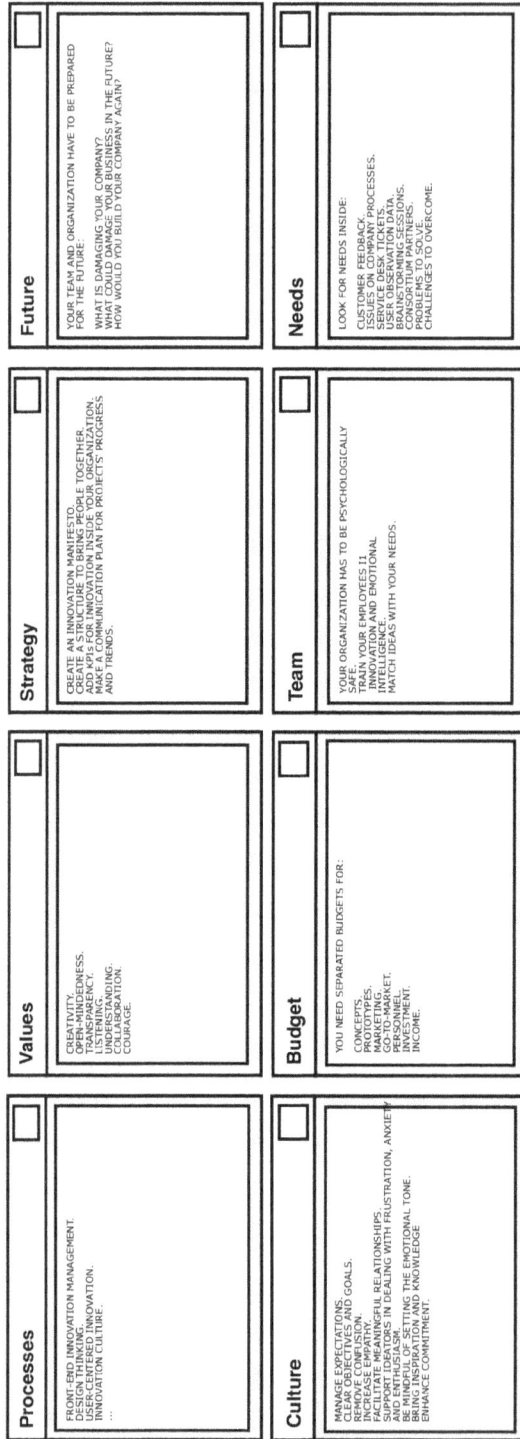

Figure 9.2: The innovation leadership canvas with emotional intelligence.

- False expectations.
- Confusion.
- Frustration.
- Responsible and professional (no personal).
- Clear objectives.
- Commitment.
- Clear and transparent communication.
- Authenticity.
- Accountability.
- Social intelligence ➜ bring people together from different teams and organizations.
- Leaders of leaders ➜ your team is the team of others.
- Reputation of innovation.

Values

Make a list of what kind of values you have as a leader, which values your organization has, and which values you think are important for innovation:
- Creativity.
- Openness.
- Transparency.
- Listening.
- Understanding.
- Collaboration.
- Courage.

Budget

Innovation has a cost, but it can create an income as well! To get there, you have to reflect on the way you can manage the finances for innovation outside the classical costs related to prototyping. You need to have a budget and separate it for concepts, prototypes, for implementation, for marketing and for going to market. Make the financial side of innovation easy by considering:
- Cost.
- Personnel.
- Investment.
- Income.

Strategy

You will find some basic strategy guidelines to follow in your organization for innovation below. But, of course, you know your organization better and should look first at the immediately urgent aspects, which have to be implemented. After the basic aspects are covered, you can align your strategy with the overall organization and translate the organization's strategy into what it signifies for innovation.

- Create an innovation manifesto to create a clear understanding of what innovation is for your team and organization.
- Add KPIs for innovation for your team and organization.
- Create structure to bring people together.
- Communication is key about projects, trends, challenges and progress.
- Train in innovation, collaboration for innovation and creativity.

Team

As you are not alone in leading innovation, you have a team that reports directly to you, but you also have a "team" which is not directly reporting to you, and you have "super innovators" everywhere in the organization or outside the organization; you have "engaged" people as well, and you have the heads of other departments. Your team is not only your immediate team when you are leading innovation.

Your organization has to be psychologically safe. Use emotional intelligence skills and train your team and employees in them as well.

- Support your teams with innovation.
- Bring ideas into a context of needs and issues.
- Deal with frustration when ideas are not selected.
- Your team has to be motivated and resilient.

Future

Every CEO has to think about the future of the organization; in some cases they create some innovation team somewhere for that purpose. So, as an innovation leader, you have to bring this conversation to the highest level and talk openly in a coffee break with the CEO. Do you remember the value of courage for innovation leadership?

Your team and organization have to be prepared for the future:

- What are the things killing your company?
- What will kill your business in the future?
- How would you build your company again?
- What technology, startups, and research are out there that relate to your business?

Needs

Why do I need innovation? Where can I start my innovation? These are the typical questions that have to be addressed immediately and put into a structure and into a proper framework (see Figure 1.4). Below you have a list of where to look for needs as an example. You have to create your own lists based on your type of organization and business.

Look for needs inside:
- Customer feedback.
- Issues related to company processes.
- Service desk tickets.
- User observation data.
- Brainstorming sessions.
- Consortium partners.
- A problem to solve.
- A challenge to solve.

How to use emotional intelligence for front-end innovation management?

The classical front-end innovation process is managing the funnel of generating ideas, defining concepts, making prototypes and implementing innovative solutions. During this process, a lot of emotions are happening, which you need to understand to make processes more effective and useful without damaging the innovation culture, and even positively enhancing the opinion of innovation in your organization. Figure 9.3 shows the emotions related to each phase of the front-end innovation process, and the emotions the "innovators" have to feel, or are feeling, and you have to manage them.
- "Idea generation" phase: Happiness and false expectations. This is the phase when you are organizing brainstorming sessions, ideation events, design thinking, hackathons, etc. In this phase you need people to be in the yellow quadrant of the mood meter (Figure 9.1) to be able to be creative and think outside the box without criticism. But at the same time, you have to manage expectations, and communicate very clearly the reason of the ideation and what will happen after this, because if nothing happens, you are destroying the trust in the innovation team.
- "Concept – collaboration and improvement" phase: This phase follows the "ideation" event when you have an idea, and you have to give it shape and create a clear concept that may already include a business model. Your task is drawing up a first draft of what this idea will be about, including the classical value chain and supply chain analysis. In this sense, the "concept team" has to feel optimism and positivity (yellow quadrant of the mood meter, Figure 9.1), and as a leader you have to manage frustration and confusion (green quadrant of the

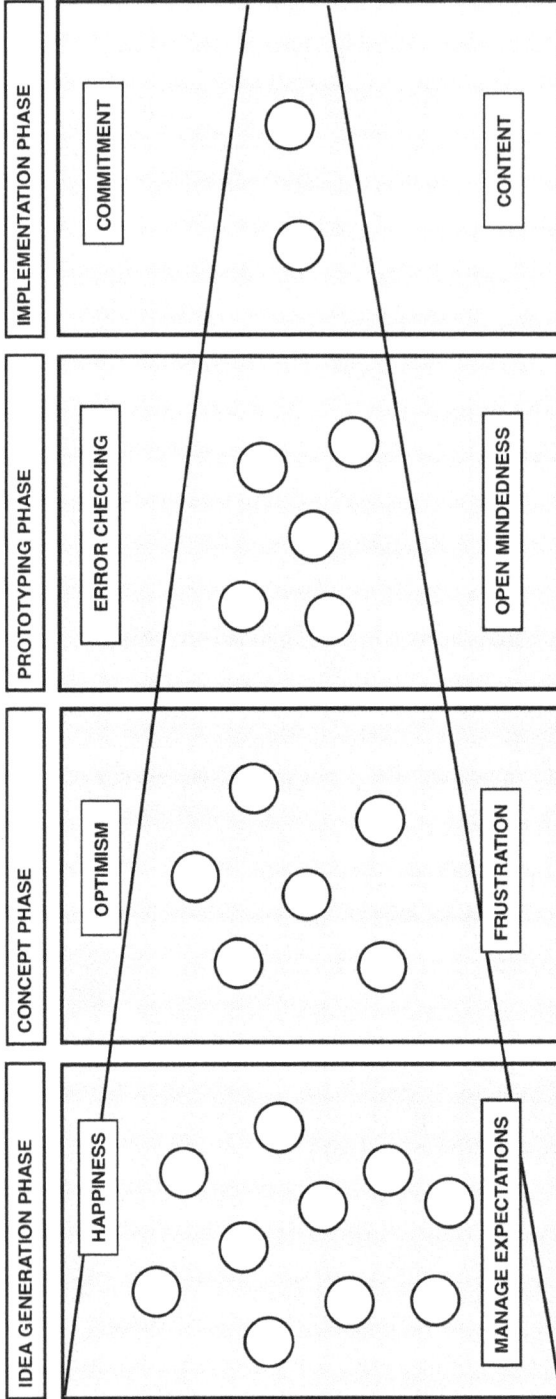

Figure 9.3: Front-end innovation process with emotional intelligence.

mood meter, Figure 9.1). Maybe this concept already exists or it's similar to another product, etc. In this case, helping the "concept team" manage frustration, increase their self-confidence, and remove confusion about the selection process will help the team better manage their expectations and learn from the creation experience.

–   "Prototyping" phase: Evaluation and selection. This is the selection process, in some cases together with a group of experts, for finding a "suitable concept" to prototype. This is the phase where the "selection team" has to be in the blue quadrant of the mood meter (Figure 9.1) because its members have to review, check errors, be realistic and objective, and as a leader you have to be in the green quadrant to feel objective, professional, content, calm and able to manage frustration from the experts and from the ideators. Again, clear communication about criteria selection and about the process will help to manage frustrations and avoid damaging the opinion about innovation.

–   "Implementation" phase: The phase when the ideator and team are responsible for implementing the idea in collaboration with other partners. The ideal quadrant will be the green part of the mood meter (Figure 9.1). Commitment, professional (not personal) motivation from the ideator's team, from the collaborators, and from the organization are required.

Communication is needed inside organizations, incubators, accelerators and hackathon events throughout the whole innovation process. It doesn't matter if this process is managed online or offline, the emotions are the same, and if you are collaborating remotely, the most important point is that you have to invest more time in building relationships, and you have to take even more care to communicate better, and see that every step, every criteria, every piece of information is clear and accessible for everyone. Rewards and recognition, as well as communication through reports with statistics and information about decision making, enhance transparency and visibility.

How to use emotional intelligence for design thinking?

Design thinking is not an activity for team building, ideation is not for team building. When you want to start a design thinking project, you have to have a budget and a commitment to making the "selected solution" happen. Here, the leader has to create a design thinking activity following the mission, vision and strategy of the organization, including discovered needs, current and future challenges. Design thinking activities are getting super popular among the innovation community, but they have to be done right, following the design principles and managing the expectations very well inside the team and organization. Clear communication with a focus on the steps of the process, guidelines, outcomes, budget, and follow-ups is very strongly recommended. In this section, the focus will not be on explaining the design thinking process, as there are other books for this. Design thinking (well executed) is focused on user-centered innovation, not because an individual has an idea and implements it, but because you are co-thinking, co-designing, co-prototyping, co-testing, co-implementing with your users. A user could be your customer, employee, a manager, supplier, etc. And because you are co-creating with others, you have to be clear about your intentions, objective, and process, and keep up constant communication with your users, or key-user group. This key user group will be your first customers, your first adopters of your innovative solution and will become your ambassadors. To be able to create this prominent level of engagement, you have to consider them part of the team, and communication has to follow this premise.

Figure 9.4 shows the drawing of a generic design thinking process together with the emotions related to the process. Let's analyze the emotions which are going on throughout the process from the participants' and leader's perspective.

- "Empathize" phase: This is the most anthropological phase where observation, active listening, and empathy toward the user are key. Participants have to know how to observe and how to actively listen. The leader has to bring the participants into the blue side of the quadrant of the mood meter (Figure 9.1) and create an atmosphere of empathy, compassion, understanding and appreciation.
- "Define" phase: This phase is still in the blue quadrant of the mood meter (Figure 9.1) because it's the phase for analyzing all the qualitative and quantitative data and information from the observation and interviews. It's a process of pensiveness and processing information to structure it.
- "Ideate" phase: This is the phase when you are organizing the ideation activity. In this phase you need people to be in the yellow quadrant of the mood meter (Figure 9.1) to be able to be creative and have a lot of ideas without being criticized.
- "Prototype" phase: If you can create several prototypes this is best because you can see different ways of creating a concept or idea, and you can combine them at the end. The objective is to bring all the creativity possible from the participating individuals and teams. The participants have to be in the blue quadrant of the mood meter (Figure 9.1) because they have to review, check errors, and be realistic and objective about what they are doing. They have to be in the green quadrant as well and feel joy; because the participants are creating, they have to be concentrated and work together. You as a leader have to be in the green quadrant to feel objective, professional, content, calm and to manage the ideators' or experts' frustration and help them to move from one emotion to the other with positivity and motivation.
- "Test" phase: Testing is the process of doing a test with the potential users, and it's coming from usability and user experience (UX) methodology. When hosting a design thinking workshop you can make a prototype on paper (paper prototype) and test it with the users or make a carton prototype and test it with

EMPATHIZE	DEFINE	IDEATE	PROTOTYPE	TEST	IMPLEMENT
OBSERVE AND INTERVIEW YOUR USERS.	MAKE A LIST OF YOUR USER'S NEEDS AND USER'S PROBLEMS.	BRAINSTORM IDEAS TO MATCH NEEDS AND SOLVE PROBLEMS.	BUILD PAPER PROTOTYPES OF YOUR IDEAS.	USER TESTING AND PROTOTYPE AND TEST AGAIN.	SELECT THE PROTOTYPE WHICH IS BETTER ACCEPTED BY USERS AND SENIOR MANAGEMENT
EMPATHY	PENSIVENESS	OPTIMISM	JOY	QUESTIONING	CONTENT

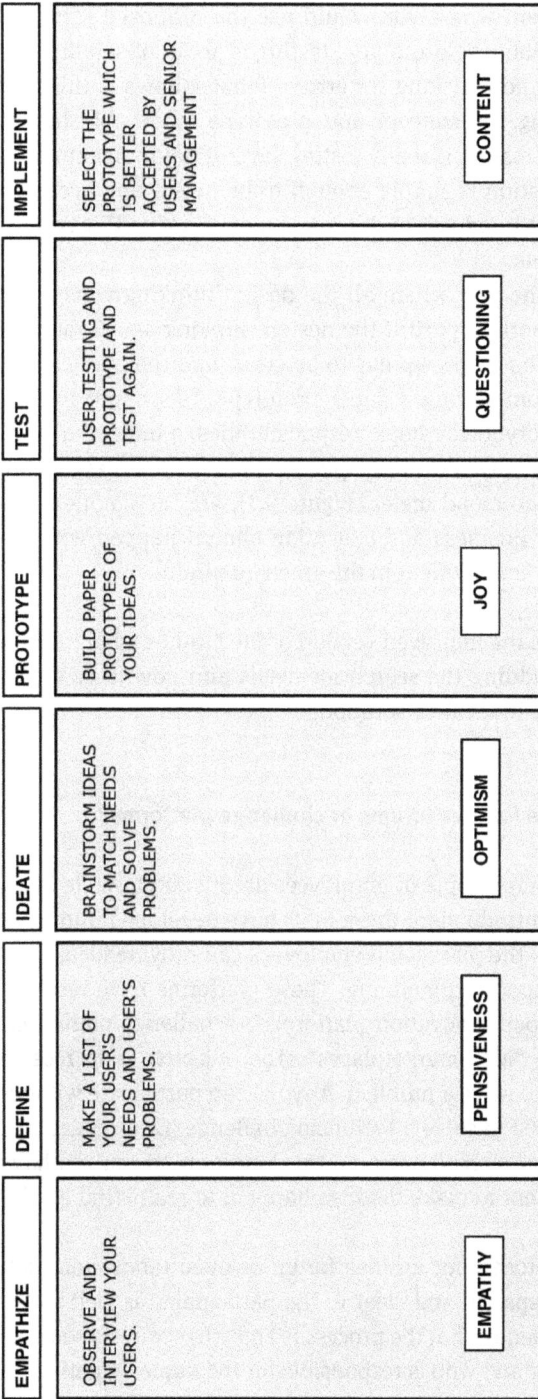

Figure 9.4: Design thinking process with emotional intelligence.

the users in a real environment where you would use the proposed solution. Besides being enthusiastic about the prototype, testing is about observing, analyzing, being disgusted by and checking for errors. What follows is thinking about solutions and changing the concept and prototype to be able to test again. Testing is not one test; testing is really testing several iterations until the version of the innovative solution is simple enough to be useful and accepted by all the potential users. The quadrant in the mood meter is blue (Figure 9.1) for both leader and participants.

– "Implement" phase: This is the part where all the design thinking workshops stop, but this is the most important part! If the design thinking activity is well defined from the beginning, the follow-up has to be clear, and the budget allocated as well. This is not about having a paper prototype; this might involve building a prototype in a factory. Clear steps, responsibilities, a budget, a roadmap and follow-ups have to be defined in this phase. Contentedness and calm, from the green quadrant of the mood meter (Figure 9.1), are the emotions for every participant and leader. Business and execution should happen with accountability, authenticity and commitment in the green quadrant.

As you can see, design thinking is the improved version of the "front-end of innovation management" because it's adding the search for needs and how to co-create with the potential final user of the innovative solution.

How to use emotional intelligence for idea forums or challenge platforms?

In principle, an idea forum is where people or employees are invited to write ideas for the organization. Since their introduction, these tools have developed into more challenge-based platforms, where the public and employees can provide ideas for a specific challenge or topic in a specific timeframe. These platforms have received different names ranging from "open innovation platforms", "challenge platforms" or "crowdsourcing platforms" to "idea marketplaces". The objective is to receive ideas from anywhere at any time to solve a problem. Anyone can participate without needing to be an expert in the area to solve a technical challenge. One caveat is of course that when you are "adding" a challenge onto this kind of platform you have to have the budget and commitment to make the idea happen, to really find a solution to implement.

Figure 9.5 shows a generic process for an idea forum or open innovation platform. This process has to be transparent and clear to the participant, as well as the participation criteria, selection criteria, what the process is and what will happen during the process, what the goals are and who is responsible for the implementation. In some cases, there is an award for the person who submitted the "selected idea".

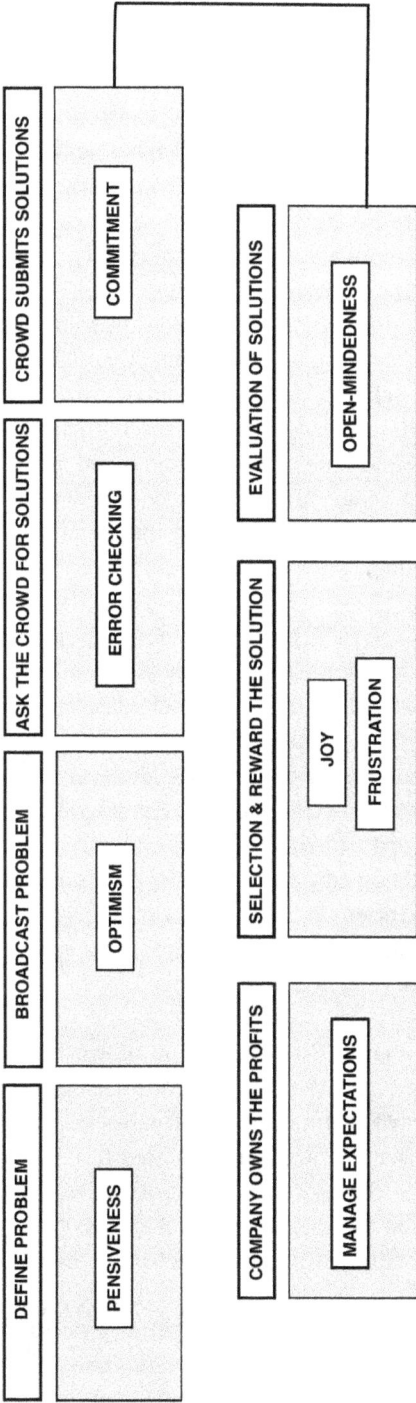

Figure 9.5: Idea forum process with emotional intelligence.

We will go through the process of using challenge platforms phase by phase to look at the emotional situation of the stakeholders:

– "Define problem" phase: This phase is in the blue quadrant of the mood meter (Figure 9.1) because it's the phase for analyzing issues and data from your organization, and discovering the challenges, issues and factors which are not working. It's a process of pensiveness and processing information to structure the information into a challenge.

– "Broadcast problem" phase: This is the point of joy and optimism (yellow quadrant on the mood meter, Figure 9.1) after preparing the challenge; but it's also about managing uncertainty because you don't know which ideas or solutions will come from the crowd, or how many, or if you will like them. The platform owner has to deal with these emotions, be self-confident and positive.

– "Ask the crowd for solutions" phase: When you are asking, the participants could be confused, nervous, stressed (red and blue quadrant from mood meter, Figure 9.1), and you as a sponsor of the challenge might feel insecure or nervous about the outcome. You have to find strategies for overcoming these emotions and take action to emphasize positive feelings when asking for solutions. Think about your message!

– "Crowd submits solutions" phase: Ideators and participants are feeling joy (yellow quadrant from mood meter, Figure 9.1) to submit their ideas, they are proud, and they are feeling very committed to solving the challenge. So, if their ideas are not selected, they will feel frustrated (red quadrant on the mood meter, Figure 9.1). One thing you can do to reduce the levels of frustration (only one idea will be selected) is to reward participation, clearly communicate the selection criteria, and communicate every step and decision to the participant or ideator.

– "Evaluation of solutions" phase: If the selection criteria are clear for everyone, the expert team will feel pensiveness (blue quadrant on the mood meter, Figure 9.1). Being objective and professional is important when selecting ideas. You can remember that if you are angry or too critical, or very happy or excited, you are not making the right decisions.

– "Selecting and rewarding the solution" phase: The ideator may be frustrated (red quadrant on the mood meter, Figure 9.1) if their idea is not selected, and happy if their idea is selected (which is only true for one idea). The rest could be frustrated. The frustrated crowd has to be managed and supported in dealing with their disappointment and frustration. Sponsors of the campaign or challenge will feel the joy of finding a solution for their problem or maybe disappointment because they don't like the submitted solutions or ideas. You have to manage those negative emotions.

– "Company owns and profits from the solution" phase: This entire process is only about getting ideas. So, if you are looking at other "front-end innovation processes" and "design thinking" workshops, the idea forum or open innovation platforms are only for the "ideation phase". Organizations or teams could be frustrated if they don't know the whole process and why you are using an idea or open innovation platform. You are using it only to get ideas. Innovation has not yet been done – in fact, it's very far from having been achieved. This is regardless of the cost of those platforms, plus the award given away.

Tools are not creating a culture for innovation, leadership is. People are co-creating the creative and innovative organization, and good innovation leadership starts with understanding the impact on the emotions, i.e., being aware and managing emotions from the crowd with proper communication and strategy.

How to create an innovative organization?

"I have begun a shift in my thinking away from innovation process models to more of an innovation mindset. It is more about how you think than in what order you do things. And I believe that it is also a useful shift for organizations to make" says Markus BensnesSenior Innovation Adviser at NorConsult (Bensnes, 2020).

An innovative organization is an organization which has embedded the innovation mindset, which is open and honest. It is important for an organization to manage emotional intelligence skills because then frustration is managed properly and the organization's members are self-motivated for innovation, making impact, working together and collaborating with internal and external partners. As an innovation manager, your job is to accompany the innovation processes with emotional intelligence, by taking care of the levels of frustration, happiness, commitment and accountability.

Innovation is a mindset, and you as a leader have the job of transforming the mindset of your organization. You have to create an innovative organization. This task could be done through the CEO or through the innovation manager, or through the head of innovation, or through a team leader, or an enthusiastic manager for innovation. The "innovative organization canvas" is shown in Figure 9.6, which I created to help you transform your organization. The pillars are people, culture, partnerships and tools.

People

Bring people together: Usually, when you have an organization with silos, this is the first step to work on – you have to break down the silos, and you have to bring people together. Below you can find the main points for taking action:
- Host a one-to-one meeting with the director of each department to understand how they are doing and how innovation can support them.

PEOPLE	CULTURE	PARTNERSHIPS	TOOLS

Bring People Together ☐

DIRECTOR OF EACH DEPARTMENT HOSTS ONE-TO-ONE
MEETINGS.
JOIN MEETINGS RANDOMLY.
HOST INFORMAL AND FORMAL EVENTS TO BRING PEOPLE
TOGETHER.
ANALYZE NON-RELATED CASES.

Education ☐

INTERNAL NEWSLETTER FOR INNOVATION.
TRAININGS FOR INNOVATION, CREATIVITY AND EMOTIONAL
INTELLIGENCE.
WORKSHOPS WITH EXPERTS.
WEBINARS FROM OTHER INDUSTRIES.

Common Understanding ☐

WRITE AN INNOVATION MANIFESTO.
USE SCORECARD FOR KPIs AND STRATEGY.
BUILD AN INNOVATION CULTURE.
CREATE YOUR OWN ECOSYSTEM AND COMMUNITY FOR
INNOVATION.
EVERYONE IS WELCOME: STARTUPS, ACADEMICS,
GOVERNMENTS, SUPPLIERS, ETC.
BE PRODUCTIVE, FOCUS ON GREEN INNOVATION AND
SUSTAINABILITY IN EVERY INNOVATIVE SOLUTION.

Internal Partners ☐

LEGAL.
PROCUREMENT.
IT.
R&D.
HR.
FINANCE.
OTHER STRATEGIC INTERNAL DEPARTMENTS THAT YOU NEED
TO BRING INNOVATION TO THE MARKET.

External Partners ☐

UNIVERSITIES.
ACCELERATORS.
STARTUPS.
CONFERENCES.
COMPETITIONS.
SUPPLIERS.
GOVERNMENTS.
ASSOCIATIONS.

Internal Tools ☐

INNOVATION MARKETPLACE.
OPEN INNOVATION PLATFORMS.
IDEA FORUMS.
INTERNAL NEWSLETTERS (ASK AS AN OPTION).
MULTIMEDIA SUCH AS VIDEO, PODCAST, WIKIS, ARTICLES.
OTHER SOFTWARE, APPS, TOOLS, WEBSITES YOU CAN USE
FOR YOUR PREFERRED INNOVATION PROCESS AND
COMMUNICATION.

External Tools ☐

CHALLENGE PLATFORMS.
COLLABORATION PLATFORMS.
IDEA PLATFORMS.
EDUCATION AND LEARNING PLATFORMS.
TECHNOLOGY FORUMS.
INNOVATION FORUMS.
HACKATHONS.
NEWSLETTERS.
PODCASTS, VIDEOS, MAGAZINES, ETC.

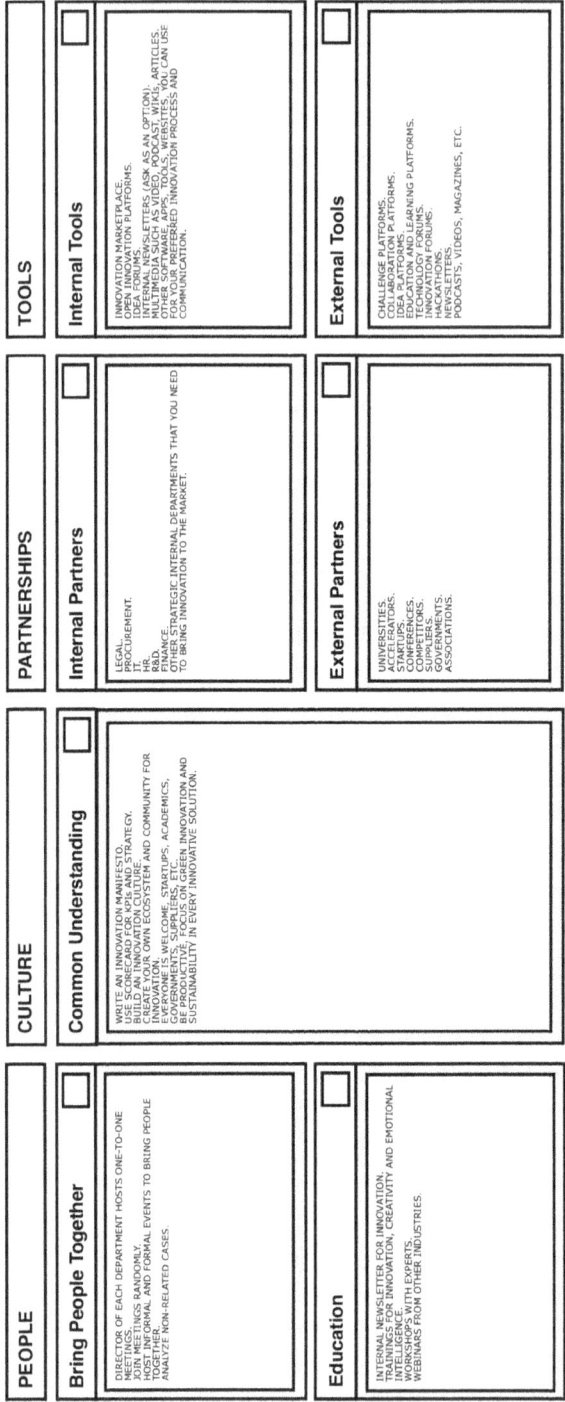

Figure 9.6: The innovative organization canvas.

- Join together randomly every month for a team meeting of the departments in which you are responsible for innovation.
- Create informal and formal activities to bring people together, such as a "Friday Innovation Coffee" or a "Friday Afternoon Innovation Tea".
- Create new activities to analyze non-related industries, challenge brainstorming sessions and observation days.

Education: Information and knowledge are decentralized which means that it is difficult to get them from everybody at any time. Consequently, you have to ensure that your organization and people are well informed and receive the knowledge they need to perform. In the following list you can find activities you can do to increase the level of knowledge about innovation in your organization:

- Create a newsletter to inspire your organization and educate people on innovation and projects.
- Offer trainings for creativity, innovation, collaboration and emotional intelligence skills.
- Organize internal workshops and webinars with experts related to your organization and your areas of interest.
- Inform people about tools, processes, methodologies and conferences for innovation.

Culture

Common understanding: Your organization has to be aligned and everyone has to speak the same language when they are talking about innovation. Here are some steps you can implement in your organization:

- Write an Innovation Manifesto to facilitate clarity about what innovation consists of for your organization.
- Align innovation KPIs with your organization's KPIs and vision. Additionally, you can use the scorecard to create the innovation strategy from the organization's strategy.
- Build an open innovation culture, which means that your organization is ready to collaborate for innovation internally and externally.
- Create your own ecosystem and community for innovation from your organization's perspective.
- Everyone is welcome: startups, academics, governments, suppliers, etc.
- Be productive, you can do two things at the same time – you can focus on green innovation and sustainability in every innovative solution.

Partnerships

Internal partners: Innovation cannot be created alone by the innovation team. The support functions are key for the good development of innovation. You cannot create a collaboration without the legal department, and you cannot adopt a new technology coming from a startup without the help of the procurement team. In the same way that you cannot integrate new technology without the support of the IT department, you cannot apply for a public grant and receive public funding without talking to the finance department, for instance.
- Legal.
- Procurement.
- IT.
- HR.
- R&D.
- Finance.
- Other strategic internal departments that you need to bring innovation to the market.

External partners: This whole book is about collaboration for innovation, and as we have learned, knowledge for innovation is decentralized; it is everywhere and not near your desk or your city. The following is a reminder, a quick list you can take into account when looking for others with whom to collaborate and work to create impact and bring innovation to life (the complete list is in Figure 3.3).
- Universities.
- Accelerators.
- Startups.
- Conferences.
- Competitors.
- Suppliers.
- Governments.
- Associations.
- Etc.

Tools

Internal tools: Regardless of whether you are a corporate, an SME or belong to a different type of organization, you can have internal tools for communication or innovation. You have to create your own list of tools you have in your organization and see which one you need to be able to communicate, create partnerships, scout technology and gather your needs for innovation.

- Innovation marketplaces.
- Open innovation platforms.
- Idea forum.
- Newsletter software (ask IT for options).
- Multimedia such as video, podcast, wiki, articles, etc.
- Other software, apps, tools, websites, you can use for your preferred innovation process and communication.

External tools: As already stated, the technology and knowledge you need is outside your organization. To get to it, you can add your needs or your challenges to other platforms to find the partner you need for collaboration. Below you have examples of external platforms you can use to "post" your needs and challenges or find startups and academics with the knowledge you require.

- Challenge platforms.
- Collaboration platforms.
- Idea platforms.
- Education platforms.
- Technology forums.
- Innovation forums.
- Hackathons.
- Podcasts, videos, magazines, etc.

How to calculate the budget for innovation?

"We need collaboration, instead of inventing everything by ourselves, why not start collaborating," says Rohit Talwar, CEO Fast Future Think Tank (Talwar, 2020).

A good transformational and innovation leader has to be able to do the math! And the innovation budget you have is what will become the enabler for your transformation and your currency for making innovation happen. The more savvy you become about finance engineering, the more you can do. Another important thing is that you may not forget the items in the "Innovation Leadership Canvas" in Figure 9.2. It features "training" and "training" has a cost related to it. While this is one of the first things that gets dropped off the planning when there are budget cuts, or no one even adds it in the first place, it is a key element! How will your organization be innovative if its employees have no idea what innovation is or how to manage innovation? You know training is important, so you have to be able to make room for this cost, always!

Let's look at budgets through the lens of the following example. Let's say you are in the market for a tech solution from a corporate which costs 100 euros and is, say, 20 cm large, and you have a startup offering you the product for 20 euros which is only 10 cm in length but is flexible and slim. Of course, you should get the startup solution! Not only for the price, and the better product, but because when you have a great opportunity in your hands to really bring innovation to the market, you are helping the industry grow – you are becoming an active member of the innovation ecosystem. As Rohit Talwar said very well: if you want to save budget costs on innovation, instead of creating everything yourself, you can spend some time looking around (for instance, on the collabwith.co platform) to see startups that have similar innovative solutions compared to what you want to create and co-work with them. Additionally, you can search for research results and technology coming from universities to apply to your company. This is much cheaper for you than starting from zero and doing the whole journey, with the costs attached to it. Do you remember Figure 7.2 about the phases in "Knowledge and Innovation Investment"? If you are in the "collaboration for innovation" mindset, you will only have the costs related to "adoption" of the innovative solution.

The innovation budget has to be in correlation with your work on the "Innovation Leadership Canvas" (Figure 9.2) and your work on the "Innovation Organization Canvas" (Figure 9.6, which both are complementary to your innovation leadership mission and strategy. Table 9.1 is the "Innovation Leadership Budget Calculator" where you can find support and useful guidelines to calculate the budget required for innovation leadership in your organization. This calculator is a baseline, you can add or remove the "categories" you need in your particular case and for your innovation leadership strategy.

Table 9.1: Innovation leadership budget calculator.

Category	Formula for calculator
Personnel	Salaries of your team members, you can include here as well the external employees you are contracting on a regular basis and working on daily operations for your team.
Consulting	Sometimes you do not have all the knowledge in the world in your team or in your mind. It's better to get the knowledge from the experts from academia or from other professionals. Here you can allocate budget for this knowledge acquisition.
Collaborations	This budget is for doing feasibility studies, innovation projects, research projects, co-creation projects, co-brainstorming sessions, experts' debates, with external partners coming from universities, startups, research centers, suppliers, governments, incubators, accelerators, ecosystems, industry associations, etc. How many do you want to do per year? You can allocate an average of 50K euros per collaboration; if the collaboration costs less, you have more in the budget for another collaboration.

Table 9.1 (continued)

Category	Formula for calculator
Investments	The classical phases of the innovation process have a cost: conceptualization, prototyping, implementing, going to market. How many ideas do you want to prototype? Or implement? Do you want to be responsible as well for this budget? You have to calculate this cost, but also you can share costs with departments you are co-creating and co-designing, or you can ask for an extra budget for specific projects. This will depend on your innovation strategy and how you want to allocate your innovation budget. Other investments could be invested and innovative solutions co-created with startups or universities. This cost has to be defined as well. Think about a minimum of 100K euros per investment.
Internal costs	If you are working with other departments, such as legal, IT, HR, R&D, finance, etc., in some cases, you will be required to pay back a percentage of this internal work. Check it out!
Tools	Here you have to add the annual fee, and the setup cost for being part of different innovation platforms such as collabwith.co, strategytools.io, foresight future, technology radar or other knowledge management platforms and innovation marketplaces, etc. On top of this, there is the cost of licensing an internal idea forum, or external services for open innovation, or for having your own open innovation platform for your employees and customers.
Training	Add the cost here for training your team and your key external team in innovation, collaboration for innovation, creativity and emotional intelligence. This includes the cost of conferences as well, as they are part of learning and knowledge acquisition. Do you need extra training on specific processes? Such as design thinking or how to manage front-end innovation?
Events	Once you have decided which events you will organize to bring people together, they have a cost – it could be a cake or a small amount of catering per month, but you have to calculate it too. If you are organizing bigger events, such as "Innovation Contexts", "Innovation Days", "Innovation Coffees", "Innovation Cooking Events", "Innovation Fairs", "Innovation Showrooms" or "Hackathons", you have to add the costs to this category.
Income	If you are applying for public funding or public grants, you will receive income for your innovation projects or activities. Or, if you are investing in new technology and startups, you can receive revenue in the form of stocks or a percentage of customer acquisitions. Do you want to commercialize a product or sell your innovative solution to an external party? This can create income for your organization.

Table 9.1 (continued)

Category	Formula for calculator
Communication	You can create videos, podcasts, newsletters, and online tools to communicate with internal and external partners. You also have to include and cover your costs for websites, social media, events, online advertisements, etc.
Travel and accommodation	The expenses you need for travel in order to perform innovation activities include travel, accommodation or public transport to attend conferences, trainings or other events.
Extra costs	Online subscriptions, books, papers, online and offline magazine subscriptions, computers, other hardware or material needed to perform innovation within your organization. Do you want to have an innovation library? Do you want to be part of a specific association which includes a membership fee (online or offline)?
Extra error and risk buffer	+20%

"We don't know what we will need in the future. We cannot prepare people for a future we know today but we must prepare them to become innovators to successfully face the many, many issues they will be confronted with in the future," says Hilligje van't Land, Secretary General at International Association of Universities (IAU) (van't Land, 2019).

The budget calculator could be developed for one year or to forecast costs over your five-year strategy. Keep in mind that you don't have to do everything the first year – make a list of priorities. You can create your own table with a five-year overview and see when you are adding which costs or what income. The perspective that innovation is not only a cost for your organization or industry is quite interesting: you can creatively create investments and incomes to support your innovation leadership strategy.

Entrepreneurship journey with emotional intelligence for startups and academics

"I was intrigued about the connection of Emotional Intelligence and business in particular in a startup context. Everyone is looking for recipes for personal and professional success and this approach might be the key for both," says Alex Gunkel, CEO Space4Good, Founder RoadEO and Co-founder SkyTree.

If it's difficult to transform an organization, you can imagine how difficult is to transform an industry or all of society. The innovation leadership required to transform an industry with a new innovative solution has a name, and it's called "entrepreneurship". This transformation cannot be done alone – it has to be supported by the ecosystem, country and industry itself. In this case, the social intelligence and emotional intelligence skills required to bring people together are mandatory for the leader. This is a journey of learning, a journey of growing and a journey to go deep into the person themselves. Entrepreneurship is a journey to becoming an innovation and transformational leader, and the success of the startup will depend on the leadership skills of the founder. In Chapter 7 about the cost of knowledge, you have Figure 7.2 where you realize the independent cost of "going to market" which is separate from "knowledge transfer" and "adoption". This cost of "going to market" was calculated concretely in Figure 7.6 with the "Calculator for Entrepreneurship (Innovation Going to Market)". This should be useful for kicking off your thinking about the investment or funding or effort required to bring an innovation solution to the market, and how important it is to learn about finance to be able to survive in the market. A startup is not a "six-month-trial-period-idea", a successful startup is an evolution of the innovation solution, it's a learning process by the founder, it's a transformation in the market, and all of those "things" take time. Are you ready to invest time and effort? Are you ready to transform the market?

Now, it's important to remember that it's your unique journey – don't follow the fake news about entrepreneurship or startups in sensationalist magazines, because they often create headlines for the purpose of exploiting search-engine-optimized clicks. They are contributing to twisting reality and, as a consequence, are increasing false expectations and enhancing frustration. A transformational and innovation leader does not have all the answers, and this leader will look for knowledge outside their area of expertise and will go out of their comfort zone as needed. Learning is one of the epicenters of entrepreneurship and collaboration is key to surviving in the process. Figure 9.7 shows the "Startup Journey Canvas with Emotional Intelligence", which has the 6 elements required to become a leader for innovation and a successful entrepreneur who is bringing positive impact to the market and creating value with an innovative solution. It's your journey, so you have to create your own path. When you are building a team inside the startup or around your startup to make "it" happen, you will find people who are not ready to follow the entrepreneurship journey and that is fine. It's not about you or your leadership skills, sometimes it's about the fact that they are not ready. You are learning and your team has to learn and grow likewise.

Below you can find a guideline for working with the "Startup Journey Canvas with Emotional Intelligence" (Figure 9.7) and how to fill in each box with your required strategy and collaborations. This canvas is not designed to be used once, it's a live canvas to have at your desk. You should review it every month or every six months, if necessary. Innovation leadership is important for simultaneously dealing with difficult conversations and situations (for instance, a problem between co-founders), with the startup team and with customers to bring an innovative solution into the market.

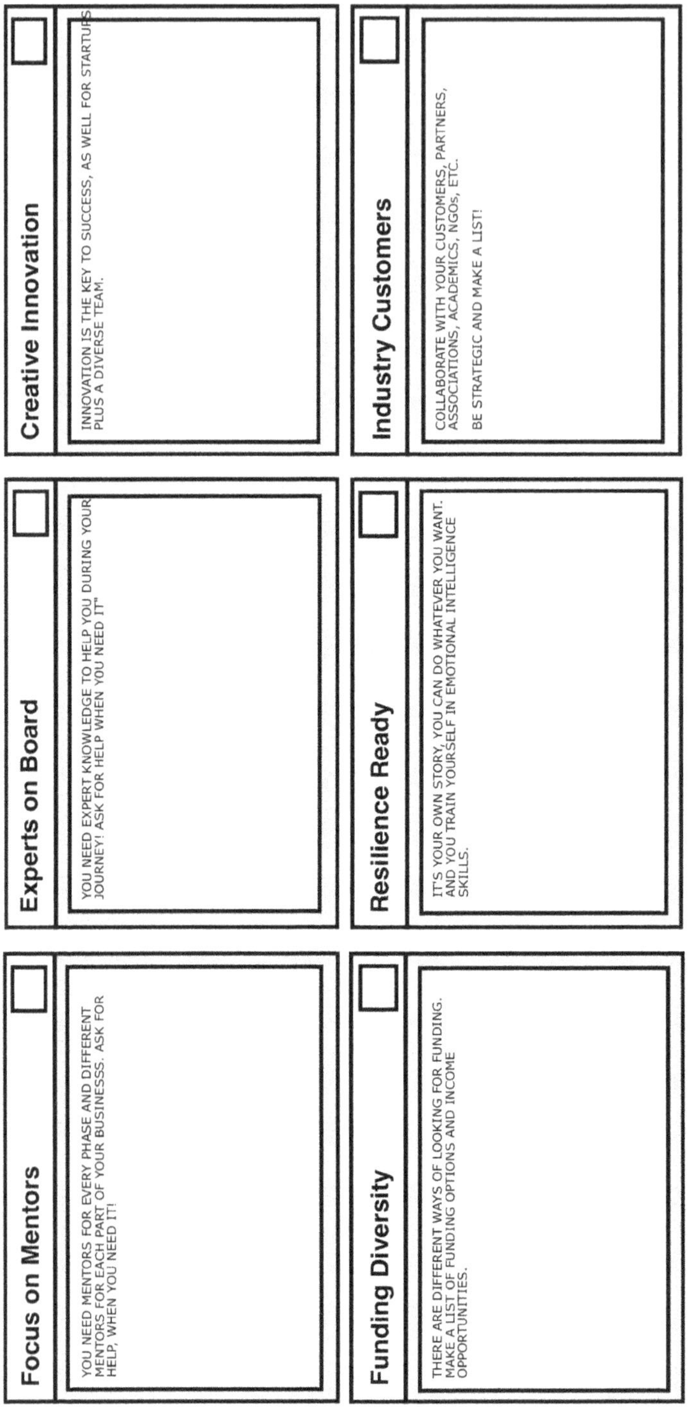

Focus on Mentors

YOU NEED MENTORS FOR EVERY PHASE AND DIFFERENT MENTORS FOR EACH PART OF YOUR BUSINESSS. ASK FOR HELP, WHEN YOU NEED IT!

Experts on Board

YOU NEED EXPERT KNOWLEDGE TO HELP YOU DURING YOUR JOURNEY! ASK FOR HELP WHEN YOU NEED IT"

Creative Innovation

INNOVATION IS THE KEY TO SUCCESS, AS WELL FOR STARTUPS PLUS A DIVERSE TEAM.

Funding Diversity

THERE ARE DIFFERENT WAYS OF LOOKING FOR FUNDING. MAKE A LIST OF FUNDING OPTIONS AND INCOME OPPORTUNITIES.

Resilience Ready

IT'S YOUR OWN STORY, YOU CAN DO WHATEVER YOU WANT. AND YOU TRAIN YOURSELF IN EMOTIONAL INTELLIGENCE SKILLS.

Industry Customers

COLLABORATE WITH YOUR CUSTOMERS, PARTNERS, ASSOCIATIONS, ACADEMICS, NGOS, ETC.

BE STRATEGIC AND MAKE A LIST!

Figure 9.7: The startup journey canvas with emotional intelligence.

Focus on mentors

You need mentors for every phase and different mentors for each part of your business:
– About entrepreneurship.
– Industry C-level.
– Startup CEO's.
– Psychologists.
– Business coaches.

Funding diversity

There are different ways of looking for funding:
– Business angels.
– Accelerators.
– Public national and European grants.
– Customer contracts.
– Partnership contracts.
– Consulting services you can provide.
– Other vertical and horizontal services you can create with your business.

Experts on board

You need expert knowledge to help you during your journey!
– Do you need to back up your idea with research?
– Do you need to get answers to your technical questions?
– Do you need to know about marketing?
– Do you need an advisory board member?

Resilience ready

It's your own story, you can do whatever you want:
– Start I: Deal with frustration and learn to breathe.
– Start II: Build resilience, manage expectations, differentiate urgent issues vs. priorities.
– Meet customer: Be calm, understand their fear, build trust.
– Manage business: Manage customer frustration, expectation and happiness.

- Fast growth: Focus on yourself, your team and your world around you. Create a psychologically safe team with emotional intelligence.
- Leadership: Listen, respect, have an open mind, be solution-driven and live togetherness.

Creative innovation

Innovation is the key to success, plus a diverse team:
- Innovation is generating value from creativity.
- Check your customer needs every 3 months.
- Be creative to create your income streams.
- Be creative with marketing, communication and brand awareness.
- Try new things fast and re-do.
- Contact a professor from a university to use your startup as a case study for their students.
- Can you create a new business opportunity for your business?
- What will kill your company in the future?
- Every year think: How would you create your company if you started it right now?

Industry customers

Collaborate with your customers, partners, associations, academics, NGOs, etc.:
- Be open-minded.
- Listen.
- Be creative about ways to work together.
- Focus on solutions.
- Understand their needs and issues.
- Collaborate with your supply chain and value chain.
- Collaborate with your customers!

As a summary, innovation leadership is not only happening and needed inside organizations, it's happening inside startups, governments, venture capitals, public institutions, ecosystems, online platforms and within every individual actor who is responsible for driving innovation and making innovation happen.

For this chapter about leadership, I chose to interview very specific and recognized leaders who are doing incredible work in their areas of innovation expertise, either inside startups, ecosystems or organizations. or at a national or European level.

Conversation with Constantijn van Oranje-Nassau about "Innovation Leadership"

Special Enjoy TechLeap.nl
    @constantijn14

How would you define leadership for innovation?

Never thought about it. I guess it is to create a culture of curiosity and a space for experimentation, where the new is not feared, where the current is challenged, and the future embraced. It means that current hypotheses always need to be challenged. That it is imperative to keep inviting new voices and interests to the table and ensuring cross fertilization between sectors, disciplines, profiles, age groups, professions, etc. And to be humble about all we know and curious about what we may become. Leading in innovation is about safeguarding that culture, but also by setting rigorous processes. Innovation is not one big brainstorm. It is not just about ideas, but about execution. Invention only becomes innovation when it really changes things and makes an impact. Potential for change is not enough. It needs to be delivered.

What are the key elements for driving change in the industry and society for innovation adoption?

Culture, money, talent, markets, technology, best combined with a big crisis that ensures all executives understand the urgency of change and are able to communicate this effectively to the organization and its stakeholders.

How do you bring people together from diverse backgrounds, cultures, and countries, and with different ways of thinking, to drive innovation?

How? If you want to innovate you better figure out how to bring different disciplines together. Diversity helps increase the span of possible solutions and a better understanding of customers' needs. To bring them together shouldn't be too difficult, as people like to meet and interact with others. There needs to be a culture of curiosity and respect, and probably a common sense of purpose. Then it is important to get the incentives right, and aligned with the required inputs, in the context of an enabling infrastructure and environment. These obviously differ in a commercial, academic, entrepreneurial, corporate or government setting.

What type of leadership is needed in those cases to transform an industry and a country to adopt innovation and new technologies to become really innovative?

A leadership that is fully convinced of the long-term importance of innovation; that has a vision of change and embraces transformation; and manages to communicate this effectively to the people that have more direct short-term interests, and can translate all of this into a culture, strategy, and organizational design.

Conversation with Maria Graça Carvalho on "Innovation Leadership"

Member of the European Parliament
   Former Minister of Innovation and Research in Portugal
   @mgracacarvalho

How would you define leadership for innovation?

I would say that leadership for innovation is all about creating the right conditions for the flourishing of the creative thinking that will lead to new concepts, products and services. This is valid for policy makers and lawmakers, central and local administrations, the academic world and private businesses. A leader for innovation is essentially someone that is creative by nature but also allows others around him to shine by removing bureaucratic barriers and rewarding "out-of-the box" thinking.

What are the key elements to drive change in the industry and society for innovation adoption?

The first element has to be the acceptance of the need to be innovative. Change does not come easy for anyone because it is often disruptive. We need to understand the reasons that justify taking the risk – or at least what we perceive as a risk – of abandoning old practices that seemed to work fine for a long time. We need to be able to understand the benefit that comes from innovation. The new technologies are an example of well-accepted innovation. We all embraced them because the advantages were obvious. Presently, the industry faces the need to be innovative in order to remain competitive in the global scene, and both the industry and the society in general are increasingly aware of the need to rethink their practices for sustainability reasons, because we cannot go on living and doing things the way we did for decades. We need to find a balance between keeping and improving our quality of life, creating wealth, and protecting our planet and the limited resources it provides us. The second element is the creation of the right environment for innovation to flourish in. That responsibility falls mostly under lawmakers and administrations. They need to develop the incentives for innovation and remove the many bureaucratic barriers that exist. At last, but certainly not least, we need a strong investment in education and science. Without a strong commitment to science, including fundamental science, without well-qualified citizens that are learners throughout their lives, we cannot be innovative.

How do you bring people together from different backgrounds, cultures, and countries, and with different ways of thinking, to drive innovation?

We live in a globalized world and, although that has confronted us with new challenges, it made clear that our differences are not as profound or irreconcilable as many believed. Another thing that globalization made us understand was that we can all profit from working side-by-side and that the differences that actually exist can in fact be an advantage. To give just an example, amongst many, the European Research Area created an environment where scientists from different nationalities and backgrounds work side-by-side on common challenges, where the transfer of technology is a reality with advantages for all. Broadening the scope, we can think of a future where different sectors, across the globe, are increasingly involved in all stages of innovation, from concept to product, from idea to policy.

How do you see the role of innovation on a European level, national level, university level and industry level? What type of leadership is needed in those cases to adopt innovation and in all new technologies to become really innovative?

This European Commission has repeatedly stated that innovation is at the core of all the pillars it has identified, from the European Green Deal to digitalization and industry transition. This is a very important principle. However, intentions alone will not suffice. The EU budget needs to have the resources that match the ambitions, namely for education and science. At the national level, in this context of response to the economic effects of Covid-19, it is also important that member states understand that the need to address immediate challenges must be balanced with mid- and long-term strategies. I have to admit that I am a bit concerned about what line of action will be followed in some countries. We are already seeing a few of them, namely Germany, making the right commitments, allocating significant resources from their national budgets to innovative policies. It is important that others follow this example. Between the recovery plan "Next Generation Europe" and the MMF, member states will receive significant funds. This is an unmissable opportunity for change. Otherwise, we will only widen the gap between nations. In regard to universities and industries, we need the sort of leaders that are willing to cooperate – namely with each other – to address current challenges and find the opportunities that come with them. I am rapporteur for the strategic agenda of the European Institute for Innovation and Technology (EIT) in the next framework program Horizon Europe. This institution needs to make some changes, namely in terms of openness, transparency and a better national and regional balance of the funds that it distributes. Nevertheless, I believe that EIT and its Knowledge and Innovation Communities (KICs), focused on different fields, from climate to energy, from raw materials to digitalization, are a good model of how universities and businesses can work side-by-side, acting in all dimensions of the knowledge triangle – education, science and innovation – training good professionals and developing innovative products and services.

What is the role of digital platforms and virtualization of innovation ecosystems for the adoption of innovation?

Digital platforms, as we have witnessed during this health crisis caused by Covid-19, are an extremely important tool for bringing people together, and my belief is that their role will only increase from now on. In a certain sense, they are fulfilling their original purpose. As we all know, the internet started out as a tool to enhance communication among specialists in different sectors and was widely used by academics since the 1980s, long before its commercial explosion. The only inconvenience that I see, particularly in digital platforms, is the fact that some of them have become so big and so powerful that, without the establishment of clear boundaries, without the acceptance of a clear set of rules and procedures, they can actually become an obstacle to innovation in many fields.

Conversation with Natalie Samovich about "Innovation Leadership"

Head of R&I Enercoutim
  Chair WG Smart Energy at AIOTI
  Co-founder Resilient Group
  @Natalie_Sam

How would you define leadership for innovation?

Innovation leadership is multidimensional, it transcends well beyond the technology dimension. It can be driven from many angles: the startups, SMEs or well-established incumbent companies. Innovation leadership has to be focused on solving scaling-up challenges from the start.

.Multidimensionality of the innovation challenge is reflected within the leadership strategy and could assist in aligning around the set missions by organizations or teams. The societal challenges context, technology roadmaps and the level of perceived urgency of the topics contribute directly towards not only what but how to achieve the set goals. Building consensus and a common vision are some of the most difficult topics within the innovation continuum: what – why – how. Hence, the biggest contribution to mission-oriented innovation leadership could stem from considerations of the multidimensional approach. This approach can include clear definitions of key performance indicators and system of system approach that is inclusive towards project stakeholders.

What are the key elements to drive change in the industry and society for innovation adoption?

All dimensions introduced above should be substantiated, communicated and the expected outcomes should be outlined. Innovation adoption is not a naturally occurring phenomenon. The utility of the solution, its short- and long-term impacts and the enabling policies cannot be underestimated. These are some of the building blocks of innovation adoption. The question is how we scale up adoption where there is an urgent need, for example, concerning climate change, reaching climate neutrality or navigating through the economic recovery. For example, at ETIP-SNET there is a working group working trying to address scaling up challenges after the research and innovation programs .https://www.etip-snet.eu/about/working-groups/wg-5/

Common knowledge platforms helping not only to identify innovative solutions, but to work on the issues jointly and with effective communication, are some of the ways to bring innovation into action to address energy transition in this case. Society is driven by global context, socio-economic dimensions. The industry is driven by policy and competition. Bringing the two together could provide another key.

How do you bring people together from different backgrounds, cultures, and countries, and with different ways of thinking, to drive innovation?

Common projects and large-scale demonstrators based on shared missions and visions might accomplish some goals of driving innovation. Global context and positive interdependencies are some of the bottom-up approach drivers. Mission and vision unite people in many different ways. From very tangible missions, such as achieving car-free historical centers zones, decarbonization of energy generation and more complex ones, such as of aiming at reaching climate neutrality goals to self-organization to act during adverse events, the mission and vision definition play an important role. Transnational research initiatives, agile local teams, cross-domain experts working on solving short-term challenges in spite of diversity and the level of challenge if driven by a common goal can organically streamline efforts. Innovation leadership is strategic marketing as to where you want to go. It needs to be coupled with a clear pathway towards stakeholders communicating a plan as to how to get there.

What is the role of digital platforms and virtualization of innovation ecosystems for innovation adoption?

The role of the platforms and the related ecosystems that these digital solutions are enabling cannot be underestimated. In the energy sector, such platforms bring the whole R&I community together. An example is the BRIDGE initiative .https://www.h2020-bridge.eu/ that brings the EU energy sector together along with https://www.eranet-smartenergysystems.eu/ and others.

I believe it is the most agile way forward; if coupled with strong policy support it can really speed up innovation adoption on the societal level. Digital knowledge management platforms if complemented by active community members can achieve the most effective results. The best practices dissemination as well the most efficient organization for addressing barriers and facilitation of policy contributions can be achieved through such organizations. Community leadership or ecosystem leadership is one form of dealing with complex cross-domain challenges.

A word of warning on false leadership . . .
It can be recognized when used to declare the support and big goals but falling short on following up or delivering the results. This can have an overall slowdown effect on the industry. Speed of leadership and effectiveness should be discussed more than the initial step of getting behind a vision or an idea. We are all captivated by big declarations, but it is executing what is timely and urgent that matters. Let's all lead during the Covid-19 recovery and energy transformation towards reaching Climate Neutrality. Maybe the leadership of all of us is needed nowadays. I would like to pose a question: should we be waiting for a few industry leaders to adopt measures and show the way? Legacy assets conflict and other barriers can exist for wide-scale innovation adaptation to take place. These barriers should really be openly discussed and recognized. Disruptive innovation is multidimensional. The leadership of ONE and EACH of us matters. The leadership of all actors in the ecosystem should be the new normal.

Conversation with Christine MacKay on "Innovation Leadership Inside Organizations"

CEO Salamandra, UK
  @SalamandraUK

How would you define leadership for innovation?

Leadership for innovation requires you to keep an open mind, have bags of curiosity and sign up for lifelong learning. At salamandra.uk, a B2B animation agency, we define leadership for innovation as a collaborative effort between the entire team to build, learn, communicate and support each other. For me personally, it's putting my team before the business and staying connected to every individual for regular human to human (H2H) catch-ups to check in on how they are doing, where they want to get to and enabling this to happen.

What are the key elements to drive change inside organizations for innovation adoption?

The feeling of inclusion needs to be nurtured to drive change, as it needs to come from within each of us. There also needs to be room for error; so, at salamandra.uk, there is no such thing as a stupid question. Employees need to feel valued and heard and my team is on board with everything that happens in the business from strategy to sales to customer engagement and I include them in important changes or pivots to the business. For example, our "Lizard Lounge" all contributed to creating and agreeing our core company values, right down to the wording. With that collective buy-in, we now base our work-life, branding, and choosing customers and staff around them.

How do you bring people together to drive innovation and to be creative from different backgrounds, cultures, countries and different ways of thinking?

I believe that a melting pot of cultures, countries and languages enriches any work or life environment. Recognizing and appreciating the myriad of nuances and perspectives these add to the workplace and to our animation projects is priceless. We have two offices at opposite ends of the UK but through technology we stay connected and collaborative.

We have two daily work meetings and often sit on Skype during the day with each other which has become important from a mental health perspective now that we are wfh (work from home). We also organize "lunch and learns" where we teach each other all sorts of new things including 3D shortcuts to model furniture making.

How do you see the role of innovation on an international level?

From a business perspective, we are now a global village. Salamandra.uk has clients all around the world, most of which we have never met, and I expect globalization to happen more as we continue to work from home and Zoom calls become the accepted modus operandi, with the costly and time-consuming need to fly overseas. Because we work in animation, what we sell is totally transportable and translatable, so it's important for us to trade overseas as well as in the British Isles. The continuous development in hardware and software enables this international growth, but I would say that the best "innovation" is to stay "human" in your approach, because people do business with people, and usually with people they like.

What is the role of digital platforms and virtualization of innovation ecosystems for the innovation adoption?

Connectivity is vital for internal and external comms and employee engagement; you never want to lose touch with your team or clients and digitization allows for remote experimentation and ideation and that is how our Eton and Dundee offices stay mentally aligned.

Virtualization of innovation ecosystems open up an opportunity to push new technologies and software in business, whether that's systems or products, and work with teams of people in various geographic locations.

Summary

To sum up this chapter, I will leave you with a number of exercises that help ground you in your innovation leadership journey.

To practice

1. Innovation leadership is about transformation, about social influence and about change.
2. Learn to forecast costs and incomes to outperform in innovation leadership!
3. The secret is about collaboration for innovation, so bring people together!
4. Bringing a new innovative solution to the market takes time and effort.

In the following chapter you will find

- Tips to understand that digital is not the only way.
- Tips on how to create a digital tool which is about emotional intelligence as well.
- Tips to adopt digitalization to outperform on collaboration for innovation.

Notes

(Grundy, 2020) https://collabwith.co/2020/03/blockchain-innovation-sw-developers/
(Rader, 2020) https://collabwith.co/2020/05/steven-rader/
(Bensnes, 2020) https://collabwith.co/2020/05/podcast-markus-bensnes/
(Talwar, 2020) https://collabwith.co/2020/05/podcast-rohit-talwar-on-the-future-after-the-COVID-19-crisis/
(van't Land, 2019) https://collabwith.co/2019/12/podcast-hillitge-higher-education-innovation/

References

Bohmer, R. Urch Druskat, V. Edmondson, A. Garvin, D. Katzenbach, J. Smith, D. Levy, P. Meyer, C. Pisano, G. Roberto, M. Royer, I. Snyder, W. Wenger, E. Wolff, S. Equipos que triunfan. Harvard business review. Ideas con Impacto. Page 37. Ediciones deusto. 2004.

Brackett, M. Permission to Feel: Unlocking the Power of Emotions to Help Our Kids, Ourselves, and Our Society Thrive. 2019.

Chan Kim, W. Mauborgne, R. von Hippel, E. Thomke, S. Sonnack, M. Hargadon, A. Sutton, R. Christensen, C. Overdorf, M. MacMillan, I. Gunther McGrath, R. Moss Kanter, R. 1997, 1998, 1999, 2000, 2001. Harvard Business Review on Innovation. Harvard Business School Press. Ideas with Impact. PAGE 74. The Harvard Review Paperback Series. 2001.

Goffee, R. and Jones, G. What holds the modern company together? The short answer is culture. But which type is right for your organization? Copyright. By the President and Fellows of Harvard College. Page 142 and 143. 1996.

Katz, R. 2003. Managing creativity and innovation. Practical strategies to encourage creativity. PAGE 33. Harvard Business Press. Harvard Business Essentials. 2003.

Kotter, J. and Cohen, D. The Heart of Change: Real-Life Stories of How People Change Their Organizations. 2012.

Kruse, K. Great Leaders Have no Rules. 2019.

Li., C. 2010. Open leadership. How social technology can transform the way you lead. PAGE 66 and 225. Jossey-Bass. An imprint of Wiley. 2010.

Samsonowa, T. 2012. Industrial research performance management. Key performance indicators in the ICT industry. Contributors to management science. PAGE 103. Physica-Verlag. A springer company. 2012.

Weisinger, H (2008) Emotional Intelligence at Work. Ed. Jossey-Bass.

"We have changed the way we do innovation, it is not only technology driven. It is how we bring things together, to create value, and create the best insights for curing diseases. There are a lot of factors that contribute, both holistically and personally, that drives our innovation"

Jeroen Tas, Chief Innovation and Strategy Officer at Royal Philips (Tas, 2019)

Chapter 10
How Digitalization is Helping to Create Value for Innovation: Digitalize All That Can Be Digital and Leave the Rest to Human Interaction

Summary: In this chapter you will learn how to lead the builders of algorithms and interfaces with emotional intelligence, how to think about technology design and the creation of new solutions with a new perspective on emotions, and that sometimes you don't need a piece of technology to make a revolution.

Any innovation leader, academic, researcher or practitioner should know some basics about technology and the impact of technology on our lives. The question everyone has to answer before designing and creating an innovative solution is: what kind of future do we want to have? Common sense, ethics and philosophy are the new domains for innovation, including psychology, neuroscience, anthropology, human-machine interaction and social studies. Really, we and you cannot leave the future in the hands of a single software developer or tech guru. The innovation leader should be responsible for bringing these experts together to conceptualize the new innovative solution. Here we revisit the point of knowledge decentralization: you need a multi-disciplinary and multi-diverse team to be able to create. Nowadays, we are at an inflection point of technology, you can do almost anything you can imagine with technology. There is a need to be critical; it's the time to reflect on human values and how we as a society, and as innovation leaders, are using the technology. Together we are responsible for making decisions for the future of our society, for the products that will be on the market. Do you want to have a store with only screens and no people? Or do you prefer to shop via your mobile phone everywhere and go to the store to have a personal experience with physical products you can test and where you can create a special bond with the brand? Technology should not remove our values as human beings; technology is just a tool to help us. The questions are getting deeper when we and you are designing new applications: how is this technology changing the values of our society? Does this make sense? Are we neutral enough? What is the price that the user is paying with his lack of privacy? How far can this technology go to change our values? What is the sense of disruption? Innovation has to have a purpose. Technology has to have a purpose and it has to have a positive impact.

On a personal note, when I was designing the collabwith.co platform, together with the team, we started to ask philosophical questions and how it would be possible to answer them technically. For instance, what is the first result of a search? Can we have a neutral result? Is it possible that the algorithm is inclusive and not discriminating against any other kind of knowledge or search result? Why do we need

https://doi.org/10.1515/9783110665383-010

to ask these questions? Because it should be the person who makes the decision about the kind of knowledge, research results, technology, and startup they want to find to work with. Which parameters and filters can we allow the user to select to personalize their search results to still be neutral? Design is not only graphic design, it's about philosophy, and therefore innovation design, and technology design and digitalization have to start with a philosophical question as well. An example is the Netflix algorithm where you always see the same films and it's very difficult to get away from the never-changing recommendations or Facebook and Instagram with their algorithm which makes you always see the same "liked" or "watched" content.

Some more philosophical and ethical questions surrounding the creation of collabwith.co: If our users hate legal documents (but they are important to protect their IP, privacy, confidential information or protect misuse of their work and research results), how can we design the process inside the platform that the legal documents (in some cases required) are not intrusive but something that users accept and think about and reflect on? At which point in the process can we add them? In which format? Then there are the questions regarding trust: What is digital trust? How can trust be created at the human level? How is trust created in other digital tools and on social media? What are the key factors in our platform that give trust? Or technical challenges: How can we display knowledge without using a neuronal-network or map style? Can we create an interface which can help people to network or to discover the knowledge and technology they need in an uncomplicated way? Everyone on the team has these questions in mind irrespective of the position and job they are doing, and these questions accompany us when we have a cup of tea or a walk!

What is digitalization?

"Digitalization is, on the one hand, a fundamental change to business operations and business models based on newly acquired knowledge gained via value-added digitization initiatives. When we think about examples such as platforms that have been developed and scaled up in the last years or about the application of big data for the maintenance of machines, digitalization has enabled numerous new business areas, but there is even more potential for future applications. But digitalization is much more. It starts in the head as a special type of mentality: the digital mindset. It is digitally enabling analog or physical artifacts for the purpose of implementing said artifacts into business processes with the aim of acquiring newly formed knowledge and creating new value for the stakeholders" (Schallmo, 2018).

Digitalization is a tool, a process, a technology, a way to innovate. Innovation is and has to be a holistic change, it's not possible to think that only one "app" (mobile phone application or Web tool) or only a small digitalization in the supply chain will bring about innovation in a broader sense. The solution has to be designed in a way that is embedded in the way you are doing business and at the core of the organization.

And as Prof. Schallmo said, "it's all about people" (Schallmo, 2018). The adoption (effective change) is the way to apply the change and create value. Digitalization is a holistic change, and all the rules from change management and a transformational leader should be applied. This is one of the reasons why it's essential to talk about innovation leadership. In the podcast interview with Jeroen Tas, Chief Innovation Officer at Philips (Tas, 2019), he stated that innovation is not about a piece of technology. Instead, it is about having a holistic view of an idea and about how to work towards this vision. In the healthcare industry, the major change in adopting artificial intelligence will happen when health insurances, hospitals, doctors, technology providers, patients, and governments are working together. The question is who will orchestrate this change, but also, what the digitalization roadmap to get there is. Is this really the future we want to have? What is the impact on our daily lives? The innovative answer has to be given together with health ecosystem actors, philosophers, anthropologists, psychologists, sociologists, academics, entrepreneurs and research organizations. The future technology is currently in academia, university and research centers. It's important to discover how to apply it with purpose.

As an example, we can have a look at the automotive industry, I remember I was in 2012 in a workshop about innovation with Prof. Piller at the RWTH Aachen University in Germany and he explained very simply the difference between incremental innovation and disruption. For instance, the Smart car, created in collaboration between Mercedes-Benz and the Swatch Group, was a disruption because it's small and focused on mobility and simplicity, instead of creating a better car with better applications and a better engine as would be seen in an incremental innovation.

Tesla is an incremental innovation (surprise!), because the electric engine was already invented by Moritz Jacobi in May 1834 in Germany (Doppelbauer, 2017a); and the first electric cars were driven in the United States starting in the 19th century and through into the 1920s. In fact, most cars were electric before the invention of the combustion engine (Doppelbauer, 2017b). Tesla has only improved upon the idea of driving electrically. What Elon Musk did very well was to position electric cars and sustainability as a luxury item and create partnerships with governments and cities to push subsidies to buy electric cars. Elon Musk is a transformational leader who is bringing innovation to the market to be adopted by society. Although we have to question whether electric cars are sustainable because the batteries are a huge pollution factor, and the materials from the car are not recycled, and electricity is still not coming from renewable energy. But it's certainly a starting point, and it's very good to position sustainability as a luxury factor and not only for hippies.

So when can we speak of disruption? How important are technology and digitalization in innovation? This is answered best when you start from a philosophical question. The philosophical question in the case of automotive disruption is about mobility: How can we go from point A to point B? This is the reason why Smart was a disruption at that time in October 1998, because it focused on the answer of mobility. If this is clear to you, then you can determine the disruptiveness of car sharing, self-driving cars (this is an ethical question about our future), flying cars (we have helicopters, planes, didn't you know?) and other forms of digitalization of mobility such as Uber, mytaxi, Flixbus, Car2go, BlaBlaCar, Greenwheels or electric scooters such as Lime, Bolt, Tier and eCooltra or shared bikes (like Vélib' in Paris or Bicing in Barcelona). Digitalization with philosophy is an innovative disruption.

Digitalization vs. innovation vs. collaboration?

Digital transformation has many advantages. It is possible to reach customers in a better and faster way. Furthermore, it is possible to derive relevant, previously unexplored information from products and services (i.e., by applying sensors and big data analytics) and to initiate processes (i.e., delivery of spare parts, maintenance). Basically, digital transformation enables companies to save time and money and to deliver a higher quality of products and services (Schallmo, 2018).

If the future technology and potential innovations are already present in our universities, research centers and in the academic intellects, how can you access to them? This is where digitalization can support innovation. Digital tools can help you access knowledge which is very far away from your local region. Knowledge you might need badly. This is the concept of knowledge being decentralized and innovation decentralization that causes the need to collaborate for innovation with academics and professionals who are not in the same city or country. And this is how technology and digitalization can support you in your innovation process and innovation creation.

You cannot simply replicate your "offline" process an put it "online". It is necessary to ask yourself fundamental questions to start a different way of thinking about digitalization. Digitalization is also an opportunity to re-think your business and processes. When you are doing technical innovation and digitalization, what does it really mean to digitalize a process? What are the benefits, what are the values? For instance, with the digital platform collabwith.co, which I founded, we digitalized the access to technology, research, academics, entrepreneurs, startups, universities, and we digitalized the collaboration process, but only the administrative side. The collaboration itself is done outside of the platform. We structured the request for collaboration for innovation, but the thought process still occurs inside our customers and our users. They are the brokers – we are only the tool to support their visionary thinking. They are the business developers, and they are the lawyers – we only facilitate their discussions and their decision making. Additionally, we supply a tool to find knowledge and technology, we empower our users, we give them superpowers for innovation. At the same time, we support our community with an educational system of articles in our online magazine, podcast interviews, videos, webinars and workshops to make a transformation of their mindset regarding how to make innovation happen. These resources help Collabwith's users with the questions of what innovation is, how to collaborate, how to implement digital transformation, what is artificial intelligence, how to use emotional intelligence for innovation, how to finance your innovation, how to network, how to use smart legal contracts for collaboration for innovation, etc. And all the digitalization and non-digitalized processes and innovative solutions were coming from conversations with real users, from our own experiences, from interviews with innovation ecosystem actors, and by asking ourselves philosophical questions about the issues, feedback and conversations we are having all the time.

Which kind of value can a digital tool bring to innovation?

My recommendation is to focus on the employees' needs and concerns. To understand what they worry about and to enable them to bring digital transformation from their hearts into their heads and hands (Schallmo, 2018).

Apart from the fact that digital tools are fundamental for optimization, effectiveness, efficiency and automation of your innovation processes (and, of course, your organization's processes and business models), digital tools have the power to transform the way you are doing business, how you are working, how you are making innovation happen and how you are collaborating. It's up to you whether to use the power of digitalization or not. There are many areas where digital tools have made a significant impact on organizations in a very visible way. Marketing with social media tools is just one example. As Prof. Khaleelah Jones, Founder and CEO at Careful Feet, explained during one of our interviews on marketing, it's about "how sophisticated digital allows companies to be with targeting and segmentation, and how much money can be saved" (Jones, 2018).

Concerning the value creation using digital tools in innovation, we do not have to limit our thinking to efficiency improvements through their use. For a concrete example we should have another look at the collabwith.co platform which I founded so that super innovators can directly contact organizations and make a request detailing what they want to collaborate on with them in less than 5 minutes.

The value proposition to its users is simple: a collaboration with another partner for innovation will make a difference in their organization regarding innovation and business growth. The way that they can make use of the collabwith.co platform is very simple, and one of its key benefits is a way to structure a request for knowledge and collaboration properly and professionally (instead of thinking about how to write an email that will trigger a reaction). You can add your data, explain briefly what you are looking for, what you need, the timelines and what you can offer. This reduces your timelines to kick off a collaboration or a new innovation project by removing emails, reducing the number of calls, easily managing expectations, and reducing the decision-making process timelines. The simple reason for the time-saving effect is that the other party can make a decision more quickly with all the required information already in the request.

At collabwith.co, community members will find a marketplace as well to discover collaboration opportunities, showcase their work, their technology or knowledge offer, and their needs for innovation. A dashboard makes it easy to follow up with potential collaboration partners to speed up their innovation process and bring their product to the market faster. Our objective with Collabwith was and still is that users can manage everything in one place instead of having several points of contact via emails, Slack, WhatsApp, LinkedIn, between their organization's team and their potential innovation partners. Users can limit themselves to only one place to manage their collaboration for innovation, including requests, contracts, payments, their collaboration network, their opportunities to collaborate and including a community ready to collaborate to innovate. Collabwith was created to accelerate innovation and network with incredible likeminded people that can be essential to their business, organization and innovation. Otherwise, they might never meet and/or know that they both have a collaborative mindset for innovation and their needs and offerings match. At Collabwith you are increasing the probability of connecting and making a request to the right person, with the right message, at the right time, exactly when needed and for the precise knowledge and technology that is required.

What makes the platform a valuable digital tool is that we have created a great environment to establish a clear call to action, ecosystem networking and innovation co-creation, including the information of what you can offer, what you need and what is your request. For instance, what if you don't know how to digitalize? Then collaborate with Prof. Schallmo or other professors specialized in digitalization and innovation. Ask for help, get new knowledge and learn how to do it. The same goes for innovation – do you need to know how to innovate? Then collaborate with an innovation consultant or a professor, join webinars and workshops, learn! If you don't know how to collaborate with a university or academic or startup or corporate or any kind of organization, you can contact the professionals and ask for advice and help.

Benefits of using digital tools for innovation

- Speed up the process.
- Remove unnecessary bureaucracy.
- Co-create with visionaries who are not in your local region.
- Increase your creativity while collaborating with others from other fields of expertise, other cultures and other backgrounds.
- Increase diversity and inclusion in your innovation process.
- Facilitate thinking outside the box.
- Increase the chances of finding the right partner.
- Save money and resources!

There are other innovation platforms and tools dedicated to crowdsourcing ideas and investment based on challenges such as inocentive, herox or inocrowd. Prof. Piller and Prof. Diener from RWTH Aachen have created a great annual report about open innovation and open knowledge for innovation (Piller and Diener, 2019) if you want to know more about open innovation platforms.

How far can we go with digitalization?

We need to find smart ways in order to connect academia and practice. In many cases, companies seek new solutions and innovative people. On the other hand, universities can provide new ways of thinking and new methods for the solution of problems (Schallmo, 2018).

You cannot digitalize everything. We are human beings, and human values and way of thinking and doing things have to be a priority. Digital tools can help you to automate processes and increase the level of trust, but at the end of the day, the outcome of any process depends on the professionalism of the people involved. Applied to using a collaboration platform like collabwith.co, the degree to which they are really willing to collaborate and to bring innovation to the market and adopt it depends on how the collaborators are as a person. For instance, a university technology transfer officer can focus more on business development, building relationships with organizations, on communication, on scouting potential collaborations instead of using time for partner research, technology scouting, contacting corporates based on trial and error, legal negotiations or always working with the same companies and organizations because it takes too long to find other corporates to collaborate with. Digital tools are built in a way that you can be much more effective and efficient in establishing collaborations, so you can focus on generating more profit doing more collaborations per year, increase your research transfer opportunities and work directly with the right organizations if they are using digital tools for collaboration.

Useful skills for a non-digital and digital collaboration for innovation

- Have a clear objective for your collaboration.
- Find the right partner to collaborate with (knowledge, technology, research)
- Understand your value and what you bring to the collaboration.
- Contact your collaboration partner properly.
- Leverage for the best possible results.
- Build a relationship with your collaboration partner.

You can imagine a startup working on the process of onboarding a new user and introducing them to their digital platform. They can do it offline, with the user going to a physical place and receiving an explanation about how it works and having the necessary software directly installed in person. In some cases, if it's a new technology and a new company this is a very good practice to start with, because you will gather information and feedback from the user which has a huge value. This can happen in small talks, direct interactions, within the on-site real-life scenario environment of your user, etc.

The user will then have the distractions of his usual surroundings when using the digital tool. At the beginning it is fine to do this, but this is not scalable, unfortunately. Of course, at the same time, you want to keep this customer conversation at the onboarding, as it is important to give a little extra value to your user, create engagement and create a competitive advantage between your competitor's solution and yours. One of the potential philosophical questions is: How can you digitalize the onboarding process with a human touch to continue to have a personal interaction and increase engagement? Is it possible to digitalize this personal touch? You do not have to remove all the personal onboarding process because you cannot physically visit your customer, you can think outside the box in a creative way and look for solutions and ideas and discuss them with your customer, even try them out and improve them along the way.

One example which personally I don't like about digitalization is when Pampers created the smart diapers (Fast Company, 2019), which is a diaper with a sensor connected to a mobile app, and it's telling you when your baby's diaper is full and has to be changed. Do you want to be so disconnected of your life and baby that you do not realize yourself that you have to change its diaper? Or do you want that your baby is exposed to all the radiofrequency waves from a wireless sensor? Is this cool? Do you want to have this future? What are the values we are changing with this technology? Does that make sense at all? It makes no sense.

Digital and online tools have to be well developed

To become useful, digital tools have to be developed correctly, otherwise the risk becomes that people will not use it! I remember being in a meeting and someone wanted to show us a page from a Web tool, and he said, "I am not logged in because it takes a lot of time." This is a true story, and it's not a problem of the user, it's a problem of design (inexistence of UX design), software development and operations, and this "bug" is impossible to find when looking at the "tickets list" from the support service and helpdesk. If you are talking to the person responsible for the platform, he might reply that the budget was for functionality development, not for commercialization. What is commercialization? If you are building a super great tool for a community, with a very good interface, a very good front-end and backend, then the community will use your innovative solution, and you will make an impact. If your platform or digital tool takes time to log into, no one will use your platform, even the administrator! If it's impossible to understand the interface, no one will use your super digital tool. It's not about commercialization. It's about good practices in software development and the creation of innovative solutions. Any kind of technology has to be well designed, well programmed and well operated to be able to make an impact.

The same goes for service and process design for digitalization and automation. If it's not well designed, you will create issues instead of making your customer's life easier or improving your business and increasing the growth of your organization. Digitalization has to be well thought out with an interdisciplinary team, and it has to make sense for your customer, your organization and your business.

Artificial intelligence vs. emotional intelligence

Nowadays, one of the technologies that is trending is artificial intelligence, which is not new, and even I remember doing an internship at the mathematics department of my university designing an artificial intelligence algorithm for student exams which would create questions based on the students' answers (I can imagine now, with the Covid-19 crisis, how important a smart exam like this one has been ☺). Artificial intelligence had a philosophical starting point when philosopher Ramon Llull created the idea of logical machines to produce knowledge and information. Those ideas were followed by other philosophers – Descartes, Hobbes, Russell – until our days when Alan Turing created the first machine of logic programming, and artificial intelligence became an academic discipline around 1956. There is a debate that artificial intelligence could get to the point of being emotionally intelligent. Machines would recognize their own machine emotions, recognize the emotions of others and communicate in a way that they can manage emotions. Does that make sense? Instead, technology can be used as a tool for understanding our emotions as human beings, for communicating our emotions, visualizing the emotions of organizations and as a tool for explaining emotions and providing tips on how to regulate emotions. There is a mobile app called the MoodMeterApp which is doing exactly that. Rafael Calvo, together with Dorian Peters, summarized the positive impact of this kind of technology for increasing people's wellbeing through technology in their book, *Positive Computing* (Calvo and Peters, 2014).

If you want to use technology for human wellbeing, it's very important to design technology with emotional intelligence; emotions are information – data that has an impact on our behavior, thoughts and physical responses to ourselves and others. One problem that most people have is that they do not understand what they feel, or they find it is hard to name their own emotions. To become emotionally aware of the feelings you are experiencing is "emotional Intelligence". Improving your emotional intelligence makes you claim control of your emotions instead of repressing your emotions. This will allow you to become less reactive and more interactive in conversations and communication. In Figure 10.1 you will find a nice framework which creates a relationship between software and algorithm development with the emotional intelligence mood meter.

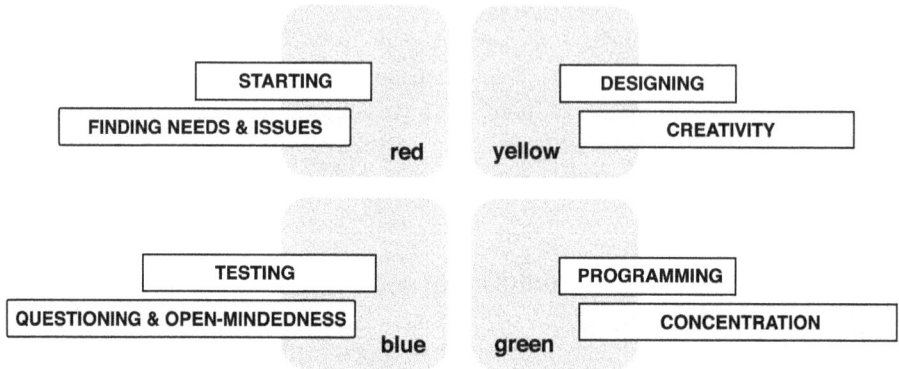

Figure 10.1: Framework algorithm and software development vs. emotional Intelligence using the mood meter.

In Chapter 4 "The Secrets of Collaboration: Using Emotional Intelligence for Innovation and Collaboration" you got an introduction to emotional intelligence skills. You have learned that how you are feeling can impact your decision making, your communication, your interactions, your creativity and your work results. Your ability to manage your emotions can have a positive or negative impact on your business, your relationships and your performance. Figure 10.1 gives a general outline of a framework to help you to understand in which emotion it is best to design, test and program algorithms and other software for innovative solutions or for any new application. The **red quadrant for anger** is especially useful to scout issues, finding new needs while you are working on a new algorithm and establishing a real problem to solve. The **yellow quadrant for happiness** and **excitement** is suitable for designing the software architecture, planning the algorithm, finding creative ways to match with the enterprise architecture and brainstorm about what the algorithm has to be in terms of design and program. When you are in a mood of positivity and optimism, it is clear that you will think with a positive outlook and with a focus on doing well with your algorithm. The **blue quadrant for sadness** is best suited for error checking. Not error checking on your emotions, mind you; this is about the task, which you can concentrate on better in this mindset. When you are trying to see if the user requirements are matched, or if the system is doing what it has to do, and it's working, you have to be critical and not accept any unwanted behavior of the code! **The green quadrant for content and calm emotions** is super useful for programming and coding, with your brain motivated and performing at its best. Being rational and objective when executing the design is key. Hence, if you are feeling stressed or disappointed, this is not the right time for software development. And this is applicable for innovation leadership, because you have to know the mood of your team that is required to create a positive application of artificial intelligence or a piece of code, but also when your team is ready to design a piece of software, and you have to support them to create the right mood at your workplace and influence the team dynamics. Technology for good, or artificial intelligence for good, start with how you, your development team and your innovation team are feeling.

AI and software development best practices

- Algorithms should be objective and neutral in terms of the results for the user.
- Algorithms should be designed, tested and developed by a diverse team of philosophers, psychologists, sociologists, neuroscientists, anthropologists, usability experts, human-machine interaction, software developers and the final users!
- The end user is not only one person or one persona.
- The end user has to be represented by a group of people from our society.
- Technology is for everyone; technology has to be inclusive.
- Just in case, even before you start developing, ask your question again: Is it really needed? Do I want this kind of solution as a future?
- Agile development with several iterations is essential – observe, concept, develop, test, concept, develop, test, observe, concept, develop, test, observe, concept develop, test.
- What kind of emotion do you want the user to feel when using your innovative solution?
- How are you feeling when you are designing, testing and programming your algorithm?
- Think twice before adding "notifications" into your plan, they are causing stress and fatigue and reducing productivity.

Innovation is serious, and the innovation team or a team dedicated to new innovative solutions should not only consist of software developers plus, if you are lucky, a graphic designer! Thinking of the need for diverse CVs, technical universities should teach philosophy, anthropology and psychology as part of the computer science master's programs and other engineering disciplines. Innovation teams and AI teams should be trained to be emotionally intelligent as well!

Digital experience vs. emotional intelligence

"Promotion of user wellbeing is a priority for technology development" according to the guidelines for positive computing in the book, *Positive Computing*, by Rafael Calvo and Dorian Peters (Calvo and Peters, 2014).

What will be the user journey and experience? What if the user has to enter data on three screens and do 10 steps before something is really happening? If your user cannot log in, or it takes too long to be worth it to log in, then your user will be disappointed, non-productive, not engaged. By way of contrast, it's a benefit for your organization if your tool is usable. It's worth looking at the emotions which your new digital tool or innovative solution creates in the user and consumer.

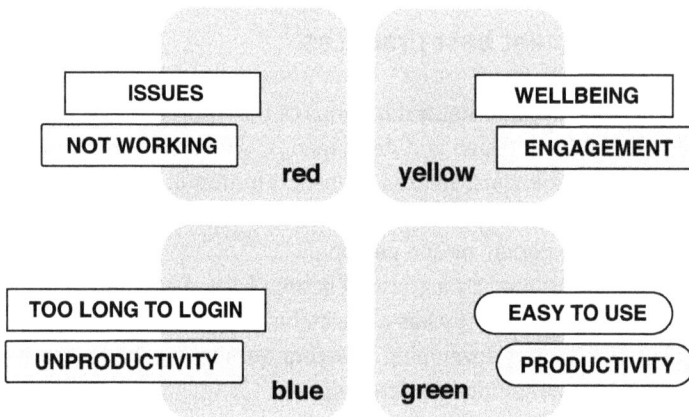

Figure 10.2: Framework – user experience vs. emotional intelligence using the mood meter.

Figure 10.2 shows a framework to understand user experience vs. emotional intelligence, and how a digital interface and tool can impact the performance of a user in a positive way and also their wellbeing. The **red quadrant is for disappointment and anger emotions.** A typical situation for this quadrant is when the digital tool, app or interface is not working, or when you are frustrated. But the red quadrant is a position to keep trying, you are feeling an intensive emotion, which is giving you power. My question is this: Is this necessary? Do we have to punish the user to use the innovative tools? This is clearly a waste of time and resources for the user, but also for the software developer and the whole operations team behind that digital tool. The **blue quadrant is for low-level emotions**, when for instance, you try to create a new account in a system, and it takes more than 20 minutes, even though it's a single-sign-on solution using LinkedIn. Another low light is to promise the user to "collaborate more easily with your team" and "remove emails" and in the end leave the user with chaos – messages inside multiple channels, full of notifications. Maybe the system is working, but you are creating stress and a feeling of helplessness as your users' experience. **The yellow quadrant is for happiness, excitement and joy**. The user is feeling optimism and positivity when using your system and this is what makes a user engaged and willing to recommend your product. It's not only about interface design, it's about the whole experience in the process of using the new tool, the outcome, the communication between the user and the interface, and having chosen suitable colors. **The green quadrant is where emotions like pleasantness, calm and peace of mind** are located. Here the user will be the most productive and concentrated on using the innovative solution. The objective is to design technology and digital tools to bring "yellow and green" emotions to your customers, partners and people who will interact and use your services and products. You need to be aware about what you are feeling in the moment, and how you pick up on the emotions of another person. Instead of reacting, you should know yourself in the situation and what you see, the interpretation you have of the situation and what you are feeling right now to respond more effectively to the situation.

On a personal note, when I was designing the first prototype of collabwith.co I had a clear vision that it had to be simple, very easy to use, and with minimal required interactions for people to achieve their goal. Operations had to be perfect, which means 99.99% accessibility and availability of the service. On the other hand, I wanted to go further with positive computing, and since day one the login page has had a "positive quote" below the login details. There are more than 300 positive quotes that randomly appear at every refresh of the login page. Positive quotes such as "The difference between ordinary and extraordinary is that little extra", "When you are open to opportunities, you find people that can change your life", "Courage is like a muscle, we strengthen it by use", etc. I strongly believe that these small details of positivism and joy can make an impact on how the people interact on the platform. Also, the platform needs to communicate in a positive way with kindness and appreciation. The colors, the font, the style of the buttons, the lines, the graphic design is intended to be calm, positive and simple to help the user to be content and relaxed while interacting with the platform. If you are thinking about contacting a very well-known academic, you may be feeling a little bit nervous or anxious, so the interface and how the information are structured are designed to reduce the levels of anxiety and to make it super easy.

It is important to be aware of what information people are communicating and how we connect emotionally. We need to understand how to match our emotional state to accomplish what we want to achieve, or what the team wants to achieve. People do not always comprehend emotions or what emotions communicate. Once you know the message of an emotion, then you can answer more effectively.

Translated into an everyday example – when I was working in a R&D lab where we were designing a system for virtual identity management, besides the details, the key issue was whether you are keeping your personal and private details all in one place. How to share your data and how to update and store it has to reduce the fear, and it has to reduce the frustration. A clean design is needed, and the process has to be clear, smooth and simple, but with enough authority to trust it. And here the philosophical question arises as well: What is an identity? What is identifying a human being? What was identity in the past and what is identity now? Is there an evolution of human identity? Do we have to digitalize our identity? How far and how much?

User experience with emotional intelligence best practices

–   Create a user journey with emotional touch points, including the emotional state of the user at the moment of using the solution, and the emotions the solution wants to bring to the user during the user journey.
–   Review which types of emotions the features and functionalities are evoking in the user.
–   Which are the key functionalities that have to outperform operationally?
–   While designing, define the emotions the innovative solution wants to bring to the end user.
–   How can you apply positive emotions in the innovation design?
–   Is your technology bringing wellbeing to the user?
–   Is your new innovative solution creating a positive impact on the user's life?

In this last chapter about digitalization and innovation, I have interviewed different professionals and researchers in this area that applied similar concepts. They are talking about AI and ethics, digitalization, UX and innovation from their unique perspective.

Conversation with Prof. Christian Haslam about "Digitalization for Innovation"

Associate Professor at Aalborg Universitet, Denmark
    @chrhaslam

What is digitalization?

Digitization is the act of applying digital technologies to add or create value for one or more actors within a given context. There can be many degrees of digitalization ranging from simply replicating an existing, analog, process in a digital medium to reimagining an entire business case by utilizing new possibilities an adopted digital technology makes available.

Which kind of value people are bringing to a digital tool?

Digital tools can be utilized to create many types of value in many different situations. Since the term "digital tools" itself is extremely broad this is not surprising. However, the relatively low cost and high degree of flexibility digital tools offer (generally speaking) makes them a useful option in many scenarios.

What is digitalization for innovation and which kind of value digitalization can bring to innovation?

Digital technologies can be powerful innovation drivers in the same way that any other new technology can affect what is possible within a given context. Digital technologies are especially interesting since they can often be developed and deployed quickly, and at relatively low cost. This lends itself well to low-risk experimentation and exploration, which is vital for innovation.

Conversation with Prof. Kimberly A. Houser about "AI and Ethics"

Assistant Professor University of North Texas
    @kimberlyhouser

What is an AI algorithm?

An algorithm is a set of steps programmed into a computer to read data and produce an outcome. Artificial Intelligence (AI) is a branch of computer science which creates programs and machines that can perform tasks typically performed by humans, such as recognizing images and making decisions based on data (Donahue, 2018). Algorithms are generally designed by humans to instruct a computer to solve a problem. Machine learning, a type of AI, is the ability of a machine to modify an algorithm on its own without the intervention of the programmer by training itself on data sets.

What does it mean to design and create an ethical AI algorithm and technology?

Ethical AI (sometimes referred to as trustworthy AI or responsible AI) requires that algorithms and AI programs be designed to create results which are accurate, fair, and nondiscriminatory. Ethical AI requires that potential harms be planned for and corrected prior to releasing an AI program for public or commercial use. For example, scholar Joy Buolamwini (Buolamwini, 2018) discovered that facial recognition programs misidentified darker skin women 20–34% of the time but was accurate 99% of time the on lighter skinned males and suggested that these types of errors can be mitigated by making sure data sets are reflective or society and the AI programs be transparent and accountable. The ultimate goal of ethical AI is that those designing AI programs are not only taking these types of risks into consideration in the creation of AI programs, but also crafting and utilizing tools to detect and mitigate these risks (Houser, 2019).

What is AI and technology for good?

AI for good is the use of technology to solve humanity's problems. For example, AI can be used to predict natural disasters, read MRI and cancer slides, locate those stranded due to natural disasters, predict where the flu will hit, source food-borne illnesses, and create objective decisions mitigating the impact of unconscious biases of humans. The potential for social good using AI cannot be overstated. For example, AI systems were able to detect cancer by examining lymph node slides 99.3% of the time compared with trained human pathologists who were only able to discover 81% of the cancers (Liu, 2018). Additionally, AI can be used to make more objective decisions regarding human rights and privileges by mitigating the unconscious biases of humans resulting in more equitable results for women and other under-represented groups.

What kind of value can AI algorithms bring to innovation?

Although many people are aware that AI is being incorporated increasingly into industry, few understand the full extent to which it benefits both commercial and societal endeavors. The main commercial value is improved productivity and reliability by automating certain functions. This not only decreases the time for the function to be performed, but also improves the consistency and accuracy of the function. While there is no doubt that AI can create more objective decisions than humans, it is also true that AI can incorporate and amplify human error. As such, many encourage the use of augmented AI which permits humans and machines to work together.

By freeing up a worker's time through automating the menial functions of their jobs, workers can then focus more on problem-solving and innovation, creating new systems, products, and ideas. Additionally, AI's ability to process massive amounts of data and detect patterns can provide insight that humans would be unable to glean on their own. The key is that innovation requires creativity, the human part of the equation. For example, AI in combination with human creativity has made leaps and bounds in areas such as autonomous vehicles. These vehicles are equipped with sensors that can detect lanes, other vehicles, speed limits, and potential hazards. In the U.S., the widespread use of autonomous vehicles will avoid the 94% of accidents that are caused by human error and save the hundreds of billions of dollars in lost workplace productivity, economic activity, and injuries and loss of life (NHTSA, 2018). Traffic flow can be eased saving the 6.9 billion hours in traffic delays each year, as well as reduce greenhouse gas emissions caused by these delays. This type of innovation would not be possible without both human creativity and the ability of AI to process massive amounts of data and make decisions. However, autonomous vehicles cannot be rolled out until the ethical issues are addressed. For example, an autonomous vehicle may be called upon to make a split-second decision of whether to run over an animal or a human, or worse, run over a pedestrian or risk the passenger's life. It is the combination of AI with the social sciences that offers the best future. We want AI to be used to make equitable and ethical decisions which can be used to overcome the limitations and unconscious biases of humans, but also must make decisions that incorporate a high level of ethical understanding, which do require human input.

Conversation with Uljan Sharka about "AI & Design"

CEO iGenius
    @uljansharka

What is iGenius?

iGenius is the scaleup on a mission to reimagine data interaction for businesses. It was mentioned as one of Europe's top 100 SaaS companies, and one of nine top names in data and analytics, by venture capital firm Accel. With offices in Italy, the USA, the UK and Switzerland, iGenius is a high-growth scaleup that thinks like an enterprise, where talented innovators can thrive, and people come first.

Some of the biggest Fortune 500 companies are already using iGenius' main product, crystal – an augmented analytics platform that combines sophisticated understanding of business data and jargon with a seamless conversational and humanized user experience. The platform allows any user, regardless of analytics training, to extract value from their business data stream and receive direction when making data-driven decisions. Putting siloed and complex data into one conversational interface, crystal answers questions and gives data-based insights via voice or easy-to-read data stories. These insights make advanced connections between data sources with the help of machine learning and enrich responses with advice and data-driven next best actions. Furthermore, this approach streams, rather than copies, data and can cut energy consumption from data computing by 50%.

How do you approach the design of AI algorithms and interfaces?

Our approach is people centric. Machines can't replace human interactions, but they can help make our lives easier, especially at these unprecedented times. crystal works side-by-side with the users, supporting them with data exploration. When building crystal's persona, we focused on competence, rather than servility, making sure her relationship with the user would be built on equal grounds. We wanted users to see crystal as a real colleague, someone to trust, rely on, even joke with, but always in a respectful and professional manner.

Why is it so important to bring good graphic and emotional design into technology development?

Though we all may start from looking at the same data – the pixels on a picture, for example – the way our individual minds put that data into context and extract value from it varies greatly. For information to have value, we need human knowledge to put it into context: humanized data in the form of visuals and natural language can help us achieve that faster and make it accessible to anyone.

What is the future of AI development?

AI cannot enable a sustainable future if it's not sustainable by design: at iGenius, we believe in designing, training and delivering sustainable AI products. These principles are also the foundation of our product, crystal.

Conversation with Virginia Vila on "The Importance of UX"

Director UX Collabwith
   @virginiavila

What is the role of the user experience designer?

This role works as a facilitator between the person using the technology and the technology itself. But what does this facilitation mean? Beyond the general belief that designers stare at the sky waiting for the inspiration or suddenly having a light bulb go off in their heads, Designers are thinkers. And UX designers are in charge of thinking through every aspect of what it is presented to a user. They are involved throughout all the project stages, not only at the beginning and most definitely not at the end when they can barely help.

Why are UX designers important for a digital solution?

UX designers think researching, prototyping, testing, talking, listening, iterating, always involving the user's point of view. From covering aspects such as how the information will be displayed, if it is readable and clear, to plan all the actions the user is able to perform in that screen and prepare for all the different scenarios that may occur. And this strategy needs to align with all the different teams within a project: business, marketing, graphic design, development, etc. Innovation cannot happen if this role is not included in digital projects. If you focus solely on the brand and the user has not been taken into consideration, what do you think it will happen with that website or app? You might have a competitive product and cutting-edge graphics but then the user will get lost using the website or app, he will not get things done and this experience will directly affect the brand.

Summary

To sum up this chapter, I will leave you with a number of exercises that help you to create a technology or innovative solution from an emotional intelligence perspective.

To practice

1. Take into account and find out the activity and presentation bias in the online tools you use every day.
2. Create your landscape of knowledge needs and sources.
3. Create your landscape of technology needs and sources.
4. Be curious and make a request for collaboration, you never know.

Notes

(Tas, 2019) https://collabwith.co/2019/10/innovation-podcast-with-jeroen-tas/
(Schallmo, 2018) https://collabwith.co/2018/12/prof-schallmo-on-digitalization-my-recommendation-is-to-focus-on-the-employees-needs-and-concern-to-understand-what-they-worry-about-and-to-enable-them-to-bring-digital-transformation-fro/
(Doppelbauer, 2017a) https://www.eti.kit.edu/english/1376.php
(Doppelbauer, 2017b) https://www.eti.kit.edu/english/mitarbeiter_2687.php
(Jones, 2018) https://collabwith.co/2018/12/prof-khaleelah-jones-on-marketing-how-sophisticated-digital-allows-companies-to-be-with-targeting-and-segmentation-and-how-much-money-can-be-saved/
(Fast Company, 2019) https://www.fastcompany.com/90378602/pampers-smart-diapers-let-you-track-babys-poops-with-tech

References

Calvo, R. and Peters, D. Positive Computing. Technology for Well-being and Human Potential. 2014.

Joy Buolamwini and Timnit Gebru, Gender Shades: Intersectional Accuracy Disparities in Commercial Gender Classification, 81 Proc. Machine Learning Res. 77 (2018).

Kimberly A. Houser, Can AI Solve the Diversity Problem in the Tech Industry? Mitigating Noise and Bias in Employment Decision-Making, 22 Stanford Technology Law Review 290-353 (2019).

Lauri Donahue, A Primer on Using Artificial Intelligence in the Legal Profession, Harv. J. L. and Tech.: JOLT Dig. (Jan. 3, 2018) https://jolt.law.harvard.edu/digest/a-primer-on-using-artificial-intelligence-in-the-legal-profession.

National Highway Traffic Safety Administration, Automated Vehicles for Safety, U.S. Department of Transportation (2018), https://www.nhtsa.gov/technology-innovation/automated-vehicles-safety.

Piller, Frank and Diener, Kathleen. The Third RWTH Open Innovation Accelerator Survey. The Market for Open Innovation: Collaborating in Open Ecosystems for Innovation. September 2019.

Yun Liu et al., Artificial Intelligence-Based Breast Cancer Nodal Metastasis Detection: Insights into the Black Box for Pathologists, 143 Archives of Pathology and Laboratory Medicine 859, 861–62 (2018).

Conclusion: It's All About People, the Planet, Collaborations and Virtual Communities

We are not in the same place after Covid-19 started, writing these last paragraphs during the second half of 2020, we are remote, and we are living a "decentralized" life. We have collectively acknowledged that we can take this crisis as an opportunity to adapt in a positive or negative way. We have in front of us a scale and we see how, depending on the way we are reacting, the scale can tip to one side or the other. This time we have discovered the power we have to make an impact, and the best manner to create a positive present and future is to be emotionally self-aware and understand these emotions, how we regulate them, and how we are able to see and sense emotions in others. Emotional Intelligence is the foundation for this recognition of what is happening for us as individuals, around us and with the planet. This consciousness produces a calm that will help us to trust ourselves, trust others, make positive decisions, be creative and take action with resilience. Resilience is the power to adapt to change and new situations and the consequence of dealing properly with frustration and fear within us and within our environment. Through this, we will be able to join together, people and planet, and collaborate in physical and virtual environments, offline and online.

Typically, when we talk about digitalization, it is construed as a way of doing things by copying reality and replicating it digitally. This doesn't work and only generates stress instead. We need to think about our human senses and go back to join our emotional intelligence skills: self-awareness, being mindful of our environment and our planet and being conscious of what we are doing. We have our own journey; we have to make sense of our actions and thoughts and drive them toward a positive action. In these unprecedented times, a crisis has made visible to us how emotions are part of our decisions in business and our personal lives, and it's important to understand these emotions. These emotions are providing us with information, and once we understand why we are feeling that emotion, we can take action in a positive way. Fear and frustration, if they are not well understood, are how we create a negative solution and a negative environment.

This is the time to creatively re-define a new reality, when the scale has to be balanced on the positive side. And this is true when we practice self-reflection and are self-aware. Especially then can we create a new innovation with intention and positive abundance and gratitude. And again, we are not alone, it's always a good idea to engage in "community thinking" and create your community of academics, startups and other organizations and actors from your ecosystem to define and build the new solutions you need. The foundation is sharing your knowledge and receiving knowledge. At the base, an important realization you have to make is that people do not only have one dimension, but are multidimensional; they are not only academics or entrepreneurs, maybe they play guitar, they are artists, they have

https://doi.org/10.1515/9783110665383-011

friends that are in other domains, they love to read biology books, they are building self-driving cars in their garage even though they are lawyers, etc. It's the time to appreciate the other dimensions to connect people and to bring them together as a community. Let's be open-minded and non-judgmental.

When I am thinking about trends for innovation in the future, the concepts you have read in this book come to mind, such as collaborative innovation, innovation leadership, emotional intelligence for innovation, collaboration and entrepreneurship, decentralized knowledge, decentralized innovation and emotional intelligence for artificial intelligence.

The next step is about innovation wellness and innovation for good where common sense, humanity, and spirituality join forces to build the next level of philosophy, intention and consciousness of our thinking, of our creativity, discussions, actions and leadership, where we are more aware of each other. The future, as the title of the conclusion says, is about people, the planet, collaborations and virtual communities to bring people together to create a positive impact that is good for us and for our planet. And the question to reflect on still remains the same:

What kind of future you do want to have?

Index of Conversations

https://doi.org/10.1515/9783110665383-012

Index of Figures

https://doi.org/10.1515/9783110665383-013

Index of Tables

https://doi.org/10.1515/9783110665383-014

About the Author

Jara Pascual, MBA and Master of Telecommunication Engineering, is founder and CEO of Collabwith, as well an author and an entrepreneur focused on innovation. Collabwith is an online platform bringing people together and encouraging collaborations online and offline. As a board member of the forum Knowledge4Innovation, her voice is heard regularly at the European Parliament discussing the topics of female investment, digitalization, "from lab to market" and academia/industry collaboration. She is also the host of the innovation podcast "Business of Collaboration". She writes about innovation and collaboration management for different online magazines, is a telecommunications engineer and has worked for 15 years in innovation management on transformational innovation culture and projects for a number of Fortune 500 Companies and R&D labs.

https://doi.org/10.1515/9783110665383-015

Let's Keep Talking: The Business of Collaboration Podcast

I created the "Business of Collaboration" where I have conversations about innovation, technology and knowledge with people whom I admire. On the podcast, I discover how my guests are doing something different, maybe for many years, often without mainstream recognition or success. I talk to well-known people, discovering how they created their groundbreaking innovation or technology that has changed lives forever. It was important for me to give visibility to their stories and the human being behind the innovation.

At the same time, I try to answer the following questions: What is innovation? How do people collaborate and work together? And who is behind the most innovative ideas, technology and knowledge? I am very curious about people, how they innovate, how they create new technology or acquire new knowledge. I added conversations at the end of each chapter in this book as a small insight into some of these incredible minds who answer portions of these questions.

The podcast "Business of Collaboration" also features conversations between a business executive and a professor who talk about life experiences and how to work together for a positive impact. I believe in connecting people on a human level to collaborate better. I believe in creating a conversation to enhance understanding and collaboration. "Business of Collaboration" gives these people a voice and a platform to share their stories, because to me they are superheroes.

You will find the podcast "Business of Collaboration" on iTunes, Spotify, Stitcher, Google Podcast and on our website https://collabwith.co.

https://doi.org/10.1515/9783110665383-016

www.ingramcontent.com/pod-product-compliance
Lightning Source LLC
Chambersburg PA
CBHW081054220326
41598CB00038B/7093